955.3
C3389
F

Presented By
The Publisher

May 26, 1929

VANISHED KHMERS

FOUR FACES OF SIVA. The Detective Story of a Vanished Race. By Robert J. Casey. Illustrated. 373 pp. Indianapolis: The Bobbs-Merrill Company. $5.

BUT in this story there is no solution of the mystery. The reader can take his choice of the several guesses archaeologists have made as to what became of the vanished race that built the majestic temples and walls and cities of Angkor, in French Indo-China, or he can decide to wait until they have discovered more facts on which to base their guesses, or he can conclude that the mystery is insoluble and take Mr. Casey's account of what he himself saw and did and learned in that region for what it is, a very thrilling and fascinating narrative. The author is dowered with an imagination and a gift of words that enable him to portray vividly and dramatically glimpses of the story of the ancient Khmers and the cities they built. But he keeps close to the conclusions of the archaeologists and the sights he saw, so that his book, for all its thrills and its dramatic scenes and interests, is an accurate and dependable account of a phase of ancient Asiatic civilization that seems not a little akin in character and mystery to our own unsolved "detective story of a vanished race" down in the jungles of Central America.

Mr. Casey has brought together, as materials for his story, something about how M. Mouhot, the French naturalist, discovered Angkor sixty years ago and amazed and puzzled the learned world with an account of its mysterious and stupendous architecture. He has sifted legends and myths and superstitions still believed by the natives; he has set down his own experiences and observations and the studies and conclusions of archaeologists who for two generations have been devoting themselves to the labor of finding out whence came the race of the Khmers who built these majestic, deserted cities and temples and what became of them. And all this the author weaves into a continuous narrative, rich with the color and feeling of the scene, intense with the mystery of its significance and moving with its constant suggestion of the vitality of the life that once swarmed through these streets and temples. Mr. Casey did a bit of exploration in the jungle himself, after hearing the story of a Cambodian road builder about still other ruins far in the jungle that no white man had ever seen. Through several thrilling chapters the reader follows him on this madcap adventure, wherein he was in constant deadly peril; is with him when he finds the ruins, and as he staggers and faints on his way back to water and help.

FOUR FACES OF SIVA

The Nation, Sept. 25, 1929

Four Faces of Siva: The Detective Story of a Vanished Race. By Robert J. Casey. Bobbs-Merrill. $5.

The mighty temples of Cambodia, rediscovered in the Malay jungle less than a century ago, are to the Old World what the Maya cities are to ours. Degenerate descendants of the powerful Khmers fear the spell of the cities where their ancestors once ruled; and modern historians have difficulty in puzzling out the story of this people. At their height the Khmers must have numbered millions; they built scores of cities, and temples with façades five times as wide as that of Notre Dame; they carved literally miles of intricate and delicate bas-reliefs in stone which must have been hauled a hundred miles by man-power and lifted, in twenty-ton units, to a height sometimes of two hundred feet. And then they died, leaving descendants with few traditions of their greatness and no explanation of their fall. Mr. Casey tells the story ecstatically and colorfully, so breathlessly indeed that the reader is sometimes at a loss to tell what is history and what is Mr. Casey's literature.

From a painting by Dan Sweeny

FOUR FACES OF SIVA

The God of Destruction looks down from the South Gate of Angkor Thom well pleased with his great jest

FOUR FACES OF SIVA

THE DETECTIVE STORY OF A VANISHED RACE

By
ROBERT J. CASEY

"And there are cities with thick walls and high towers and beautiful temples up there in the jungle, Monsieur.... cities that no white man has ever seen."
—THE CAMBODIAN ROAD WORKER

INDIANAPOLIS
THE BOBBS-MERRILL COMPANY
PUBLISHERS

COPYRIGHT, 1929
BY THE BOBBS-MERRILL COMPANY

FIRST EDITION

Printed in the United States of America

PRESS OF
BRAUNWORTH & CO., INC.
BOOK MANUFACTURERS
BROOKLYN, N. Y.

To The Memory of
GEORGE PUTNAM STONE

CONTENTS

CHAPTER		PAGE
	PROEM *The Hidden Cities*	xi
I	TOWERS IN SILENCE *Concerning, Mainly, the Corpus Delicti*	15
II	THE MYSTERY OF ANGKOR *The Detectives Arrive and the Tigers Depart*	29
III	THE ROAD TO CAMBODIA *Trails Converge upon a Mighty Enigma*	36
IV	BANNER-BEARERS AND ROAST PIG *The Quest Begins*	51
V	WRAITHS IN THE MORNING *A Nervous Native Talks of a Curse*	58
VI	GOLDEN SPIRES AND ECHOING BELLS *The Long Trail Goes Northward*	69
VII	HOME OF THE HIGH GODS *The Clue of the Great Temple*	78
VIII	KING KAMBU AND THE SNAKE LADY *The Relevant Case of Dak, the Forest Dweller*	88

CONTENTS—(Continued)

CHAPTER		PAGE
IX	WHO WERE THESE PEOPLE? *The Foundations of the Mystery*	101
X	BURIED TREASURE *The Hint of a Possible Motive*	112
XI	KINGS AND PRINCES AND LITTLE QUEENS *A Dead Man Gives His Testimony*	122
XII	MOON MAGIC *The Resurrection of the Enchanted Apsaras*	139
XIII	THE DANCING-GIRLS *Echoing Footsteps Out of the Past*	153
XIV	THE OLD CRONE, THE FOUR HENS AND THE UNFORTUNATE THIEF *Whispers Out of the Old Market-Place*	160
XV	PNOM BAK KHENG AND THE DOZEN DAUGHTERS OF ANGKOR *Voices in the Horror Chamber*	175
XVI	FOUR FACES OF SIVA *Old Gods Hold Their Tongues*	189

CONTENTS—(Continued)

CHAPTER		PAGE
XVII	THE CAPITAL OF THE KING OF GLORY *The Puzzling Works of Yaçovarman*	202
XVIII	A CINEMA IN STONE *The Legend of the Leper King*	214
XIX	NECROMANCY AT PRA KHAN *The Reassembling of a Skeleton*	228
XX	THE LESSER TEMPLES *Clues in the Lengthening Twilight*	244
XXI	THE DEAD CAPITAL OF PARAMACEVERA *Here Lingers the Aura of Lost Glory*	253
XXII	ANGKOR VAT *A Nation's Spirit Is Made Captive in Stone*	267
XXIII	MARCH OF THE DEMIGODS *A Light Goes Out*	278
XXIV	THE TALE OF THE HIDDEN CITY *Fairy-Stories Sound True by Moonlight*	291

CONTENTS—(Continued)

CHAPTER		PAGE
XXV	INTO THE WILDERNESS *Progress of a Fool's Errand*	305
XXVI	THE PHANTOM CAPITAL *A Ghostly Metropolis Lies at Journey's End*	316
XXVII	THE SHADOWS OF BABYLON *Sambour Writes Its Story on Dusty Bricks*	327
XXVIII	SHRINES OF THE VASTY DISTANCE *Parallel Mystery in Java*	339
XXIX	THE LONG TREK TO NOWHERE *The Khmers Walk into the Great Silences*	363

LIST OF ILLUSTRATIONS

Four Faces of Siva: The God of Destruction looks down from the South Gate of Angkor Thom, well pleased with his great jest . . . . . *Frontispiece*

Facing page

Angkor Vat: Over the western causeway came the nations of the East 26
Angkor Vat: Southern wing of the Western portal . . 30
Angkor Vat: Here through the Western Gate walked the elephants of the kings 34
Saigon: General view of the port 48
Saigon: Boulevard Charner 48
The Royal Naga: Seven-headed cobras which guard the bridges of Pnom Penh 72
Pnom Penh: A building of the royal palace group . . 72
Angkor Vat 86
Angkor Vat: The mystery of the temple 86
Angkor Thom: The terrace of the Leper King . . . 106
Angkor Thom: Here may be the wreckage of the royal palace 106
Angkor Thom: Elephants shoulder through the stone of the enceinte 120
Angkor Thom: The Gate of Victory 130
Angkor Thom: The royal terrace 130
Angkor Vat: The dance on the terrace 148
Angkor Vat: The same dances that were performed on the temple steps nearly a thousand years ago . . 148
Angkor Vat: The little Apsaras 154
Angkor Vat: Little ladies of the dance 158

LIST OF ILLUSTRATIONS

Facing page

Environs of Angkor Thom-Pnom Bak Kheng: One of the sandstone lions 178
Angkor Thom: Desolation now marches through the wall of Yaçovarman's capital 190
The Bayon: One long scroll of war 204
The Bayon: The lions peer haughtily at the world from the eastern porch 208
The Bayon: Lions keep their endless vigil at the east portal of the crumbling shrine 208
The Bayon: Through this northern portal walked the kings 212
The Bayon: The four faces of Siva peer from every crumbling tower 216
The Baphuon: Whose vaulting stages gave to the Khmers the promise of the great temple of Angkor 222
Prah Khan: A building whose vault was supported by massive columns 230
Prah Khan: One of the towers of the north part . . 230
Bantei Kedei: Eastern portal of the inner wall . . . 236
Neak Pean: The shrine of the sacred Naga . . . 236
Ta Prohm: The chapel of the royal treasure house . . 240
Ta Keo: A shrine said to have been dedicated to human sacrifice 246
Beng Mealea 250
Angkor Vat: Where the precipitous stairs leap up to the Holy of Holies 268
Angkor Vat: Ceremonial basin 274
Angkor Vat: The towers and their connecting galleries 280
Angkor Vat: The profile of the temple 286
Angkor Vat: A tapestry of stone 286
The Hidden City: The trail drives blindly through the bamboo to nowhere 318

LIST OF ILLUSTRATIONS

Facing page

The Hidden City: Telescopic view of the wall detail	318
Sambour: The Tower of the Lions	336
Sambour: A Greek temple	336
Borobudur: The great Javanese temple	350

PROEM

The Hidden Cities

The tiger smell is in the breeze that wanders lazily through the heat waves in the flats. Gibbons are chattering in the bamboo and fromager and banyan. Elephant tracks are in the marsh ground ahead. The jungle is humming with mysterious voices that seem to be echoes in silence, and out of the green distance rise the vast bones of a forgotten city.

Towers seemingly as tall as those of Angkor lift their cyclopean heads out of the trees. Walls enmeshed with writhing roots carry on the forbidding barrier of the forest. At their foot is the green scum of what may be a moat or the arm of a marsh.

And here is enthroned a desolation the more terrifying in that no mortal eye has looked upon it from this vantage point for hundreds of years.

Perhaps a white man is seeing it for the first time. Perhaps it is one of those weird relics of the East that has not echoed to the sound of footsteps since a great and virtually unknown population set out through its gates on a long journey into the blue.

At any rate there it stands . . . amazing proof that the story of the Cambodian jungle is not yet told . . . that the sleeping towns of Asia are still asleep . . . that there is still romance to be found in the world while inquisitive souls are willing to risk another few lives in a region that already has claimed so many.

White roads are weaving an unfamiliar pattern of Occidental civilization across the lower reaches of Indo-China. Northward—ever northward—come the tides of rice.

Water-buffalo plod inland from the rivers dragging plows behind them, and half-naked men and women stand knee deep in paddy-fields where once the jungle marched, and the tiger and elephant were the undisputed overlords.

As in the recurrence of a cycle, civilization has come back to Cambodia and is sweeping onward irresistibly, but not yet is its advance complete. In the North its mighty current spreads out like a surf that beats impotently against the dike of the forest. What lies beyond man will know to-morrow. To-day he can only guess.

The jungle guards its secrets closely—as it has always guarded them, and it is only when some one steps off the trail and sets his feeble curiosity against the distressing might of the wilderness that the world hears a whisper of its mysteries.

FOUR FACES OF SIVA

FOUR FACES OF SIVA

CHAPTER I

TOWERS IN SILENCE

CONCERNING, MAINLY, THE CORPUS DELICTI

LIKE a procession of giant skeletons, the bone-white fromager trees came down to lave their gaunt roots in the lily beds of the great lake. Ghostly figures moved in the deep green shadow. Wraiths made animate by the heat waves quivered at the water's edge. The Great Ones—the wild elephants which claimed the jungle as their hunting-ground—crashed through the bamboo at their play in the unseen distances, and gay parrakeets fought noisily in the tops of the coconut palms.

Across the waters which seemed to steam with the molten metal of the reflected sun a sampan made its silent way, and under the banyans a naked fisherman stood watching it with surprise akin to dread.

The sampan merged with the greenery of the bank and five men debarked—a pale-faced stranger, the like of whom the fisherman had never seen before, and four dark-skinned Cambodians girt with loin-cloths.

The pale stranger was dressed in amazing garments of white and wore a white casque on his head. The fisherman would have fled in panic had it not been for the greater terror of the Tiger which stalked the bush, and for the fact that his boat lay beached on the other side of the point. In trembling awe he stood his ground as the party approached.

"Who are you?" demanded one of the Cambodians, apparently speaking for the figure in white.

"Chan the Fisherman," the native replied. "I live on the upper edge of the Tonle Sap and I am the friend of all who dwell in the far Southland where the river goes into the sea."

The Cambodian spokesman translated for the benefit of the Pale One whose lips parted in a ready smile. Chan the Fisherman was startled to see that the man had teeth,—clean white teeth like those of a young child,—nor was there any trace of betel juice in his graying beard. Truly a marvelous person. The white skin probably had come of some sort of illness, for in all his travels about the great lake, Chan the Fisherman had never seen another like it. The clothes of the stranger were odd and uncomfortable, but Chan knew that different tribes had different customs in this regard. . . . And the man seemed friendly.

"Where do you come from?" inquired Chan.

"From down the river," replied the Cambodian.

"This noble stranger who is with us comes from a land which they say is beyond Pnom Penh—a land over the sea."

This time Chan smiled. He was too old now to listen to such fables. "What do you seek?" he asked.

"My lord, whom you see here, has had a touch of the sun," the interpreter explained. "He seeks the tiger and the leopard and the gibbon and other animals of the forest."

Chan shuddered. A lamentable and terrible malady, this!

"Why should any one seek My Lord the Tiger?" he demanded. "Does not the tiger come to find him in the night as he has always done?"

The Cambodian shrugged his lean brown shoulders and reknotted his sampot.

"Who am I to say what these rice-faced strangers are thinking about? He says that he would go to seek the tiger. So we go to seek the tiger."

"Then you have found him. This forest is his home . . . his and the elephant's. Pray to the old gods that you may be spared from the accident of meeting with him."

The white stranger signaled to his attendants who brought a number of queer objects out of the sampan and proceeded to make a camp. Then, through the interpreter, he joined in the conversation.

"We would go into the forest from here toward

the north," he said. "Do you know anything of this district? Would you act as our guide if we were to pay you many measures of rice?"

Chan shook his head.

"No," he answered slowly. "It is not good to go into the woods. The woods are filled with mysterious things. The tiger that hunts by night and the panther that hunts all the time are bad enough. It is not good to affront My Lord the Tiger. . . . But there are worse things back in the bamboo thickets. The woods are full of ghosts that lead one astray and strike him down with deadly fevers."

"I have met such ghosts before," commented the white man. "The swamp ghosts that bring the fevers are old friends of mine. They have never harmed me."

"These ghosts are different," protested Chan. "There are thousands of them . . . kings and princes and weeping queens on misty elephants . . . and priests in robes of gold, and soldiers in brass, and millions of men and women and little children driving southward through the jungle. . . . Armies of them, and they make no sound."

"Have you ever seen these ghosts?"

"No, but that is because I have the great fear of them. I do not wish to see them. My grandfather saw them one time when he had come here to catch fish and had lost his boat.

"He went into the forest that night and he saw

them and he was found here the next morning completely out of his mind. He talked of the ghosts until the day he died."

The Pale One seemed unimpressed, but the Cambodians, who had overheard the story repeated in their language, trembled violently as they went about the work of preparing camp.

"Why should these ghosts walk here instead of at Pnom Penh or in the delta of the Mekong?" The Pale One asked. "What is the peculiar potency of this region that calls men back from their ashes?"

"Who can say, my lord? The curse of the high gods is on this forest as it has been for hundreds of years. As far back as my people can remember there has been a curse on the forest. . . . Else why should the great cities be standing there empty? Why should the people who built them be lying there under the stone mounds asleep?"

"What cities?"

"Surely my lord has heard of the great cities. . . . All the world must know, even beyond Pnom Penh whence my lord has come, that the cities are there in the jungle. . . . The great cities that the giants built when the kings of the seven-headed cobra ruled in this valley."

The Cambodians hung their heads as if they wished it to be evident that they were taking no part in this conversation. The Pale One who had been seated on a fromager root got up and looked keenly at Chan the Fisherman.

"Is this something else that your grandfather talked about after he had wandered in the forest and seen the ghosts?"

"He saw the cities, yes. . . . But he had heard of them before he saw them. The story is very old among my people, my lord. The giants built the cities. That is what every one says and it seems so reasonable. For they are vast cities, just the kind that giants would build, and they are made of tremendous stones that only giants could have carried.

"The giants ruled in the forest. They did not have to fear the tiger nor the elephant nor the ghosts . . . if there were any ghosts in those days. They were very strong, these giants, and they did just as they pleased.

"They came here when the land was young and the lord of the Cobra was still king. And they liked this land because of its fertility. So they decided to stay here. The lands in the mountains from which they had come are very rugged and it is difficult in such a country to raise the rice necessary to feed so many giants. That is how the cities came to be built, my lord. I have heard of it many times.

"They say that the cities are mountain high with towers on which are pictured men and elephants and dancing-girls and the birds of the air, and that the stone roads which run through them are made of massive blocks that the giants brought with them out of their own country. This is also reasonable, my lord, because there are no such blocks to be found anywhere hereabouts.

"There are walls about the cities and tall spires where the faces of the gods look out upon the world. . . . That is the story, my lord. I have never seen these places, but that is the story."

The Pale One yawned, which may have been due to the fatiguing heat or possibly to a loss of interest in the amazing tale of the cities that the giants had built. He sat down once more on the root of the fromager tree and began to kindle a fire with a miraculous apparatus that he had taken from his haversack.

"If the giants built these cities that you speak of so eloquently, why did they leave them?" he inquired.

"That is one of the most mysterious things about it," answered Chan the Fisherman. "They became proud and offended the high gods who had allowed them to prosper. So the gods cast a deep sleep upon them and buried them under the mountains which are beyond the jungle. They are still there, waiting to be called back.

"And that is why there are ghosts in the forest. Other people came here and found the cities. The guardian that the gods had left at the gate told them that there was a curse on the place. But they laughed at the curse and at the gods, and they killed the sentry.

"They moved into the cities—the kings and the princes and the little queens, and the priests and the soldiers and the great army of people. The gods were very angry about it so they put a second curse on the cities. This time the curse was much stronger, and all these people who had come to take possession of the palaces that the giants had built were stricken dead, except only a very few who were preserved to burn the bodies as the law of the gods requires. They say that it took two hundred years for the body-burners to do this work. . . . And that is how the ghosts come to wander through the jungle, crying out to the gods to be merciful and let them go on to another incarnation—even as dogs—that they may profit by their lesson and gain merit."

The Pale One invited Chan the Fisherman to remain and share the meal of rice and fish that the Cambodians were preparing. For a long time he traced strange characters, which Chan could not understand, in a little black book.

"The region in which we are now traveling is rich in floral and faunal specimens. A superstitious dread of the jungle has kept it free from natives and so, under the protection of a taboo, the wild life probably has flourished as nowhere else in the world.

"The story of the district is quite like that of other regions of Indo-China. The forest is haunted by a million ghosts and it is bristling with enchanted cities. But that fact seems hardly worth recording inasmuch as any uninhabited place will be bristling with enchanted cities as long as men have the fecund imaginations necessary to construct them out of moonshine and star-dust.

"Elsewhere I have heard yarns about palaces of Cambodian Sleeping Beauties veiled by the forest up here on the shores of the Tonle Sap, and the only point of interest in the narrative of the fisherman who is my latest informant is that he adheres closely to the details given me farther south.

"One hears these reports so frequently that he begins to doubt his own common sense—I write it apologetically even though this journal probably will never be seen by eyes other than mine. It seems a concession to ignorance that I should be wasting this much time and space in recording a fable that is so lacking in originality of plot and refinement of expression.

"La Fontaine's version is much better. The old story of the lovely princess asleep in the forest-grown city until Prince Charming broke through the thorny ramparts to put a kiss of love on her brow is undoubtedly a gift to us from our Aryan ancestors and came here as it came to us out of the uplands of Hindustan. But under the treatment of Occidental intelligence it has fared better than here where it ceases to be a fairy-tale and is confused with fact on the one hand and fear on the other.

"I regret that it should have taken so obvious a hold on the native population inasmuch as its recital seems to have affected even the men whom I brought north with me out of Cochin-China, and it is going to make trouble for me when I need guides.

"A thoroughly unpleasant prospect this—that a scientific expedition which has come this far only through intense hardship should come face to face with its end because of a preposterous myth. . . ."

Through the night there were weird sounds back in the jungles, but the Pale One paid no attention to them. He lay asleep by the fire with an iron staff under his head while Chan the Fisherman and the four Cambodians huddled together and shivered and whispered until the dawn. They turned fascinated eyes toward the black shadows in the bamboo and repopulated the forest with the wandering wraiths of the old folk-tales. They could almost see the passing of the kings and princes and little weeping queens. They required no imagination to hear the crashing noises as the phantom elephants marched through the underbrush.

Their strained vision seemed capable of penetrating the black and reconstructing against the background of the night the tall towers and massive walls of the cities that the giants had built. . . . They had come so close to this mystery. . . . And the story as recalled by the fisherman had seemed so true.

The Pale One awoke to find mutiny well on its way. The interpreter announced in a trembling voice that he felt the fever coming on and that he did not seem equal to taking part in the proposed penetration of the forest.

The Pale One who yesterday had seemed so weak

and frail to Chan the Fisherman, flushed angrily and spoke his unusual language with the deep sharp accents of a master who will not be disobeyed.

"No fairy-tale is going to stop me now," he announced. "I have been in forests all over the world—beyond Pnom Penh—even beyond Siam. And there is no danger in them. If you come with me I shall protect you with the iron rod that kills the tiger. I have magic that is effective even against ghosts and sleeping giants. But if you desert me here I shall sink the boat so that you can not get away, and then I shall go into the jungle anyway. And if I die there I shall come back to harass you as long as you live. Besides which, if you do manage to get back to Pnom Penh without me, the white soldiers who are there will kill you."

"This seems to be no quarrel of mine," remarked Chan the Fisherman. "And I shall be getting back to my family which I left on the upper shore of the Tonle Sap. I am sorry that I can not take any of you in my sampan when I go. But, as I say, this is no quarrel of mine and I do not wish to be bothered with the ghost of this pale-faced idiot. May the gods deal with him as they see fit. He reminds me of my grandfather who did not say an intelligible word until the day of his death."

So Chan the Fisherman got into his boat and sculled away. The Pale One, having spoken, gave no sign that he recognized the possibility of opposition. He rolled up his haversack, put away the miraculous machine used in the making of fires, picked up the staff that kills the tiger, and turned his face to the jungle. The four Cambodians shouldered their burdens and came reluctantly after.

The sun rose, and with its rising, the dank, unbreathable heat of the forest enveloped them. They broke a trail along a little river, tripping over tangles of roots and blinded by sweat. In the open spaces was a deadly light that pale skin and blue eyes could not endure. In the bamboo thickets were dense blue shadows that seemed endowed with a baneful personality and gift of movement. It was plain to the Pale One that Man never had passed that way before.

That night they made camp on the bank of the river and the stranger from beyond Pnom Penh wrote more of the odd characters in his little black book:

"The story of hidden cities in this part of the world becomes more and more absurd as one penetrates the jungle, even though one hesitates to admit that the ultimate in this respect had not been reached in the fisherman's tale by the Tonle Sap. It is manifest that there has never been any civilization in this region. The jungle here is virgin—just as it was after God breathed upon the face of the waters. . . . Native taboos, persisting probably through untold cycles of years, made of this valley a region proscribed, and so the great cultures of the East—the migrations of

ANGKOR VAT

Over the western causeway came the nations of the East to marvel at this, one of the most grandiose works attempted by man since the Tower of Babel

peoples and the missionary movements of the intelligentsia—passed it by. If there are cities in this wilderness they must date back to some time before Adam."

The next day they moved on again, pausing to look at insignificant flowers and at flaming birds and chattering gibbons. Sometimes they caught glimpses of striped cats and once they came upon the wide path that an elephant had made for himself. On the third day they turned northward from the river into the very heart of the unknown jungle land where manifestly the foot of man had never trodden before.

Blistering heat . . . aching eyes . . . numbed feet . . .

They staggered on and on, while the forest quivered in the waves of the sun. And then suddenly ahead of them appeared a vast and awesome miracle. Five massive stone towers were rising dizzily into the molten sky. The carved roofs of a step pyramid were shouldering their way out of the fromager and coconut palm. . . . Mirage or reality, the most astounding spectacle that man had ever looked upon.

"God save us!" breathed the Pale One. "The enchanted city."

And he rubbed his eyes to remove this vision that would not be removed. . . .

And this, for all that it is a hearsay story, reconstructed on the dusty foundations of a tradition so often repeated that it partakes of the character of a myth, must be very nearly a historical recital of the manner in which Mouhot, the French naturalist, came to Angkor and brought back to the world the amazing puzzle of the Khmer civilization.

CHAPTER II

The Mystery of Angkor

THE DETECTIVES ARRIVE AND THE TIGERS DEPART

It is some sixty years now since the stunned eyes of Mouhot looked upon the magnificent heights of Angkor. . . . Sixty years since the greatest detective story in the history of the world was laid out with its million stony clues to puzzle the elect. Today, with all its principal remains classified and ticketed, its inscriptions translated and its monuments lifted out of the jungle, Angkor is still the vast and silent mystery that it was in the beginning.

The world knows more about it now. Splendid automobile roads, cut through what was once a thicket of bamboo and is now an endless rice field, bring the traveler on regular schedule and in little personal discomfort from Saigon at the foot of Asia to the bungalow on the edge of the Angkor moat in a very few hours. Yearly hundreds of visitors from all parts of the world are seeking out this odd corner and carrying away with them amazed reports that will lure other hundreds.

And yet were it not for the fact that these tremendous ziggurats remain virtually intact, defiant of time and weather on the edge of the Tonle Sap, the incredible tale of the civilization that built them and vanished would rank, as it did in Mouhot's time, as a none too cleverly constructed myth.

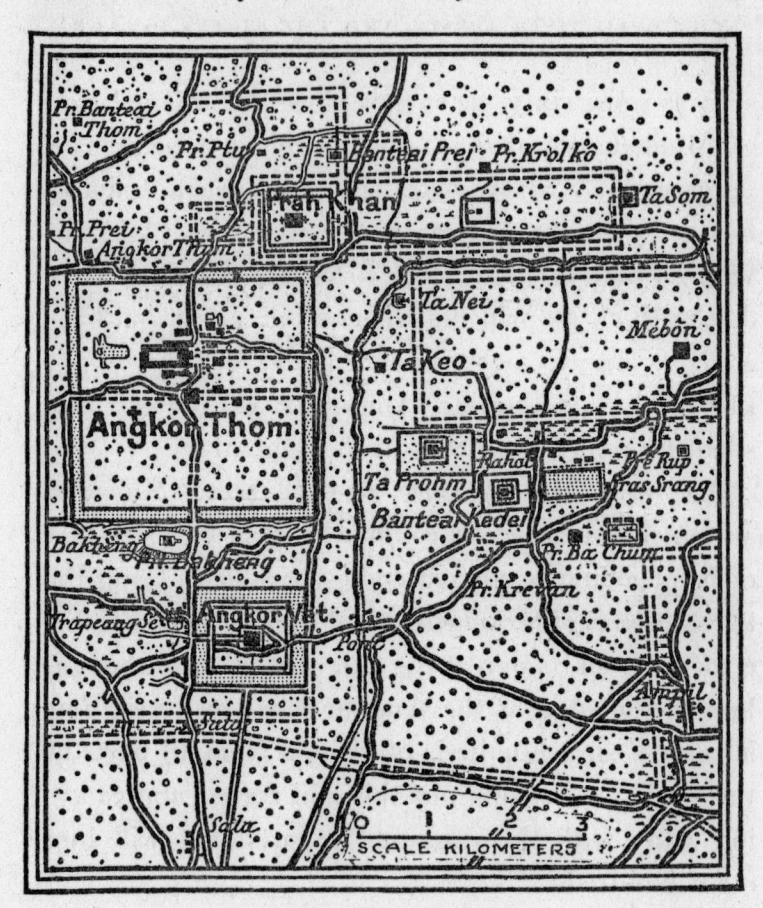

GROUND PLAN OF ANGKOR GROUP

But the monuments are there and no mere shutting of the eyes will dispose of them: Angkor Thom,

ANGKOR VAT

Southern wing of the western portal—first stage

a walled city within whose metropolitan area at one time must have lived more than a million people; and Angkor Vat, supreme architectural effort of this strange culture, not only the most grandiose temple of the group but probably the most stupendous undertaking attempted by man since the corner-stone was laid for the tower of Babel.

About Angkor Thom are scattered the remains of earlier erections and far in the jungle are capital cities built and abandoned with that prodigality which seems always to have been characteristic of Oriental monarchs. Traces of this lost civilization have been found wherever a lean tributary of the Mekong branches out toward the north, and there is plentiful evidence now that the temple builders were part of a population which must have reached a total of thirty millions.

Here at Angkor was the finest metropolis in Asia—a town whose barbaric splendor is permanently embossed in temple wall and tower and terrace. It was the perfect expression of a race of conquerors and must have been as wealthy as Babylon under Nebuchadnezzar. And yet, for some cause at which the archeologist can only guess, the populace walked out of it and never came back. The jungle moved in and engulfed it for five centuries.

There begins—and there ends—the mystery of Angkor. Little enough is known about the origins of the race that evolved the culture which centered in Angkor Thom. The people were called the Khmers and were either of Hindu extraction or the diligent pupils of Hindu teachers.

That about sums up the available information concerning them. What became of them is a puzzle much more intriguing and apparently much less likely to be solved.

There is mention of a kingdom under Hindu direction, if not domination, in Indo-China as early as the year 238 of our era and there is evidence that the Khmers flourished during the thirteenth and possibly into the early fourteenth century. But, strangely enough, their civilization, wonderful as it was, made little impress on neighboring nations. It seems impossible that a culture such as the one which built the pyramid of Angkor Vat could have perished without a word of its demise reaching the civilizations with which it must have been in constant touch. But such seems to have been the case.

Two generations ago the world had never heard of Angkor. A dense forest of bamboo, fromager, banyan and coconut palm spread across Indo-China. French trade was confined to the coast and there was no commercial traffic on the Mekong River north of Pnom Penh for the reason that Cambodia's resources—that had given this region identity as the Golden Chersonese of legend—were as deeply carpeted with useless verdure as the hidden cities of the North.

Pnom Penh, capital of the Kingdom of Cambodia, three hundred miles north of the Mekong Delta, was a village of nipa thatch and bamboo, a comic opera metropolis where a despot ruled in fear for his life over a semi-savage if not completely barbarous people.

Saigon, the present capital of French enterprise in the East, was just rising out of the marshes south of Annam. French soldiers were still engaged in that pursuit later described as "civilizing 'em with a Krag." The hardy Annamites and Cambodians were still entrenched back in the bush, resisting the inevitable advance of culture, and savage warriors were being brought over in sizable troops from the Philippine Islands to carry on the jungle fighting with the weapons of the jungle, the bolo and the kris.

What might be hidden in the masses of foliage to the north no one knew. The world had heard but had forgotten the tales of Portuguese missionaries of the seventeenth century that marvelous cities with vaulting towers lay dead among the trees at the edge of the Tonle Sap. Wherever there is unexplored territory one is certain to hear of such cities, and the world had grown too wise and too skeptical to pay attention to such nonsense.

It was manifest to all antiquarians that if there were beautiful cities of carved stone in the jungles of

Indo-China, then there must have been at one time a great civilization in Indo-China. And it was obvious that such a civilization could not have been founded, risen to power and expired without any one having heard about it. Civilizations do not die unhonored and unsung, and great races of cultured people do not carry on the rôle of a conquering power in secret.

True there had been a Chinaman—probably an imaginative soul—who had written what purported to be a chronicle of his service as ambassador to some kingdom in the south of the Mekong Valley.

It was conceded that the writer might actually have seen some such service, but it seemed obvious that in his description of the marvels he had found in his dubious kingdom he was merely a pleasant liar. If the Cambodians were to be considered as the inheritors of these theoretical grandeurs then the lie stood proved. For the world had seen something of Pnom Penh, the one aspiration of Cambodia toward civilization, and Pnom Penh seemed to be a great deal like any other bush town on the face of the earth.

During which troubled times Monsieur Mouhot passed up the great river into Tonle Sap and made his astonishing discovery.

Archeology, already thrilled by the translation of the Rosetta stone and the unbelievable bit of detective work which led to the decipherment of the As-

ANGKOR VAT

Here through the Western Gate walked the elephants of the kings

syrian cuneiform inscriptions, turned its attention at once to this new field. The tigers and elephants which for centuries had made their home in the forests of the Mekong suddenly found that the jungle was becoming overpopulated with bearded and bespectacled gentlemen who wandered about without thought of danger or personal discomfort. They moved northward and left the Angkor district to the savants, and word by word the fragmentary history of the Khmers was pieced together.

The district then belonged to Siam. It was not ceded to France until 1907. But science declined to recognize any frontier. The galleries of Angkor Vat were cleared of the massed shrubbery. The inscriptions on the walls and pillars of Angkor Thom were copied and deciphered, and for sixty years learned men toiled here unceasingly to prove at length only what had been suspected from the first: That a highly intellectual people had built up in this valley a civilization, and that, however inconceivable experience might show such a thing to be, their marvelous culture had been sunk without a trace. . . .

CHAPTER III

The Road to Cambodia

TRAILS CONVERGE UPON A MIGHTY ENIGMA

From the United States the road to Angkor is long but fairly direct and traversible with little or no personal discomfort. Most of the trans-Pacific boats follow the same route—San Francisco to Yokohama and Kobe, thence to Shanghai and down the Chinese coast which slants southwestward to Hongkong. At Hongkong one changes for the Messageries Maritimes or one of the Japanese lines to continue along the coast to the point of the continent. There in a fertile delta only a few hundred miles from the equator is Saigon, capital of France in Asia.

Saigon is nine hundred and fifty miles southwest of Hongkong and about the same distance from Manila. It is six hundred and thirty miles northeast of Singapore and six hundred and forty miles by water to the southeast of Bangkok.

French Indo-China starts where China proper leaves off. In point of fact the Chinese culture is virtually continuous all the way down the east coast to Cochin-China and Saigon. The French colony is a peninsula, the west side of which is bounded by the Gulf of Siam and the Siamese kingdom. The east side of the peninsula is the ancient Kingdom of Annam. The west side is Cambodia.

Southward through the plain of Cambodia flows the Mekong, a broad river recalling the Nile in its effect on the lush vegetation along its banks, and, like the Nile and the Tigris and the Euphrates, the principal influence in the founding of a civilization. Three hundred miles from its delta the Mekong is joined by a tributary from the Tonle Sap, the great lake, and up near the head of the lake, four hundred and fifty miles above the mouth of the river, is Angkor.

The boat from Hongkong reaches the mouth of the Saigon River after about five days' steaming along a fringe of blue mountains. Almost before one is aware of it the sea is gone and palms are rising out of marshy flats on either hand. The course is through a maze of small islands fashioned by the hydra-headed river . . . a dizzy course that is constantly turning back on itself, sometimes in leisurely curves, sometimes so abruptly that one seems to be heading out to sea again. For hours the spires and towers of Saigon are blazing white in the hot sun but seem like a mirage ever receding.

And one seems still no nearer when at length the pilot tires of his endless hide and seek and permits the tugs to come alongside and swing the ship about to a wharf. Somewhere, off beyond the fringe of palms, is the Saigon of the white spires. . . . Here at the dock is a row of corrugated iron sheds, unpainted and unlovely amid a St. Vitus's dance of heat waves. French officials in linen or khaki and cork helmets or heavy felt hats are coming aboard for the routine inspection of passports. Rickshaw men, pony drivers, half-naked coolies, perspiring welcome committees—the usual population of a wharf in any port of the Far East—are elbowing one another for space amid a cargo of iron pipe in the dizzy violet shadows of the building. . . . A tired, hot customs official pulls open one of the sliding doors of the shed nearest the gangplank and prepares for business, his eyes half shut against the glare as he scans the ship for disembarking passengers.

Yesterday out on the China Sea there was a stiff cool breeze and the distant hills looked almost glacial. To-day a few miles inland comes the heat that is more peculiarly the breathing spirit of the region than any other feature of Indo-China. One might know that he had arrived in Saigon if the ship had docked in the middle of the night instead of at high noon with the sun flaming overhead in a blue-white sky.

One accepts Saigon as he accepts the other miracles of the East, almost without comment, but that does not make it any less a miracle. It is magic akin to that of the slaves of the lamp that this town should be here on the shimmering verge of the South China Sea. For Saigon is like nothing else that one will find in Asia from Harbin to Singapore.

It is Nîmes, or any of the other lesser Parises of Provence or Languedoc, plucked up by the roots with all its brave imitation of Versailles and the Tuileries and the Boulevard Haussmann, and set down here in the ancient hunting-ground of the tiger . . . a puzzled sort of Nîmes that preserves nothing of its old atmosphere in transplantation save a willingness to sleep.

It yawns under the arching trees of the Rue Catinat and gazes out upon the still waters with half-closed eyes through a veil of dust. Once, that France so far away out in the blue may have hoped that this town in exile might live up to its immodest title: the "Paris of the East," and that it might inspire the dozing tropics with something of the gaiety, the nervous activity and spiritual energy of the city whose architecture it so painstakingly copied. But Saigon has ceased to be concerned with the modes of Paris. The French official guiding a pen over documents that have become pulp under his perspiring arms dreams of Paris as he might dream of heaven.

But he would no sooner think of copying the gait and garb of the Place de l'Opéra than he would think of copying an angel.

And indeed it would be difficult for this little Nîmes to look authentic even if it cared to, for the streets are filled with rickshaws, a Chinese city is its principal suburb and its metropolitan life is a surging mélange of all the yellow and brown races in the world.

Past the terraces of the Continental Hotel all day long walk little Annamite women with bare feet, black cloaks, black head-coverings and black umbrellas, a procession that might be a march of pensive nuns. And there come Cambodian women with close-cropped heads, wrapped from armpit to knee in gay sarongs, and Chinese women in white jackets and black pajamas . . . barefoot soldiers in khaki uniforms with blue puttees and lampshade hats, coolies in the scanty modesty of the diaper-like sampot, sunburned Caucasians in white linens and cork helmets, exiled daughters of France in frocks less than a month removed from the Rue de la Paix . . . Malays, Lascars, Filipinos, Tonkinese, Siamese,—all the children of the sun have their representation here in this pageant of glistening bodies. No, come to think of it, Saigon is quite different from Nîmes.

Physically, of course, the spirit of the rural Versailles persists. It always does where the lonesome

French congregate to think of home. There is the Hotel des Douanes with that familiar combination of arches and mansard roof which marks its nationality at once . . . The white stone façade of the Hotel des Postes which requires no tricolor on its staff to link it with hotels des postes innumerable from Marseilles to Finistère . . . The tall, round-topped windows of the rambling Hotel du Commandant de la Marine, which suggest the architecture of shivery barracks that one remembers having tenanted in France. . . . The greenery of the Rue Catinat stepping up from the wharves through a tunnel of trees to the steps of the Cathedral . . . The cathedral itself, a great pile with twin spires dominating the town as French cathedrals have always dominated their towns . . .

The boulevards are not so much the boulevards of Paris as of its aspiring and hopeful sisters. They were laid out at a time when space was plentiful and land and labor were cheap, and their designers were more concerned with landscape-gardening than with traffic requirements. One comes upon them continually in a ramble across Saigon's broad open spaces with trees at the sides and green garden plots in the middle. Like such parkways in the cities in the south of France, these seem just about ready to give up the struggle with the sun. Probably they are green enough during the wet season. Between rains they are a sere, moth-eaten carpet scarcely distinguishable in color or texture from the pavements which zone them, and over them floats a phantom of dust to be stirred by every lazy breeze.

Saigon did not grow up by any such series of fortuitous circumstances as those responsible for its progenitors. It was built to order on ground where no city had stood before. So its design is geometrical and its streets are straight. The boulevards, whatever the condition of their gardens and grass plots, are no mere haphazard ornament but part of a civic plan. They sweep forward through the violet shadows of the tall trees, a compelling vista, that reaches a climax in the blazing façade of some public building. Thus the Boulevard Charner marches in dusty magnificence to the cloistered front of an administrative hall and the broad Boulevard Bonnard comes to an appropriate terminal in the high vaulted front of the French theater.

The theater is the focal point of social activity in this capital of empire in the Orient. Its broad white stairs come down in an imposing cascade into the Boulevard Bonnard, while in front of it, on its course from the river to the cathedral square, lie the shaded reaches of the Rue Catinat.

To the left as one looks at the theater building from the boulevard, is the Continental Hotel with its broad cool terraces, a rendezvous that rubber planters dream about during the long, lonely months of their exile back in the bush. To the right are the imposing fronts of stores—principal shrines of Occidental culture. Around the corner is an opium factory where poppy leaves, brought in pressed balls from India, are steeped under pressure in a stifling atmosphere for the benefit of the visiting Chinese. Saigon like the towers of Angkor is a thing of many faces.

Saigon is prosperous. It is one of the principal rice markets in the world and is speedily taking its place as a distributor of rubber. So by day it is definitely active despite the lethargic influence of the tropics. Rickshaws, pony-carts and automobiles flash by continually in the Rue Catinat, and here at least is energy, for the automobile is not concerned with the heat, the little hairless horses would die without it, and the rickshaw puller has never learned to move at a gait slower than a dog-trot under any circumstances.

Along the water-front totter wayside restaurateurs with their stoves balanced at one end of long bamboo carrying poles and their utensils and stock-in-trade at the other. Before the plate-glass windows of the stores stand groups of little Annamite women, pretty enough in their native costumes, gazing enviously at Paris gowns that would destroy their charm for ever. Naked children play in the streets.

Mothers still free from the taboos of civilization nurse babies on convenient door-steps.

Dusty coolies cluster about sidewalk cookeries where for five cents (gold) one may get a bowl of soup, a bowl of tea, a dish of rice, a scrap of meat and a cigarette, without hat-check fee or tip. Water-buffalo plod along at the edges of the boulevard drawing carts wide enough to fill the street, piled to the curving awning with sacked rice. Beside them are other carts, scarely less heavily laden, with the straining bodies of men as their motive power.

So moves life through Saigon, slow-gaited but powerful—a continuous procession of Jaganath that must take a considerable toll. While they live and labor to push forward Indo-China to a place in the sun—which seems to be about the last thing it needs—these men are well fed, well governed and seemingly happy. That they die prematurely is a matter of concern only to those who look upon long life as an asset. Death has never been considered a calamity in the East.

Here is a picture: The Rue Lefevre at high noon; a small Chinese boy, possibly three years old, coming home from the market with two fish. It is typical of the Orient that a child of his age should be entrusted with as important a matter as the purchase of food. It is less typical that he should be wearing a pair of pants and manifestly concerned with the preservation of his modesty. That other small boys on the street roundabout him would not assay a pair of pants to the dozen has no effect on his problem or his attitude of mind.

His particular trouble seems to be a matter discovered by one Isaac Newton quite a long time ago—the force of gravity.

He is learning that trousers left to their own devices have little or no stamina. Whatever one may do in the way of prayerful aspiration has a negligible effect on them and they tumble down with surprising results.

Lacking suspenders one may hold them up with a convenient hand but when one is carrying a somewhat slippery fish in each fist the problem, obviously, becomes more complicated.

The small boy probably was no analyst but he knew immediately when his trousers fell down and snared his feet. He stood for a moment in thought while the breezes, if any, played about his undraped form. He was not hasty in dealing with the difficulty. Now that the worst had occurred, with a total collapse of modesty there seemed to be no object in temporary measures. The thing to do, obviously, was not only to correct the present situation but to prevent its recurrence.

He tried to transfer one of the fish and hold both of them in one hand, leaving the other free for contragravitational experiment. This was not a success. A three-year-old hand lacks the area which the foremost authorities consider requisite for the carrying of two fish at once. So, with a decision that would have done credit to a much older mind, he laid both fish down on the grimy pavement, seized the trousers with both hands and struggled back into them. Then he leaned over to pick up the fish and the pants fell off again. There are some puzzles that defy scientific solution.

Less determined persons might have confessed themselves defeated then and there. They might have shouted for reenforcements or abandoned the fish to the army of lump-tailed cats that had come from nowhere to exhibit more than a mild interest in the performance. But this lad was no weakling. He had determination and courage, to say nothing of a knowledge of what might happen to him if he should come home without the fish. So he tried it all over again and at the end of the experiment stood once more with his trousers about his ankles.

No Occidental could look upon a spectacle such as this unmoved. It seemed no more than right that persistence and ingenuity should not be allowed to go unrewarded. So a strap removed from a camera case was impressed into service as a belt, the refractory trousers were hoisted once more to that elevation which a finicky civilization decrees to be proper for trousers. . . . And presumably the fish reached their destination. The disappointed cats yawned and went back to whatever work lump-tailed cats do in the Orient. The loss of a dinner meant little to them. They had lost other dinners.

At noon most of Saigon closes its doors and goes to sleep. There is a theory that the tropic sun is particularly dangerous in the early afternoon, though why it should be less virulent in the late morning is not immediately evident. Also, there is a theory that one can best preserve his strength and resist the deadly fevers if he takes a nap in the middle of the day. There may be some truth in this, but at any rate, whether the siesta is a precautionary measure or a result of the very influence it is supposed to guard against, it has taken a definite place in the social scheme. From luncheon until late afternoon one is supposed to be in bed under the draft of a fan, though, of course, one may work out his penance by passing the hour of the siesta over iced drinks on the Continental terrace. Every man to his own method.

Save in the very hot season, the nights are not difficult to endure. With the departure of the sun the muggy oppression seems to leave the atmosphere and there are hours when the breezes that wander aimlessly upland from the sea are really cool. Whatever the temperature, Saigon turns out to its evening functions as to a sacred rite.

By seven o'clock the hotel terraces and the sidewalk tables of the cabaret adjoining are crowded and there are pictures under the gaudy coloring of the lamps. Officers in horizon blue, functionaries in a variety of full dress varying from the heavy broadcloth of Europe to the starched duck and silk bodice of the Eastern mode, naval dignitaries from the cruiser out on the river, rubber planters with skins like cordovan and coats of shredding pongee . . . Women, all the white women in this end of the Orient . . . Fresh young beauties eager-eyed and too keenly interested in their new environment to feel any sense of their exile . . . Less lovely matrons with the stamp of the tropics on them, who have lived too long away from Paris to remember it save as something out of an old dream . . . Women whose eyes are still red because a ship slipped out today . . . And lazy philosophers with gay smiles and booming voices who stay in Saigon because they like it . . .

The night beyond the ring of the lamps is black and solemn, and billions of stars press down on top of the palms whose vague silhouette is patterned against the sky. A jazz band is playing pieces that two months ago were being applauded in New York, and Saigon's lotus eaters are tracing the design of

SAIGON
General view of the port

SAIGON
Boulevard Charner

an eminently modern one-step across the floor of the Parrakeet Dance Club. Dozens of rickshaws are lined up at the fringe of shadow in the street beyond the outer row of tables. And the rickshaw men—come to rest after a day of dog-trotting over hot pavements—sit on their dashboards with hand to chin gazing appreciatively at this spectacle and marveling at the saxophonic sounds which this odd culture from the West considers music.

If there is a play at the theater the population of the terraces will troop over in time for the curtain and trail a peacock tail of silken color over the white steps as it converges under the high arch of the central door. Between acts it will emerge again to return to the café tables or the dance floor while the Parrakeet orchestra plays for the entr'acte.

Gaiety here as complete and effervescent as one might expect to find in France . . . a greater drama in its plot and setting and acting than anything that the wandering players will ever produce on the stage across the street. A person feels that he could sit all night watching it. . . . And then suddenly he realizes that he is alone. One by one the rickshaw men have risen up between their shafts and have moved off into the dark. One by one the tables have cleared, and now the orchestra is putting away its instruments, and the waiters are clearing the chairs from the sidewalk. . . . It is eleven o'clock!

Saigon is quiet now. The Rue Catinat is a black band under its trees save for patches of blue light under the distant arcs. The Boulevard Bonnard is empty, and, except the white towers that bulk here and there out of the gloom and into the cold path of the stars, the town might be blotted out and this the jungle where My Lord the Tiger stalked before the coming of the Pale Ones.

One knows that to-morrow men and women will be in the street once more, that the town has not been effaced by any magic more potent than the ennui which always follows the white man into hot climes. But for all that there is an eery ghostliness in the whispering silences and the emptiness of the broad avenues. One feels that in little one has witnessed the reenactment of the mystery of Angkor.

CHAPTER IV

Banner-Bearers and Roast Pig

THE QUEST BEGINS

Drums are sounding—dull-noted, loose-headed tomtoms in timeless cacophony. Brazen cymbals with all the fierce, insistent harshness of the crack of doom fill the street with shivering echoes. Pipes are shrilling the eery wail of a lost soul. And business in Saigon has ceased while a distinguished Annamite is taken on his last march through the city streets and out to the burial place that the soothsayers have decreed most likely to preserve the peace of his soul.

Whatever may be said of the life of the Annamite it is certain that he dies gorgeously. This funeral stretched back for a mile beyond the Rue Catinat and left a spirit of glad holiday in its wake.

The head of the procession was made up of marchers divided into groups of two, each pair carrying a small table surmounted by a mast and a vertical banner. The banner-carriers apparently were in the procession for business reasons only. They were not dressed for the occasion. Some of the men wore shirts and trunks. Some wore merely the trunks and looked like something out of a copper frieze as the sun etched high lights on their glistening bodies. Nor were all the marchers men. Almost every other table was carried by women or small boys or baby girls.

One duet of banner-bearers consisted of a mother and her little four-year-old daughter. Both seemed overtaxed by the weight of the table and the tall pole it supported. Came presently two little boys about seven years old carrying a sort of four-legged sedan-chair, the occupant of which was a roast pig, brilliantly glazed. And after the pig came the pipers, drummers, wailers and gong-beaters without number.

After about three hundred of these paraders had passed there rumbled into view an ornate cart architecturally similar to the American circus wagon bearing a quantity of devil-chasing paraphernalia, and close behind that was the hearse.

The hearse was sui generis. It consisted of a Ford chassis surmounted by a gaudy superstructure that stuck out six feet in front of the hood and the same distance behind the rear axle. A platform had been fitted over the seats and on this, beneath a canopy of red and gold and fragments of glass, rested an enormous coffin draped with dingy brocade and two or three red blankets. The chauffeur, almost hidden under the decorations, was seated with his back

BANNER-BEARERS AND ROAST PIG 53

against the end of the coffin. A large crayon portrait of the distinguished principal of the affair hung at the front of the canopy over his head.

After the hearse came a number of women in white robes with white scarves over their pointed hats. They were wailing with convincing intensity and persistence, although hardly able to make themselves heard above the gongs and pipes.

Possibly a hundred men followed them in a variety of costumes in which white duck and sun helmets predominated. At the end of the procession came rickshaws and empty carriages—lacquered boxes perched over rather than between the wheels, and drawn by little hairless ponies.

Most of the populace was in the streets to witness the passing of the cortège. It was obvious that nothing so near to a carnival had been seen in these parts since the death of the last wealthy Annamite. And the tinseled pomp and wailing pipes seemed to offer a clue to the puzzling attraction of this capital: The odd appearance of ancient China in this replica of a French Catholic city. Without the Annamites, the rickshaws, the wide-gage ox-carts, the hat-box carriages, the little ladies in pajamas, the betel chewers, the naked babies, the coolie restaurants, the glare of white uniforms, the barefoot soldiers with their blue puttees and khaki blouses and breeches, this place probably would be just another ambitious town trying to resemble a greater. But with things as they are this is Saigon. It could not possibly be mistaken for anything else.

Theoretically the principal business of Saigon is rice. Near the Rue Lefebvre is the rice market through which last year cleared one million, two hundred thousand tons of this cereal for export, not counting the vast amount that was returned up-country for native consumption. And because of the rice business fortunes have been made through the importations of jute bags from India.

However, trade has been reduced to no such simple formula as the bare statistics might imply. There is a complicated banking quarter in which all the financial houses of Asia, and one or two of New York, are represented. There is an extensive business in shipping and oil import and milling machinery. Rationing of the great coolie class has given employment to hundreds of food venders who carry their stoves and equipment about with them.

The Annamites control the business of feeding themselves. They will generally go hungry rather than eat alien cooking. The Chinese are the Greek restaurant keepers of Cholon across the river; but, for all their kinship with the Chinese in culture and possibly in race, the Annamites will have nothing to do with them. They say, and possibly with logic, that the Chinese don't know how to cook.

Corollary to this business of sustaining life is the no less important business of disposing of the dead. The Annamites follow the Chinese customs closely in this respect. They look upon the cremation practised by their Buddhist brethern of Cambodia as a source of great inconvenience to the soul of the departed in its wanderings after death. Hence their grandiose funerals with suitable equipment for the disgruntlement of the devils that are always lurking on the edge of the spirit world, awaiting a chance to mislead inexperienced wraiths.

As an offshoot of this funeral cult has come the development of a trade made necessary by two- and three-story buildings with narrow stairways—the trade of coffin-handler, a highly technical calling similar in some respects to the more or less familiar piano moving of the Occident.

Always considerate of the feelings of the dead the Annamites discovered long ago the scientific principle that it is very bad joss for the corpse if the coffin is stood on either end while being removed from the house. To make sure that no such disaster occurs it has long been the custom to place a glass of water at the head of the coffin and another at the foot. The task then is to get the coffin out and into the hearse without spilling the water.

The problem was not so serious in the old days when there was plenty of room and folks lived in one-story houses. But nowadays, with the Annamite districts becoming more and more congested every day, houses of two and three stories are common and most of them have narrow winding stairways.

Human brain and human skill, however, have proved equal to the change in conditions. Coffin movers under the direction of a leader with a boatswain's whistle are now available on short notice and are trained to carry the heaviest box down the most complicated staircase without rippling the water in the glasses at the head and foot. Their talent in this respect is said to have a soothing effect on the corpse. At any rate there have been no complaints.

The sun had not yet risen when the Chinese room boy came to leave a pot of the chicory infusion which passes current in these parts for coffee and to take down the baggage for shipment to Singapore.

From the window overlooking the Boulevard Bonnard one gazed through the slowly disintegrating blackness to see Saigon wheeling out its rickshaws to meet the new day. Troops were drilling in the square behind the theater, Annamite infantry, barefoot as usual. Automobiles were streaking out into the purpling dawn with the men who really have to work in this region and therefore must be at their desks and well through their day's routine before the climacteric of the heat. Coolies were stirring themselves out of their mats in the lower gallery at the side of the theater. Women in black with pottery on their heads were picking a slow and dignified course across the street. And the black mosquitoes, routed by the light, were swirling about in ravenous swarms.

There were clouds in the east and a hint of chill in the air. An hour later, in the weird light of the false dawn, a car was darting westward to take up the trail of the vanished Khmers.

CHAPTER V

Wraiths in the Morning

A Nervous Native Talks of a Curse

Yin, the Cambodian chauffeur, drew his weathered khaki coat more closely about his thin shoulders and shivered as he glanced nervously into the unplumbed greenery along the road.

"It will be daylight soon, Monsieur," he said as the finger on the speedometer crawled past ninety and on toward one hundred. "It will be daylight soon and then we can proceed more slowly."

Yin's French was too good to permit the supposition that he had meant something else. But even in Cochin-China the theory that one should do his speeding when the visibility is low savored of novelty.

"If you hit a water-buffalo in the dark you will achieve precisely the same results as if you hit him in daylight," observed the Pilgrim to Angkor. "And at a hundred kilometers an hour you will probably miss a curve and finish in a paddy-field almost any time now."

Yin showed signs of worry.

"It isn't that," he said. "It is even more dangerous to go rapidly on this road in the dark than it is when the sun is up and there are no shadows on it. But always when I go up toward Angkor I have the fear. I do not like this place." . . .

"What are you afraid of?"

"I can't tell you that. I know that when I am deep in the forest and the tiger comes I feel that he is near. The good priests in the school at Saigon have told me that it is the instinct of my people who were always at war with the great cats. But there are no tigers in here. There have been no tigers this far south for a hundred years. But the feeling is the same."

There was a shuddery conviction in his tone and manner that instantly peopled the dark coconut groves with untold mysteries. Back behind the car a rose light was spreading out over the palms, water squares in rice fields hitherto unseen were glowing luminously and scarves of white mist were trailing across the red road.

"Hundreds of years ago," said Yin, "my people were Khmers. They lived here in this delta—millions of them—and they founded the greatest nation in the world. Up in the north end of the Mekong Valley they built the cities which you shall see. . . . Great cities, sir. Greater even than Saigon and Bangkok. Then they were cursed and driven out.

They were condemned to walk the face of the world and never to come back. But you have heard all of this, Monsieur. I talk too much."

The speedometer had come down to eighty-six and Yin seemed calmer when he talked.

"But what has that to do with the fear?" persisted the Pilgrim to Angkor.

"I am wondering," replied Yin. "I am of these people. Their traditions have been handed down through hundreds of years, and I know, Monsieur, that every time I go to Angkor I have the fear. I feel that I am violating the taboo that was placed upon them and that I should flee as they fled.

"Here all about us these people lived and tilled the soil and went out to battle on elephants. Millions of them died and were burned and their ashes were strewn endlessly over this region. They are part of the dust that is rising from the road behind us.

"For this was their road, Monsieur, though the French engineers may say not. The traditions of my race tell of the highway that led across the delta to the great river and carried the great concourses of people up to the cities of the North.

"Once I had the fever in Saigon and for days I could see the Khmers coming back along this road to die in the old homeland because of the curse. They were thin and weary and naked and had deep staring eyes. And of course it is very silly, but I see them again every time I pass this way through the shadows. I have been to the school in Saigon and I know that all this is just superstition. But, praise God, the sun is coming up."

Not even the most hardened skeptic would have permitted himself a smile at that. . . . And hardened skeptics have no business on pilgrimages to Angkor.

This youth was no mere savage freshly culled from the bush. His reluctance in confessing his superstition marked him as one a long way removed from it. Whether the result of environment or atavism, his fears were real and deeply grounded. And when he talked of them they were contagious.

Probably there is a psychological explanation for his recurrent desire to flee from the dead cities of the Khmers. Stories whispered to him by his little brown mother and now forgotten may have been stored up in his subconscious memory to link him with the curse of Angkor. And, without such a background, the suggestion of death in those silent halls, falling to pieces in the sun, could not but have its effect on any lad with imagination.

Whatever the cause of the shadowy resurgence of this empire dead for so many years, it seemed logical enough here in the weird dawn of the tropics. The Pilgrim to Angkor was never again to walk on the red road through Cambodia without seeing, as Yin had seen, the fugitive wraiths driving down through the black.

With the light the landscape took on an entirely new aspect. Verdure no longer crushed the edges of the highway. The course was straight and smooth through a wide flat countryside carpeted with rice. Mostly the bearing was west with an occasional jog to the north. But change of direction brought no change in scene. Always the road led across a region of marshes, continuous areas of rice with here and there a clump of banana trees or the shell-shocked surface of an Annamite graveyard to break the monotony of the green.

There were few villages. Considering the tremendous acreage of the cultivated fields, the population seemed quite sparse. Habitations were far apart and only an occasional group of workers could be seen in the marshes.

The color of all this was a wavering green whose intensity depended mostly on the stage of growth in the rice fields. Agriculture in the delta seems to be independent of planting seasons. Some paddies were mere lakes of water; others showed the yellow shoots of new plants; immediately alongside which might be other squares of grain ready for the harvest. Save for the fact that coconut groves and occasional patches of banana came down to meet the red highway, the vista from horizon to horizon might have been the wheat district of Kansas or the alfalfa belt of Nebraska.

The native houses were the typical Malayan structures found all over this part of the east from the Philippines to Sumatra—nipa matting, sometimes on stilts, sometimes not. In particularly opulent ménages there were two buildings to a household, one for cooking purposes and another to sleep and gossip in.

Villages were distinguishable from the rest of the countryside only by the sudden appearance of trees. Behind stalks of bamboo or palm one saw the shadowy outlines of nipa houses set well back from the street—a flickering, unreal assembly. In such places poinsettias and rhododendrons flamed at the roadside, and an odd cactus rose up to make a hedge.

The children were clustered in the shrubbery. They learn at an early age in this part of the world to keep off the highways. They were all quite naked. The men, who occasionally wandered across one's vision, seemed partial to the sarong, a strip of colored cloth wound about the hips and knotted, as against the baggy pants favored by the proletariat about Saigon.

Rice gave way to sugar-cane and cane thinned out to present a vista of banana plantations. Then once more came the rice—this time with groves of coconut palms scattered through it, breaking its flatness.

The road to Angkor is interrupted by numerous ferries most of which are already nearing replacement by bridges. A group of rowers takes one across the first arm of the Mekong Delta, a narrow placid river that is virtually without banks and is distinguishable from the rest of the landscape only by its color.

Beyond the opposite terminal a butte, blue-black and hazy, rose out of the green like a volcanic cone—a bare lone peak that was presently left behind. No other heights were visible for nearly an hour and a half and then the rising ground that seemed almost mountainous from the distance turned out to be three jagged little hills that in any other locality might be taken for a slag dump. . . .

Flat and green, flat and green. . . . Cane and coconut and banana and bamboo and poinsettia and rhododendron and rice . . . and rice . . . and rice. . . . And through it all the long, straight, red road: a hundred kilometers, a hundred and fifty kilometers, two hundred kilometers.

The second ferry was more interesting: A dusty sign, "Saigon one hundred eighty-six kilometers," stretched across the road in the sun-starred shade of a palm grove. On either side stretched the nucleus of a village, nipa restaurants and refreshment stands with open fronts and rows of tables displaying a sample array of bottles. Dried fish and cooked shrimp and strips of fat and basketed eggs and bread hung from the rafters. Women squatted on their heels by the side of the ramp, where the red road dips into the river, selling prawns out of wicker baskets and oranges and green coconuts from piles in the dust in front of them.

Somewhere a phonograph was playing, an eery repetitive wail that recalled the atmosphere of the Japanese No Play. A car swirled out of a red cloud and deposited six Buddhist priests dressed in yellow robes and carrying—all of them—begging bowls wrapped in yellow scarves and yellow umbrellas lined with green. They wandered into one of the restaurants and sat down.

Babies, naked and seminude, played in the roadway—a safe pastime here where all traffic must halt or go into the river. One, in a futile attempt to fall off the little bluff above the water, caught his chin on two upright posts. He began to cry lustily and was imitated sympathetically by a two-year old with Annamite eyes and a costume made up in its entirety of two medals of the Blessed Virgin hung about his neck. A fair-looking girl with a white towel about her head took herself away from the prawn market long enough to rescue the child wedged in the posts. Her sisters in trade went on chewing betel nut and gazed with lips parted in hemorrhagic display until the baby was quieted.

The ferry consisted of a scow towed by a steam-launch, for the stream is quite wide here—one of the principal outlets of the Mekong. The river, sluggish and brown, flows down between low green shores. Beyond is the rolling verdure of trees with foliage like tufted wool. In the approach to the boat poinsettias and sumach spilled down the bluffs.

One crosses the Mekong into a new country. For a while there is a typical patch of jungle land, a "pi" of foliage and root and branch, creeping up to the red road and threatening to swallow it. Purple hyacinths bloom in great banks in marshes along the highway. Purple flowers, and red, and tiger lilies of orange and yellow break in unexpected floral fireworks out of the green.

Siamese temples, with elephants' trunks waving from their gables and spires that rise in a succession of tapering cones, appeared suddenly in the clearings. Languid birds perched on the backs and heads of muddy water-buffalo. And through all this one comes at last to the ferry just beyond which is Pnom Penh, the capital of Cambodia.

This ferry was another man-power affair. A dozen rowers worked feverishly to move their scow a few hundred feet up-stream, after which they rode slowly down on a cross-current to the opposite side.

It was a tedious process in a hot and uninteresting setting. The only divertisement was furnished by three small boys in a dugout canoe.

There was a hole in the bottom big enough for any one of the three to stick his head through, and manipulation of the craft was a hazard. The hardy mariners, unhampered by clothes, would patch the hole with mud and shove off. Two would man the paddles while the third baled with no visible success. And so went the amusement until the boat sank—as it always did. Then the sailors would dive after their boat and swim ashore with it.

Eventually the ferry made its perilous trip from the right bank and the crossing was completed. For two kilometers the road led through clustering gardens above which presently appeared the lofty golden spires of the capital.

Once—and not so long ago—the journey to Angkor could be made only by boat, a tedious passage that took some five days. The stories of travelers who made the pilgrimage in those days are a long recital of hardship and a continuous description of impenetrable jungle.

There is no reason to believe that these accounts were at all inaccurate. In point of fact they are probably meticulously correct. But conditions change with amazing rapidity in Indo-China. A lace pattern of paved roads has been traced all across this end of Asia. Motor transport, more flexible than the typical Oriental railroad and faster, has brought the upper reaches of the Mekong Valley to within a few hours of Saigon. And paddy-fields, spreading out and beyond the old horizons, have pushed the jungle steadily northward. To-day one may ride for hundreds of kilometers without seeing any trees save in far-scattered clusters. And it was only yesterday that the tiger and elephant walked here, unmolested inheritors of the physical kingdom of the Khmers.

CHAPTER VI

GOLDEN SPIRES AND ECHOING BELLS

THE LONG TRAIL GOES NORTHWARD

SEVEN-HEADED cobras guard the bridges. Spires of gold and stupas of stone rocket out of the greenery and into the vivid blue sky. Clean white buildings doze in the sun by the banks of the great river. And this is Pnom Penh, reliquary of the culture that was Angkor.

There is a fascination about Pnom Penh that one does not realize from descriptions of it given by casual travelers in the days when the Messageries Fluviales boats were the only transport to the North. It is a town of wide, well-shaded streets with a royal palace, a pretty park, and a vast and pictureful array of markets. But to a voyager who has come here after a long trip down the Chinese coast it is something else—it is a part of the country.

The cities which imagination always associates with the Orient, are usually not Oriental at all. Shanghai, Hongkong, Manila, Saigon, Singapore—most of them are mere transplantations of Occidental communities with Occidental buildings, administration and customs. They are dwelling-places in exile for Caucasians, and, save for the apparently inconsistent spectacle of yellow people milling through their streets, are towns that one seems always to have known.

Unless he goes inland some distance from the coast the tourist in the East sees nothing at all of the native life in the lands he visits. One port city is quite like another save for the accent in which one speaks pidgin-English. Shanghai and Hongkong are English; Manila, American; and Saigon, French. Pnom Penh, on the other hand, is Pnom Penh, and its parklike avenues are places of continuous surprise.

True there are plentiful evidences here of French influence. If the legends are true the old capital of Cambodia was merely a haphazard enlargement of the usual nipa village. It had no streets recognizable as such, was as deeply imbedded in jungle growth as Angkor, and its commerce consisted of sporadic barter with the boatmen of the river. That it is a city to-day is due of course to the directing energy of the "elder brother" who stands not too well concealed behind the gilded throne of the puppet king. But with French impetus, French artistry is to be found here as elsewhere in Cambodia, the more remarkable because unobtrusive.

Save in the European quarter—which is to say,

French quarter—on the north end, there is no particular form to the architecture of the town. Along the water-front are a number of hotels and administrative buildings which resemble those of Saigon. But the greater part of the shop structures and homes are merely square blocks of white with gently sloping tile roofs. They might belong to any city on earth. They seem clean, well lighted and roomy, and there is evidenced the hand of the Occident.

But nowhere so much as in Pnom Penh is there such conclusive evidence that buildings as such have little to do with the atmosphere of a city. There are hundreds of open-fronted shops operated by Cambodians for Cambodians. Men and women in sarong or pajamas stand in them as proprietors and clerks. Other men and women, similarly attired, come all day long to haggle over their purchases. The streets are filled with itinerant food shops where haphazard chefs roast bananas over charcoal braziers or ladle flaky rice out of the steam-pots of portable stoves. Women walk the water-front. . . . Strange women with betel-stained teeth and close-cropped hair, who can be distinguished from the men only by their superior grace of carriage. Like the men, they wear the sampot, a sarong caught up diaper-wise between the legs and knotted at the belt, and their faces are hard and masculine as they were in the legendary days when the females of Cambodia turned a tide of battle against the Thais and gained the right to ape the dress and appearance of warriors. There are hundreds of Buddhist priests here. In bands they journey across the town trailing the flame of their yellow robes through the twilight of the shaded streets.

By day the capital is Cambodia in panorama. By night one lies awake listening to the heart-beat of tomtoms, the plaint of pipes and the weird melody of the bamboo xylophone as the spirit of the Khmers is conjured out of the dead ages by the necromancy of unseen dancers.

The principal building of Pnom Penh is the royal palace. It is not so much a palace as a group of palaces, temples and administration buildings. It is a modern erection as such things go in a region like this, but it gives one the impression of a close relationship with the antiquity of Cambodia. This is probably because the architectural motifs of Angkor, which have become most familiar to the Occidental world through pictures brought home by travelers, are to be found here in lavish use. The seven-headed cobra, for example, is seen here in its ancient service as a balustrade. Cambodian dancing-girls, who in the life are the twin sisters of the Apsaras in the Angkorean bas-reliefs, are reproduced in stone as caryatids upholding the glittering roofs.

THE ROYAL NAGA
Seven-headed cobras which guard the bridges of Pnom Penh are accurate copies of the architectural motif invented by the vanished Khmers

PNOM PENH
A building of the royal palace group

For the rest the buildings are more Siamese than Khmer. They are all a glistening white with conventionalized snakes on their gables and gilded spires at their summits.

The palaces are at their best when viewed from the outside. The throne-room has all the tawdry unreality of a stage setting seen too close at hand—an imitation magnificence of brass and gilt. It contains two thrones, one for the king, another for the gilded image of his late predecessor.

Elsewhere on the grounds is the royal treasure-house in which is stored the famous jeweled sword of Cambodia. The sword is an elaborate affair the dull radiance of whose gems causes one to be politely doubtful of their authenticity. The treasure-house is filled with an odd mélange of trinkets ranging in value and interest from Napoleonic relics to the diamond-studded derby hat of the recent king.

One temple on the grounds, visited only after much questing for keys and permits, contains a golden Buddha. The palace guide declared it to be of solid gold, which perhaps it is. He was similarly emphatic concerning the ornate floor whose tiles are supposed to be solid silver. One of the tiles, rubbed by the swinging of a badly hung door, showed an expanse of copper under the silver but what is the good of paying attention to a thing like that in the face of universal evidence!

At night the moon came up out of the Mekong like a great silver drum. In front of the hotel the river is about half a mile wide and placid, and without movement save where clusters of green foliage float down from the jungles of the North. Fernlike trees stand on its brink and tiny points of light flash where green turns to black on the opposite bank.

With the moon at its height, water and sky are of precisely the same tone of glowing blue. Palm-branches, sampans and the silhouette of a banyan tree give the scene its only shadows.

Little lizards have come in out of the night to ramble about the walls and ceiling.

Out in the blue darkness the drums are beating and the xylophones go on and on with their tuneful hysteria, and the mystery of Cambodia is deepening. Three hundred and twenty-six kilometers to the north the red road ends at the gates of Angkor.

Once more the caravan set out with the dawn. The first streak of sun had put out the sampan lights on the Mekong and the morning was singularly chill. Yin, shivering in his meager costume, disdained the offer of a coat. He had shivered many another morning in this valley and probably would shiver again, and he had not quite outlived the tradition that sturdy manhood ought to be independent of clothes of any sort.

For the first few miles the road followed the right bank of the river through a region of banana, bamboo and cane. In those few miles one saw something of the jungle life that once was the principal feature of this landscape. The green foliage rose in sheer walls on either side of the road, and bamboo and fromager trunks flashed past like columns in a long colonnade.

But in the background flashes of the sun revealed clusters of nipa houses standing on high stilts and as close together as they could be built without common side-walls. Here was the mysterious life of the tropic forest—a teeming population within a few feet of a great highway, and so well hidden that only an accidental trick of the morning light revealed it at all.

All one's advance information leads to a belief that in a moment the highway will be a mere slot between masses of trees and liana and immense ferns. This weirdly secretive forest along the river can be only an insignificant foretaste of what lies ahead.

But in a few miles one comes to another ferry and crosses the Mekong once more to find a region that differs from the delta country only in its location on the map. From Saigon all the way to the edge of the moat of Angkor Vat, French Indo-China is just one continuous field of rice. There are clusters of coconut occasionally and for a few miles between Kampong Thom and Siem Reap there are one or two uncultivated spots where scrub palms and creepers and one or two shrubs, tall enough to be classified as trees, give a hint of the desolation that once descended upon this peninsula. But the jungle has gone like the Khmers whose works it devoured.

The whole region is reminiscent of the Galveston Bay district. It is so flat that Yin did not have to put his hand to the gear lever for something over two hundred miles. It is probably as fertile a land as there is on the face of the earth but so completely cultivated that wild tree-growths are to be found only in occasional acres given over to ant-hill burying-grounds or arroyos that do not lend themselves to terracing. One sees hundreds of square miles of Cambodia as he journeys northward, and they are all alike from one hazy sky-line to another, an endless green lawn.

Small wonder that this valley propagated a wealthy and powerful civilization. The Mekong is another Nile but in its territory a greater Nile. Cambodia is another Chaldea but more fertile. And History is a singularly unimaginative workman. What it has done in one place it repeats virtually without change in another.

Even without the second sight to which the imaginative Yin was born, one senses the presence here of the millions who are gone. Once they stood out there in the marshy fields as these newly arrived Cambodians are standing, laying out irrigation ditches in the same pattern, transplanting the rice shoots with the same laborious hand process, plowing with the same old wooden plows and wearing the same negligible scraps of clothing.

The ancient realm of King Kambu gets no older. Here in the rice marshes it has been restored again as Siva, its destroyer god, was said to restore the crops of the harvested fields. In a moment the men and women of the paddies will be leaving their work, dropping their sickles and their wicker sieves, to take the road in a pilgrimage to Angkor as they journeyed in that forgotten existence when Siva was younger.

CHAPTER VII

Home of the High Gods

THE CLUE OF THE GREAT TEMPLE

Beyond a bank of water-lilies in the still moat,—beyond a cloistered wall that seems to have no beginning or end,—the great bulk of Angkor Vat drives its stone wedge into the sky. A pilgrim who came here because of a torn picture that he saw many years ago in a trench on the Western Front knows now why writers innumerable have failed to convey an idea of the atmosphere of this vast temple. One looks upon it through misty eyes and with an odd constriction of the throat, for there is only one Angkor. There is no such monument to a vanished people anywhere else in the world.

The sun is setting now and the gold has come back to the vaulting minarets. The lace-work of rock is fragile as cobweb in the gathering shadow, and with the half-light of early evening the central pyramid has taken on an awe-inspiring size. It seems futile to record its grandeur. One doesn't describe an Angkor. One just gazes at it in silence and amazement.

Yin sits on the stone curb of the moat, staring fascinated at the five towers. The old fear is back with him once more, but the urge to flight is not so strong as the urge to remain and watch his personal ghosts pass in review through the twilight. He is trembling and would be in tears if the inhibitions of Asia were not so strong within him.

"I suppose Monsieur will think me very silly," he observes in his high-school French. "But the first time I came here I felt that I had seen all this before—that I have seen this place alight with temple fires and have ridden with the dark elephants across the causeway.

"I have seen the towers with the morning sun behind them, and I have walked about them at noon, and many an evening I have sat here as I am sitting now wondering at them. Sometimes I get up in the night and come here. I have the fear but I come here. I can not explain it, Monsieur, but all this seems to be so much a part of me."

He does not have to explain. He fancies that his emotional reaction to the stupendous beauty of Angkor is peculiar to him because of his race. Rather it is a matter of psychological stimulus through senses that can not comprehend the legerity, the delicacy of so terrific a mass.

As for the feeling that one has seen it not once but many times before—that is not common to the descendants of the Khmers. One experiences the same sensation as one gazes at the Grand Canyon or the dusty bones of Babylon or the sheer loveliness of the Taj Mahal. It seems to be the concomitant of emotional surprise . . . which may explain why the doctrine of reincarnation appealed to so many races of the age that produced Angkor.

As one glimpses Angkor Vat from the road after turning northward through the native village of Siem Reap a mile away, the temple is like something that the slaves of the lamp built for Aladdin. It rises to its heights in a steady masterful sweep. Heat waves give it a shivery unreality, and the eye has difficulty in focusing on its pinnacles.

It is the history of Angkor Vat that no beholder can guess accurately how high it really is. The towers are loftier than the tallest palms of the jungle but they are lifted still higher by tricks in perspective that form the most interesting part of their design. In the mass Angkor is as impressive as the great pyramids of Egypt, more striking as an artistic ensemble than even the Taj Mahal. But it is not for these attributes that the dazed pilgrim would classify it as the most fascinating place in the world.

. . . The sun has vanished. The last trickle of gold is gone from the carved façade. A cloud of birds has come up out of the forest and is sweeping

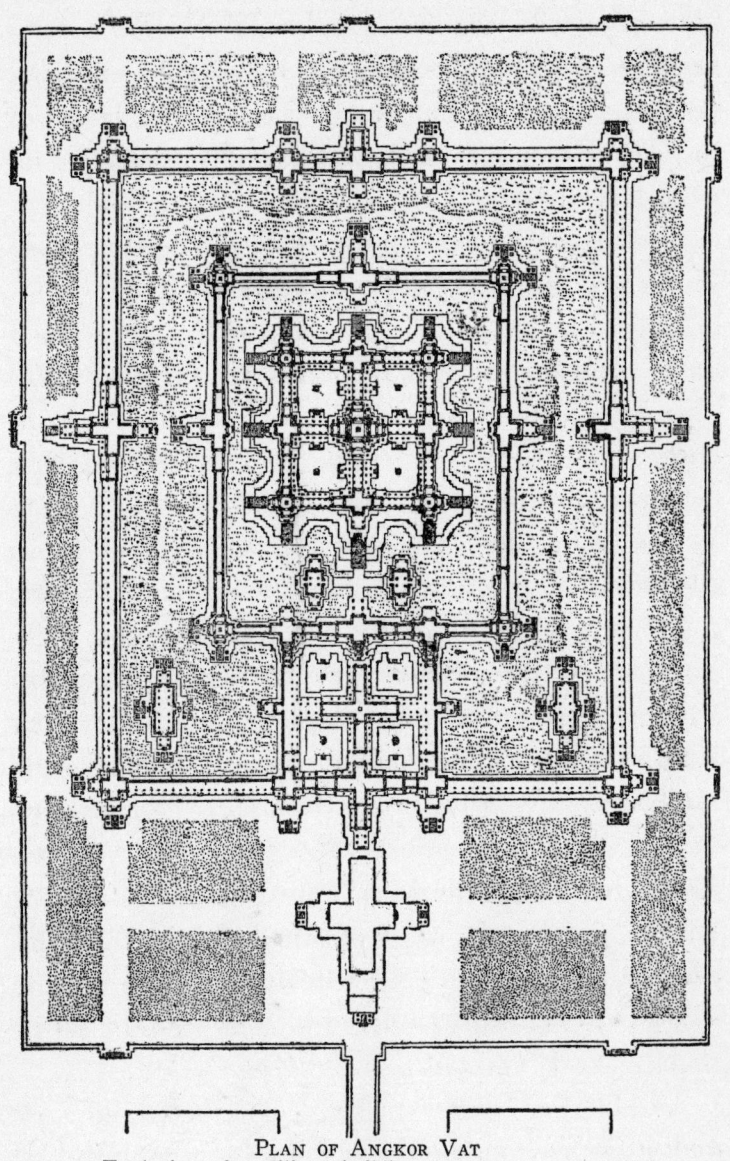

PLAN OF ANGKOR VAT
Exclusive of auxiliary buildings, causeway and wall.

across the face of the central pyramid. The towers are wrapped in silence and loneliness. . . . And one realizes that whatever gray-bearded science has done to trace the origins of Angkor, its mystery remains, grim and unsolvable. . . .

Monsieur Pierre Furneau, of the French road engineers, came out of the bungalow hotel and stood for a moment looking across the moat at the arrow point of the central spire. "It reminds me," he said, "of the mystery of the *Marie Celeste*. . . . You know the story . . . The ship that was found deserted on a calm sea with all the sails set and a fire burning in the cook's galley and the table set for dejeuner. . . . Not a soul on board nor a hint of what had happened.

"That is Angkor Vat for you. It is no ruin. The carvings on the galleries are complete. The roofs still turn the rains. The walls are as solid as they were when the Khmer masons put them there without binder or cement. And one can not but feel that only a few hours ago it was palpitating with life. The torches were burning about the altars. Companies of priests were in the galleries chanting the rituals. Dancing-girls were flitting up and down the steps. . . . That was only an hour or two ago, Monsieur. . . . It can not have been more.

"And now all these people are gone and the temple is still although it seems to echo with the sounds they left there."

This, to any one who has ever looked upon Angkor Vat, seems no more than the truth. It is this mystery of Angkor, the feeling that people did things here and will presently be back to do them again, that is the temple's great attraction. One is not so much concerned with the identity of the people who erected this incredible monument in the plains of Cambodia. He can decipher something of that from the tablets they left and he can guess the rest. But what became of them is a different question. Why did they desert Angkor and with it their culture? Why did they leave their cities to the malevolence of the jungle?

Year by year more of the Pale Ones are coming from over the seas to look upon these ruins. Automobile transport throughout the lower end of Indo-China has made the journey from the coast less of a task than the trip from Cairo to Karnak, and certainly more comfortable than the desert route from Damascus to Bagdad. A new road is under construction around the north end of Tonle Sap from Angkor to the Siamese border, a short-cut that will save some seven hundred kilometers in touring from the land of the Khmers to Bangkok. Yesterday unknown and far off the lanes that sightseers follow in knocking about the world, Angkor to-day is a show-place that attracts hundreds of tourists. Tomorrow it will be one of those places that one visits through a sense of duty and afterward confuses with all the other places that he visited through a sense of duty.

The jungle has been pulled out of the carved galleries. Causeways have been rebuilt and the massive gates restored. The long vistas of the temple areas are for the most part unimpeded by the bone-white trunks and entangling roots of the fromager trees. It is possible now to see twice as much of the Angkor

ANGKOR VAT
Longitudinal section, after Fournereau

district as when Pierre Loti came here twenty years ago and with less than half the effort. But all of this has merely complicated the puzzle of archeologists over the rise of the Khmers and their untold fate.

Angkor Vat, the finest effort of this lost civilization, has been pictured so often in Occidental magazines that it is generally believed to be the only work of the Khmers still existing. As a matter of fact it is only one temple in an uncountable group.

Close by is Angkor Thom, a walled town which in

its heyday was a metropolis even as a modern understands the word. About Angkor Thom are scores of temples, presumably the centers of suburban districts, some of them excellently preserved. And out in the jungle to the south and east are the hidden cities of a tremendous empire, some of them discovered as Angkor was discovered and mapped and classified. Others, no doubt, still sleeping in the shadows of the jungle are to be found when the rice fields move northward along the Mekong.

Basing a computation on the size of the walled area of Angkor Thom, the capital city, one may well suppose that the rural population of this civilization at the time of its power was something over thirty millions. There was no jungle here then. An extensive irrigation district carried the waters of the Mekong and the Tonle Sap through the entire valley and the region was then what it is fast becoming now, a continuous field of rice.

A road extended from Angkor to the east for nearly one hundred miles, linking up the capital with the northern cities. Traces of the highway have been found and plans are already under way for its restoration, so that tourists may roll at eighty kilometers an hour through a district where now the hardy explorer pushes through mile upon mile of bamboo in constant danger of his life and unending fear of the tiger and wild elephant.

There is a theory that the cities so far located along this royal road to the East were protected by another row of walled towns which served as fortresses rather than grain markets on a line some distance north. If so, these outlying citadels are still to be brought to light. There is no record of them in Cambodian traditions and repeated expeditions into the brush have failed to find them. It does not do, however, to doubt their existence. One has merely to think of Angkor screened by the forests for five hundred years to believe any tale of enchanted capitals that the magicians of the French archeological service may suggest.

The lost kingdom of the Khmers is still in the midst of the twilight that enveloped it when the builders departed long centuries ago. The haze is thinning a little. Strange gods, placid and smiling, are peering out of open spaces among the trees to welcome the inquisitive Pale Ones who have found their hiding-places. Little by little the story of the sons of Kambu is being pieced together from the pictures they carved and the inscriptions they left on the pillars of their temples. Little by little their ghosts, which two generations ago were merely shapeless, nameless wraiths, are beginning to take form. But back in the wilderness of the East are other ghosts whose diaphanous outlines are as yet suspected rather than seen. . . . The ghosts of war-

ANGKOR VAT

ANGKOR VAT
The mystery of the temple, its vastness and beauty are seen in this reconstruction of it as it stood in the days of its might

riors who made empire rather than temples . . . The great silent horde who stood sentry on the north frontier holding back the invader while the chisels of the stone carvers clanked unceasingly in the valley of the Mekong . . . The terrible host which marched beyond the forests and beyond the mountains, painstakingly spreading a desolation as great as the one to which they themselves succumbed . . .

The evidence of Angkor was unbelievable enough when the puzzle centered in the temple and town. A modern world could not conceive of the possibility that a cultured people might have walked out of a place so magnificent never to return. Even when one looks at it close at hand Angkor Vat seems to have no existence outside of a fairy-tale. And now one must account not only for the desertion of Angkor but for the hegira of an entire nation out of its lands and cities and into the perilous unknown.

CHAPTER VIII

KING KAMBU AND THE SNAKE LADY

THE RELEVANT CASE OF DAK, THE FOREST DWELLER

THE world was not exactly young, but on the other hand it was not so old as it is now by a matter of some two thousand years, when Dak the Forest Dweller came down to the big river. He had made suitable prayers to the Great Serpent that is the father of all creation, and he had offered such gifts as happened to be at hand to My Lord the Prince Cobra. And in a dream there had come to him information that things were not going to remain as they had been in the great forest for all these hundred of years.

Dak was concerned about it for he had been very comfortable with a palm-leaf roof above and a bamboo floor below. It rained occasionally and the tigers and elephants came to cause trouble more often than he cared to think about. But on the other hand there were berries to be found in the shadowy marshes and no worries save an occasional bush war and the voluntary tax for the placation of the Great Serpent.

Now, according to the vision of the dream, he was

to plant a kind of grain in the mud of the river bank, and he was to give up war and hunting and fishing while he sat quietly and watched what magic might develop therefrom.

He had great misgivings about the success of so silly a venture but one does not go contrary to the wishes of the serpents that control human destiny. So he arose and said good-by to his family as he had been directed.

"Where are you going?" demanded the woman his wife.

"I am going down to the great river," said Dak. "I do not know exactly where it is but I shall find it as the dream said I should. And there I shall plant a grain and I shall sit endlessly on my heels to watch it grow."

"That sounds like an occupation for which you have manifest talent. But what is to become of us?"

"I am sure I don't know," replied Dak truthfully. "There are many things that could happen to you before my great mission is accomplished. The tigers and elephants are so numerous hereabout. But of course that concerns you more than it does me. I shall be sitting on my heels waiting for the fulfillment of the magic I have started and I shall frequently think about you."

"And after the completion of this juju, what will you do then? Will you come back?"

"No, I don't think I shall come back. It has been revealed to me that I am to take a stranger to the palace of the Great Naga, son of the moon and monarch of the snakes. And after that I probably shall marry a princess and become rich."

The woman his wife set up a great wailing.

"Dak," she informed the interested neighbors, "is going away to work magic and marry a princess. And he is going to plant a grain and sit on his heels watching it grow and something terrible is sure to come of that. I have no faith in these newfangled notions."

The neighbors were duly sympathetic. They realized that her loss was great. For Dak had been one of the handsomest men of the region when he took the woman to be his wife. He was small enough to get through the dense parts of the forest with great ease. His eyes were hardly large enough to be noticeable which made him something to look at among the big-eyed men of the tribe. And he knew where the best berries were to be found in the greatest profusion. The woman had been very proud of her man and now he was leaving her. It was very sad.

However, the woman was a good worker. She could weave mats out of palm leaf and carry water and bring wood for the fire, and once she had wounded a tiger in a fair fight. So somebody married her. His name is not recorded.

KING KAMBU AND THE SNAKE LADY 91

Dak went out through the forest and traveled for many days till he came to the great river. There he discovered the grain and planted it as he had been instructed. After that he sat down on his heels, a process in which he required no instruction.

After a long time the grain sprouted and grew like jungle grass. And after another long time it headed out and turned yellow. Dak cut it down.

What to do next was a puzzle. The dream had said nothing about disposing of the products of this magic, and, come to think about it, the magic didn't seem to be very important.

At this juncture he looked up from his work and saw standing behind him a sad-faced man who, instead of baring his skin to the sun as the gods had intended it to be bared, was encased in something that might be matting except that it was very white and very soft. He was further wrapped in some shining stuff that seemed very hard and was unlike anything that Dak had ever seen before.

"If this is what has been produced by my magic I can't say much for it," observed Dak. "Something must have gone wrong with the charm or you wouldn't come burdened with a lot of coverings like that. Who are you anyway?"

"My name is Kambu," replied the shining stranger. "I am a prince of the Arya Deca, and Siva, the great god, is my father-in-law."

"He may be your father-in-law," admitted Dak. "I never heard of him, but of course he may belong to some other tribe than ours. However, you are mistaken about his being a great god because I have been instructed in such things by the best juju workers of our vicinity. The great god is the son of the moon and king of the Nagas whose name I shouldn't dare to repeat even if I remembered it."

The stranger seemed unimpressed. He was looking at the little bit of grain in Dak's hand.

"What have you there?" he inquired.

"Magic," replied Dak. "I was instructed in a dream to do certain things on this spot and this is the result of it. I am not as disturbed about it as I might have been. I have squatted on my heels for several rounds of the moon, but then if I hadn't come here I should have been squatting on my heels for the same length of time anyway. So it all comes to the same thing. What shall I do with the stuff, throw it away?"

Prince Kambu, the shining one, shook his head.

"No," he said. "It is more potent magic than you suspect. All the world about here is sere and desert. The gods have been angry with it for a long time. In my own country the hot winds have withered everything that the people might eat and all are dead including my beautiful wife whom Siva, the great god, gave to me."

"He isn't the great god," Dak reminded him, impatiently. "I thought I made myself clear on that point. The great god is King of the Nagas and the lesser cobras. He . . ."

"Let us continue the theological argument some other time," suggested Kambu. "The point is this. I have been wandering far from my native land in search of another where the breath of the angry destroyers would not make a desert of the countryside. And here it is. I can look at the magic you have made here and I can look into the future and see a nation growing up here in this valley—a nation with great palaces and temples and lofty towers."

"What are all those things?" politely inquired Dak. "You don't seem to speak the same language I do."

"You shall learn in good time," Kambu told him. "I intend to stay here and teach you and all the other naked oafs of the neighborhood how you can make use of the gifts that the gods have showered upon you. This magic you have wrought is no stranger to me. I saw much of it before the hot winds came down and slaughtered my kingdom. It is called Rice."

"What does one do with it?" pursued Dak, convinced now that the stranger was a little mad.

"One eats it," explained Kambu.

And that proved the point in so far as Dak was

concerned. Why in the name of all the sacred cobras should one bother to eat this stuff when he could find plenty of berries in the forest? He began to regret the impulse that had led him to obey the command given him in the dream. He might have stayed at home while his wife got berries and wove matting and cut wood and made fires. However, he felt no animus toward the gods. The rest had done him good.

"Let us talk now of this unnamed god who is the son of the moon and the monarch of the snakes," said the stranger. "Tell me about him."

"I don't know that it is proper to talk about him," said Dak. "But on the other hand this is a very special case and one can not stick too closely to the rules when he is this far from advice. The King of the Nagas lives north of here by a great lake. He lives in a vast cave where there are thousands of shiny stones and he is totally surrounded by his courtiers, who are cobras as big as pythons with seven heads that branch out like veins in the banyan leaf to make a fan. He is very powerful, and he and his people own all the great wood you see behind me and all the valley beyond here. We are allowed to live in the forest because we are a pious people who have always worshiped the snakes."

"In that case," answered the stranger, "I had better see this god. Take me to him."

Dak was on the point of refusing. Not within the memory of his people had any mortal dared to visit the home of the gods. It was a country that he had heard described—a stony country beyond the great lake and beyond the forests. Not a tree nor a shrub grew there and the sun beat down in a continuous flame. Once, so the doctors of magic declared, a man had penetrated this country and had loved to tell about it. But the messengers of the cobra had sought him out even in the depths of the forest and had killed him. A cobra had bitten him,—thing unprecedented among these forest dwellers,—and he had died of a little thing like that.

Then, just as he had opened his mouth to tell the stranger that he would have no time to lead such a stupid expedition, he remembered the rest of his dream. Somehow it had slipped his mind during the long rounds of the moon while he was squatting on his heels. He was to lead a prince to the court of the serpents and he was to marry a princess and be a great chief.

"I was just thinking of going up there myself," he said. "I have been praying to this god a long time and have never seen him. We'll start right away."

So, after many days, Kambu and Dak came to the land of rocks beyond the great lake and beyond the forest where the monarch of the Nagas dwelt in halls of crystal beneath the ground. The bare skin of the forest dweller shriveled under the blistering sun and he began to regret once more that he had ever sought to dabble in magic.

There could be no doubt that a god dwelt in this place. No mere mortal could stand the heat. Back in the forest it was hot enough but the sun never penetrated to the depths where Dak had built his little house. He remembered the little house and the ease of living in it. They came to the entrance of a cave, and Dak collapsed in the shade.

"I shall go no farther," he said. "After all, I have had very little dealing with gods. You can go in and transact your business, and I'll stay here until the sun goes down. After that I think I shall go home."

Kambu, who apparently had journeyed under the sun before, showed no ill effects from the journey. He still seemed eager to meet the King of the Nagas and without further argument he entered the cave.

He wandered down a long cool passage where crystals rose up from the stone floor and festooned the walls and hung in spear-points from the top of the gallery. All about him were hissing sounds but he could see nothing.

The passage opened into a large chamber where the crystals were more numerous and made a dim light of their own. In a moment Kambu was surrounded by hissing serpents each of which lifted seven heads in a fan to look at him more closely. And

KING KAMBU AND THE SNAKE LADY 97

the largest of the serpents spoke to him in a terrible voice.

"What do you mean by invading the land of the Nagas?" he inquired. "What excuse have you to offer before you are put to death?"

"I came to ask help," replied Kambu simply. "I am Kambu Svayambhuva and in my own land of the Arya Deca I was a king. Mera, the beautiful, foster daughter of Siva, the great god, was my wife. But I have been in great trouble.

"Siva, the Destroyer, had one of his whims and blotted out the crops in my land and my people died. Even Mera was taken back into the bosom of Siva and I was left alone in a great desolation. So I wandered on toward the east, across high mountains and across desert plains, until I came here to the great river that runs through your forest, and there I found a magician named Dak with a talisman in his hand which is called Rice. I should like to stay here and use this talisman to rear up a nation of servants to the high gods, but if you do not will it you may kill me because I am unable to go farther."

The King of the Nagas considered the matter for a long time.

"Well," he said, "for many centuries I have been put to the work of being god for this region and a thankless task it is, let me tell you. I've heard about you and your wife, and although Siva, the Destroyer, has no jurisdiction over immortals like us I have always heard him well spoken of.

"In addition to that I have a daughter who saw you on your way here several days ago and made up her mind to marry you. All the rules indicate that you ought to be put to death but for the sake of peace in my own household I shall have to overlook your social error in coming here. We shall make a marriage for you. You as a mortal can not take our shape, but she will not mind taking yours and in her human appearance she is said to be even more beautiful than she is as a Naga. I shall look with interest on your experiment of building a nation. . . . As for your magician, bring him in. I shall find a new wife for him and reward him suitably for responding so readily to the charm my daughter put upon him. Usually she is quite second rate as a wonder worker."

So Kambu married the Princess of the Nagas and settled down in the valley of the great river to make a new kingdom. His people were called the race of Kambujas, the sons of Kambu, and eventually that name was distorted by the tongues of aliens into Cambodge or Cambodia.

In its essentials that is the native legend of how the Angkorean kingdom got its start in the valley of the Mekong. Admitted that the dialogue may not be entirely accurate, admitted also that the existence of serpentine demigods called Nagas is open to serious question, none the less, there is a faint hint of historical significance in this fairy-tale.

To begin with, it tells of how an Indian prince came to this corner of Asia after the blight of drought and famine had ravaged the land of Arya Deca as indeed it does to this very day. His name may or may not have been Kambu. It is just as likely that Cambodia took the name of one of its own myths as that it was so christened in honor of its first king. But whatever the authenticity of detail, the story indicates that ancient tradition in the valley of the Mekong ascribed the culture of the Khmers to an Indian origin.

Kambu may have been one lone prince as described, or he may have been an allegorical type representing, in the figurative literature of the Khmers and their descendants, a great movement of people.

That the tradition of the Nagas was as firmly grounded in the people as the tenets of Brahmanism is evidenced in the motif of seven-headed cobras to be found in the balustrades of all their works. The "small-eyed people who worshiped snakes" were undoubtedly the aborigines of the region.

The monuments about Angkor, the inscriptions over which archeologists have labored for sixty years, and the texts of old Cambodia preserved in Pnom

Penh tend to show that the story of Kambu for all its resemblance to a reversed form of "Beauty and the Beast" must have come close to the truth. And why should not the history of the Khmers be told in a fairy-tale when Angkor itself is a myth that somehow became petrified.

CHAPTER IX

WHO WERE THESE PEOPLE?

THE FOUNDATIONS OF THE MYSTERY

OUT of the sunset with faces toward the blue hills of the East marched a people—the kings with their elephants, the priests in their golden carts, the warriors on horseback, and the lame and the sick and the halt and the blind and the otherwise inconsequent with nothing at all save a great hope and burning feet. They poured in a sluggish brown eddy over the arid wastes of the lowlands. Chanting their hypnotic hymns, they plodded along roads whose dust was white and dry as a Yogi's ashes. In millions they clambered up the blistered foot-hills and over crags as sharp as dragons' teeth to pit their nakedness against the snows of the mountain passes. Endlessly they came down over the foot-hills. Recklessly they thrust themselves against the might of broad rivers. They crashed through the darkness of matted jungle lands. And behind them a trail of whitening bones marked their progress for hundreds and hundreds of miles.

Out of the land of Arya Deca they came—across the foot-hills of the Himalayas, across the sources of Mother Gunga, the sacred river, across the mysterious wilderness of Upper Burma and across the land of the Thais which is called Siam, and so at last to the Golden Chersonese. Women who were fair when they turned eastward out of India were wrinkled and old and praying for death before they came at last to the valley of the great river. Mothers died with the warmth of the firelight in their eyes because they knew that their children would grow up in a land of plenty where there would be no drouth. Children were born by the side of that unmarked road. Some of them lived. Some added their mite to the terrible debris over which the vultures hovered so constantly.

A whole people started on the long trek into the wilderness. . . . The young and the old, the sick and the well, the graybeards and the beardless ones. But only Youth remained in the ranks. . . . Youth lean and naked and hollow-eyed and haggard but still resilient, still able to look toward the stars . . . when the last camp was pitched in the unnamed country of the East. Only the strong had come to look upon this promised land and to lend their strength to the founding of a new nation.

Such is the archeologist's version of the story of Kambu and the Nagas. A vivid picture of a social eruption such as the world saw frequently in the days when communities were isolated and famine was an imminent peril, it may lack something of the convincing quality of the old Cambodian narrative, but it has at least the merit of tangible evidence. It has been pieced together, a mosaic of infinite minutiæ—the tablet of a king, a broken stele, a note of dedication on the wall of a temple, a picture carved in stone. It has ignored legend on the ground that such testimony is not to be trusted. But for all its atmosphere of veracity it is not yet history—nor complete.

Whoever the Khmers were . . . whatever happened to them . . . wherever they went . . . they left behind them inscriptions in an alphabet derived from the Sanskrit, an alphabet similar in all respects to the one which immediately preceded that now in use in Madras in southern India. Archeologists needed no such talisman as a Rosetta stone to read them. And even without this evidence any tyro ethnologist would have been able to trace a Hindu influence in the images of the gods who came to their twilight in the crannies of the crumbling temples. Whatever the raw material out of which the Khmer civilization was forged, it had in it the metal of learning brought into Cambodia some time before the fifth century of our era. The puzzle to which rival archeologists find varied solutions is the manner in which the wisdom of Mother India was transported.

The culture of Cambodia was tempered by indigenous thought, just as the architecture of the Hindus reflected the influence of the "little-eyed men who worshiped snakes," before it became the new and virile thing that produced Angkor Vat. After sixty years of study and argument the derivation of the parent race of the Khmers is still open to discussion.

Monsieur George Groslier, curator of the museum of archeology at Pnom Penh, and probably the foremost authority on Cambodian antiquities, believes that the stock which developed the Angkorean civilization was aboriginal in Indo-China, or that at any rate it came into the district far in advance of the so-called Brahman invasion.

The theory of a great migration out of north India and across Burma and Siam has had the support of innumerable authorities who cite similar movements in the Mesopotamian plain and farther Asia to show how frequently such things occurred. Other archeologists, agreeing that there may have been a general migration, have pointed out the Khmer alphabet to show that the source of the movement was not north India but Madras . . . that the yearning progenitors of Angkor journeyed first by boat through the Straits of Malacca to Java and there lingered a while before moving onward to the valley of the Mekong.

That there was undoubtedly some connection other

than a mere relationship of ancestry between the Khmers of Cambodia and the temple builders of Borobudur and Prambanan in Java will be seen later. That a whole people, moving as a unit, had a part in establishing this connection is open to debate. The United States of America may be cited as an example of how a few small colonies may expand to make a nation of tremendous size and importance in a single century, without involving any wholesale transfer of peoples except as individuals.

There is a growing belief, thoroughly logical in its foundations and supported by considerable legend, that India's conquest of Cambodia was intellectual rather than physical—that a few Brahman missionaries came to Indo-China and obtained the mastery of the natives through their superior wit. On the dubious aboriginal stock they grafted the ancient learning of India and so arose a civilization as distinct from the parent culture as Saigon is from Paris.

The new people flourished, gained strength and moved like another Assyria into the North to get the slave labor necessary for the accomplishment of their grandiose building plans. They erected mighty cities—not only Angkor Thom, best known of their capitals, but other towns of brick and stone—all across the peninsula.

They had an immense priestly class, as witness

their scores of shrines. They had a written language. Their bas-reliefs show that they knew something of music. They were probably the greatest engineers of their time. They must have had a remarkable guild of artisans, otherwise the intricate carvings of the Bayon and the royal terrace of Angkor Thom and the pyramid of Angkor Vat can not be explained. Their culture was at least the equivalent of that of the people who built Westminster Abbey and Notre Dame, and it was founded earlier. Their heyday was reached while stupid barbarians were still flowing over the frontiers of western Europe to batten on the dead bones of Rome. Their capital was the finest and wealthiest in the Orient. It was the largest in the world. Imagine these people as they were and one despairs of solving their mystery. They walked out of Angkor and died.

Monsieur Groslier offers many proofs that the Khmers were in no way a different race from the Cambodians who now inhabit the region. His photographic studies of Cambodian types, compared with the images of the bas-reliefs show that in physical appearance, at least, the modern dweller in the valley of the Mekong is the counterpart of the Angkorean. All of which does not seem to change the real puzzle. The Cambodians may be the inheritors of the Khmer blood but if so they are merely physical shadows of

ANGKOR THOM

The terrace of the Leper King

Here may be the wreckage of the royal palace. Legend is silent and archeology finds no definite clue

a greater people. The civilization that made the Khmers a nation went out like a flame. . . . The blocks of Rheims scattered by shell-fire are the same blocks that made a magnificent cathedral, but they are not Rheims.

If the people of England were suddenly and totally transported from their island to some uninhabited portion of the earth they would still be English. In a few years they would establish an educational system. They would keep alive their arts and sciences and, in so far as possible, their contacts with other peoples. Assuredly they would keep alive their traditions.

It is inconceivable to the modern mind that a culture could move away a few miles from the place of its birth and then expire from inanition. The Khmers tested by any standard were highly civilized. The modern Cambodian comes very close to savagery.

So much for theory and debatable evidence. The world may never know exactly who the Khmers were or what became of them. What they were is carved on the gray-green walls of a hundred temples and a thousand towers. They were a race of builders with an intelligence equal to, if not far in advance of, that of any nation coeval with them in Europe. They were a race of conquerors whose talents in forcing subject nations to serve as instruments in their great projects made them seem brothers of Babylon. And, in departing, they left the world's most astounding collection of monuments to attest to their glory.

Out of the half-light that surrounded the dawn of **culture in Cambodia** one comes to the period of recorded history. As history, the written traditions of that period are still lacking in sequence and credibility, for the myth of Kambu and the Nagas, and other legends of equal merit, seemed like simple fact to these early chroniclers.

Like the records of India and Burma and China these are a naive combination of truth and fancy, kingly boasting and pious aspiration. Sometimes the lines of cleavage between the components are fairly evident. But not always. One may doubt, for example, the magical and malevolent powers of the queen of the Yeacks who took out the eyes of the twelve concubines of Angkor. But in a chapter of conquest narrating the overthrow of whole nations and the enthusiastic slaughter of mighty armies, he has no criterion by which to judge whether or not the incidents occurred as related, or if, indeed, the antagonists ever had any existence at all. Births and deeds of kings are interspersed with the miraculous occurrences deemed suitable in such chronicles, until after a time the student is concerned not so much with the possibility of a monarch having had supernatural powers but quite a lot with the possibility of his ever having had an existence.

It is with some surprise, therefore, that one gropes his way through the hazy shadows of these early centuries to discover that, with or without the aid of the King of the Serpents and Prince Kambu and the lovely snake lady, a kingdom has established itself in the Mekong Valley, and can prove it. There is no denying that in the early centuries of the Christian era there was a working principality in the delta south of the present site of Pnom Penh. Of a sudden the records cease to lose themselves in allegory and make specific mention of this place as Fou Nan. And as one is puzzling over whether this turn toward candor means anything or is merely a trick of the royal historians, there comes verification from an unexpected source.

Chinese record-keepers—the file clerks of their period—received reports from some unnamed envoy to the Kingdom of Fou Nan. And excerpts from his letters were copied for the guidance of future envoys. The files are fragmentary now, but enough of them is left to show that with the advent of Fou Nan into the story of Cambodia the plot of the piece becomes less fantastic and more credible. The Chinese and the Cambodian chronicles agree on most of the salient points.

The envoys came to the king who dwelt in the delta of the Mekong in 228 A.D.—which is important as the first definite date in all the mass of legend regarding the Khmers and their origins.

There is reason to suppose that the settlement of Fou Nan was quite distinct from that of the Tonle Sap region. The chronicles mention a principality to the north under the government of an Aryan ruler and imply that Fou Nan also was governed by a prince from India. Modern commentators believe that Fou Nan came into existence through an invasion from Java. One group of visitors stayed in the Mekong Delta while another traveled east and north to found the race later known as the Chams.

A prophet who is able to go back many years can find plenty to thrill him in this dim vision of a human tidal wave breaking over the foot of Indo-China. Cambodia the mighty was still learning to walk in the crystal caverns of the snake monarch. The hand of India was making odd little figures out of brown warriors who had come up with their wives and chattels from the islands beyond the seas. And the tide of invasion was dividing into two main streams, one turning east, the other west and north. And here were all the components of Destiny, cut up into weird patterns like parts of a jig-saw puzzle. The entire history of the Khmers was spread out there in the delta, but no man was then alive who could read it.

Fou Nan was destined to be an important element in the production of the great nation of the Khmers. The Chams, originally blood brothers of the Fou-Nanese, had another mission. They were to acquire the culture of the Chinese and eventually become the deadly enemies of Cambodia—the instruments of Siva, the Destroyer, in preparing it for obliteration. . . . A turn to the left and they would have melted with Fou Nan and the Kambujas; and, who knows, had they done so, the elephants of the kings might still be marching across the causeway of Angkor Vat and the entire fate of the Orient might have been altered. As it happened they turned to the right and their descendants slept on their arms for hundreds of years in fear and detestation of Angkor—one day to rise and smite it and leave it helpless prey to the mysterious Destiny that was to wipe it out for ever.

CHAPTER X

Buried Treasure

THE HINT OF A POSSIBLE MOTIVE

"And in Yacodhapura, which is the Great Capital of the Khmer people and the finest city in all of Asia, there is a statue of the lord Buddha sitting upon the coiled cobra which is the emblem of that race. And this statue was fashioned out of emeralds so cunningly matched and cemented together that the whole work seems as one solid emerald and shines with a green light so intense that none but the faithful may look upon it."

So runs the legend that one still may hear in the market-places of the East from Keijo to Cholon. "Yacodhapura, which is the Great Capital of the Khmer people," vanished as a social entity so long ago that many of the ancient cities of Asia were young at the time of its passing. What it was and where it was are mysteries to the tale spinners, but its memory persists because it was the shrine of a statue as mythical as the serpent lady who became the wife of Kambu. Sometimes the story is distorted. Sometimes gossip speaking with the voice of authority places the emerald Buddha in Java. Sometimes one hears of it in Japan and Formosa. Disappointed looters searched for it among the ormolu clocks, mechanical toys, brass beds and other amazing junk in the treasure-houses of the Forbidden City.

The Siamese, who are descendants of the Thais, said by many to have been the wreckers of Angkor, assert that the greenish idol enshrined in Bangkok is the only true emerald Buddha. And so go the stories endlessly. One would be surprised were he to find no whispers of them in the echoing vaults of Angkor itself.

. . . It was Yin who mentioned the matter. . . . Yin, still uneasy as he walked under the forbidden arches or stood defenseless beneath the accusing eyes of Siva's four faces . . .

He stood looking across the marshy ground toward the myriad towers that contribute to the chaos of the Bayon. "I have never told you," he said, "but somewhere under that temple are the treasures of Angkor . . . the gold emblems of Siva . . . the emerald Buddha. . . ."

One might be permitted a yawn at this point. The emerald Buddha is at once so omnipresent and intangible. And wonders stale a bit with repetition. But Yin's tale of old Angkor was somehow different from the rest. He told it in the slow monotone of a man who speaks without hearing himself. He seemed to be hypnotized and possibly was. But as he spoke one saw unfolded in ghastly detail the dread cinema of the last days of the Khmers. The elephants were once more charging across the great square. The warriors were on the walls and a powerful conqueror was hammering on the North Gate. . . .

Down from the valley of the Menam in the land of the Thais—down from the hills that are beyond the valley of the Menam—came the tide of spears that had been held back for hundreds of years.

The Khmers had despised these Thais in all their branches and had laughed to drag them captive to Angkor that they might justify their existence in such useful work as hauling rock for new temples. The Thais occasionally had shown unexpected strength and had now and then devastated the northern lands and burned the cities on the coast of the Gulf of Siam. But those were fortunes of war which Angkorean strategy and resourcefulness had always been able to correct.

Recently there had been troubles with the Chams,—just the usual trouble,—little wars with varying successes that fell short of the objective sought so painstakingly by both sides: total ruin of the opposition. If the Khmers had not been entirely victorious in these little wars at least they had not been definitely defeated. So harvests bloomed in the fields about Angkor just as they had always bloomed and kings and priests and dancing-girls trooped magnificently up the steps of the great ziggurat. Angkor Thom was still the strongest and most wealthy capital in all the East—the "city terrible and impregnable."

There had been rumors of a new threat on the part of the Thais—rumors that the clans were gathering in the North as they had never been gathered before—that these tribes of north Siam, ignorant, poor, pitifully equipped and hungry, were fired this time by no such silly ideals as had actuated them in previous uprisings—such abstract notions as liberty, equality or self-determination. This time they knew what they wanted. They wanted loot, and Angkor looked like a suitable place in which to search for it. The Khmer generals could not but admire them for that. This time the Thais were fighting as a nation should fight, for some material object. Purposeless wars, such as those with the unspeakable Chams, were a good deal of a nuisance.

However, there seemed to be no necessity for doing anything about it. The army was a little tired. The elephant supply was a bit low as a result of recent campaigning. The suggestion that the warriors of Angkor take up the old familiar course northwestward and meet the invaders half-way was rejected by the generals. It seemed silly to walk all that distance for a war that the Thais were willing to deliver.

Angkor at that time was a little more battered than it had been a hundred years before. The building projects of the Khmers had languished a bit for it requires hundreds of thousands of slaves to put up a really good temple, and the drain of the wars with the Chams had stopped, temporarily at least, the expeditions that would have brought in plenty of such cheap labor. The cultural level of the capital possibly was not so high as it had been when Angkor Vat was dedicated. But even so the luxurious magnificence of Angkor Thom was without parallel anywhere in the East.

The temple terraces dripped with treasures of jade and emeralds and rubies and precious metals. The robes of the priests were more splendid than those of monarchs in less-favored lands. The belts and tiaras of the dancing-girls were scaled with beaten gold. Golden gods looked down from their niches upon a world of wealth. The palace of the king lifted a canopy of jasper over floors of silver, and strings of rubies draped the throats of the royal concubines.

One day a messenger came staggering to the North Gate with the story that the Thais had invested a city to the north and massacred the garrison.

"If you are telling a lie you should be executed," decreed the general to whom he made his report.

"If you are telling the truth it does not seem fair that you should escape after all your comrades have died." So the messenger was beheaded in Ta Keo as a sacrifice.

The sacrifice failed of its purpose. In two days the elephants of the Thais were crashing through the forest along the eastern side of the great lake.

Inside the great temple and on the royal terrace of Angkor Thom the priests and princes met to take counsel.

"Things are not going so well as we had expected," the king reported. "We had counted on some interference by the gods before the Thais could get this far. They have never come within striking distance of us before in recent memory.

"It is impossible of course that they can make any headway against our brave troops. But, on the other hand, it is best that we should consider all possibilities. If, by any odd accident, they should succeed in breaking through we naturally do not wish them to get all the riches that we have taken as tribute from foemen during so many glorious years. It seems natural that we should start to get the treasures under cover at once and it remains only to decide on a suitable hiding-place that will not be known to too many people."

One of the priests whispered a description of a suitable hiding-place, and before the massed throng of the Thais hurled itself on the walls, all the golden Buddhas and altar furniture and priestly regalia had been brought in from Angkor Vat, and Ta Keo and Ta Prohm and Pra Khan, and Neak Pean, and Bantei Kedei and left in a gallery of the Bayon. The old priest who had whispered the secret of the hiding-place to the king worked for two days carrying the treasures away into the dark halls of the temple through labyrinthine ways that only he could penetrate.

Far in the depths of the central pyramid was a crypt whose existence none but the high priest of the Bayon ever guessed, whose original purpose even he did not know. In this crypt he piled up the wealth of Angkor. Then with his own hands he carried in blocks of stone and built a wall across the entrance. When that job was completed he called upon the king for a detail of slaves to haul more rock and fill up the stair-wells and underground passages. The slaves were put to death immediately afterward and none but the king and the old priest suspected what had become of the treasures when a few hours later the North Gate sundered and the conquering Thais swept into the city.

The king escaped. The Thais found the old priest sitting quietly in the Bayon, and, after cutting his tongue out, they questioned him about the disposition of the temple treasures. They realized almost at once that they had acted too hastily and they left him to die. . . .

Yin's half-closed eyes were seeing all this vividly as he spoke. The hatred of the Thais was in his face, for all that the Thais who looted Angkor—if one may accept the theory that they really did loot it—have been dead hundreds of years.

"And so the treasures escaped them, Monsieur," he declared. "They lie there to-day as the old priest buried them in the crypt, five stories beneath the ground in the middle of the central pyramid.

"You wonder why no one has found them? I will tell you. My people feared to come back to Angkor at first. The curse was on the city. But they did not forget. The secret of Angkor's existence may not have been known to the common people of Cambodia. But the kings always knew of it. The modern kings of Cambodia are of royal blood descended in a direct line from the dynasty of Angkor and they were well educated in the traditions.

"But what could they do about it? Cambodia which had been very rich became very poor. It would have been impossible for a king of Cambodia to organize an expedition of the size that would be required to excavate the crypt under the Bayon. Moreover, the Siamese who are the descendants of the Thais would never have permitted a treasure hunt in a territory which they controlled.

"As you know, the jungle engulfed Angkor Vat and Angkor Thom, and that added to the difficulty of the problem. The exact location of the city itself was forgotten. And now with Angkor disclosed to the world once more the French are in here and they have forbidden private investigation of the temples.

"I heard this story from an old friend of mine who was an adviser and close associate of old King Sisowath. He learned the secret of the Bayon from the lips of the king himself and he has promised me that some day he will come here and unearth the buried treasures. In the meantime they are where the old priest hid them hundreds of years ago, Monsieur, down under the pyramid where Siva smiles."

Well . . . perhaps. In Angkor one does not quarrel with legend of any sort.

There may be hidden treasure under the Bayon. There may be even such a thing as an emerald Buddha.

It is certain that the early French explorers found the temples empty, a condition which they took as evidence that the city had been conquered and looted. That Angkor was the wealthiest city in Asia shortly before the moment when its people disappeared is a supposition based on considerable evidence. That the guardians of the temple and royal treasury should have taken some steps to protect their gold and jewels from an invader is logical.

ANGKOR THOM

Elephants, eating appropriately of the lotus, shoulder through the stone of the enceinte

So one might not be surprised to hear some day that a wandering archeologist had stumbled upon a fabulous treasure trove in these musty galleries. No miracle seems entirely incredible here in the shadow of Angkor Vat. The old factotum of the palace at Pnom Penh, babbling of the golden gods, has at least the advantage of a suitable setting for his tale. A modern who would attempt to find an answer in the sphinx-like face of Siva or in the black maze of the Bayon must wonder if, after all, the ancient's dream may not be true.

CHAPTER XI

Kings and Princes and Little Queens

A Dead Man Gives His Testimony

When the Khmers took their last lingering look at the four faces of Siva and set their tired feet on the long uncharted path that was to lead them to Nowhere they took with them nothing but a hope and a memory of culture. The memory of culture, as we have seen, was lost somewhere between the great lake and the delta; the hope remained to puzzle early archeologists and to gladden the lot of the Cambodian. According to the legend of the descendants of the Khmers:

"In the forests are the ruins of our cities. In the valleys of the rivers and on the great dry plains are the bones of our people. Our kingdom is dust and ashes and desolation.

"But our glory will return. Some day there will come from across the sea a man of a new race to take up the thread of our story, to restore our cities and make Angkor once more the marvel of the world."

The legend to one who looks at Angkor now may

sound like a pleasant yarn invented by a grateful people to lend supernatural significance to the discovery of the lost capital. So important an undertaking as the rescue of Yacodhapura from the nets of the jungle must of necessity have been foreordained by the high gods. What more natural then than a quotation from the gods to that effect? One might smile at the naive simplicity of the legend and point out its obvious modernity were it not for one fact: the story was in circulation before Mouhot started northward through the valley of the Mekong. Since Mouhot French scientists have recorded it in conversations with tribes so deeply imbedded in the brush that they had never heard of the developments at Angkor and still considered their lost cities as they did the mythical region of Indra's heaven and the caverns of the Naga demigods.

The French came into Angkor and began to read its secrets. And Cambodia recalled the old story and saw its fulfillment. These Pale Ones from beyond the seas were undoubtedly rebuilding the cities. They were undoubtedly bringing to the attention of the world the glories of the Khmers. Manifestly one might classify them as the chosen of the gods. The rating of Mouhot and Delaporte and Aymonier and Groslier as necromancers would seem to be pretty well established. And yet there was a magician who came before them . . . a more potent magician who rediscovered and refurbished not only the stone walls and golden pavilions of the capital but something of its glittering life.

Tcheou-Ta-Quan, when he was in the service of the Emperor of China, in 1296, was a conjuror who knew nothing of his own powers. He lived the normal life of one favored by the emperor, did a bit of traveling, a bit of scribbling and was gathered to the illustrious company of his ancestors with suitable modesty. He had no way of telling that in seven centuries his voice would still be echoing in the world and that he alone of all the millions who had walked through the gate of the four gods at Angkor would be able to speak authoritatively on what manner of place was the capital of the Khmers.

Tcheou-Ta-Quan came down to Angkor over the Mandarin road of the East with a huge retinue of camels, elephants, litter bearers and guards, as befitted the dignity of one who represented a great nation at the court of one perhaps greater. He was an ambassador duly accredited and privileged to wander about the shrines of the gods and the palaces of the king. For many years he lived at Angkor Thom and what he saw there puzzled or amused or amazed him. At any rate, he put it all down in a little book that was lost when he died and found again centuries afterward. Angkor was still covered by the jungle when the record came to light. The story of Tcheou-Ta-Quan was seized upon by students of Oriental folk-lore as a highly imaginative fairy-tale and was on the verge of being lost a second time when Mouhot broke through the jungle before the moat of Angkor Vat.

To-day one who would look upon the private life of the shadows who live in Angkor Thom must do so through the astonished eyes of this Chinese reporter. And doing so he will be impressed, as Tcheou-Ta-Quan was impressed, with "glories such as no man had even seen before" and witness the fulfillment of a dream.

Sitting here on the elephant terrace in the shade of a banyan one reads M. P. Pellot's French translation of the old Chinese and instantly slips into the atmosphere of the history written by the Brothers Grimm concerning a city that was turned to smoke and preserved in crystal bottles. One looks upon Angkor Thom with something of the feelings of the prince who found the city of smoke, uncorked it, and stood spellbound while the hazes took shape as palaces and temples and towers and minarets—diaphanous at first, then strong and real.

The magic is the same here. The sun has made a dancing miracle of the Bayon and the great square and the lesser temples. There are misty lights in the spaces beyond the fromager groves. Monkeys are quarreling in the trees at one's back and Angkor seems to be in the midst of a great emptiness. Then comes a voice speaking in an odd accent . . . the voice of Tcheou-Ta-Quan, the sorcerer. Instantly the walls are strong and new again. The gray towers of Siva are now flames of gold leaf and copper. The palaces of the king spread back through lovely gardens toward the step pyramid of the Baphuon. There are people in the streets,—thousands of people,—and marching elephants shake the earth of the public square.

Out in the fields beyond the North Gate are foemen who seem to be gathering new strength in repeated defeat. The Angkoreans so far have repulsed them and have maintained their capital and its riches intact.

But even as Tcheou-Ta-Quan looks upon it Doom is waiting at the Gate of Victory. Angkor was standing as Rome had stood at the crossroads of Empire, still mighty, still confidently superior but weakened by repeated triumphs. Tcheou-Ta-Quan had come just in time to make his observations. In a very short while there would have been nothing left for him to observe.

"I came into the town through the gate of the Five Buddhas."

Thus wrote the Chinese ambassador. Buddhism was strong throughout the East at the time of which

KINGS—PRINCES—LITTLE QUEENS 127

he wrote, and in the faces of Siva he saw the smile of the god he knew best.   Perhaps Angkor itself had

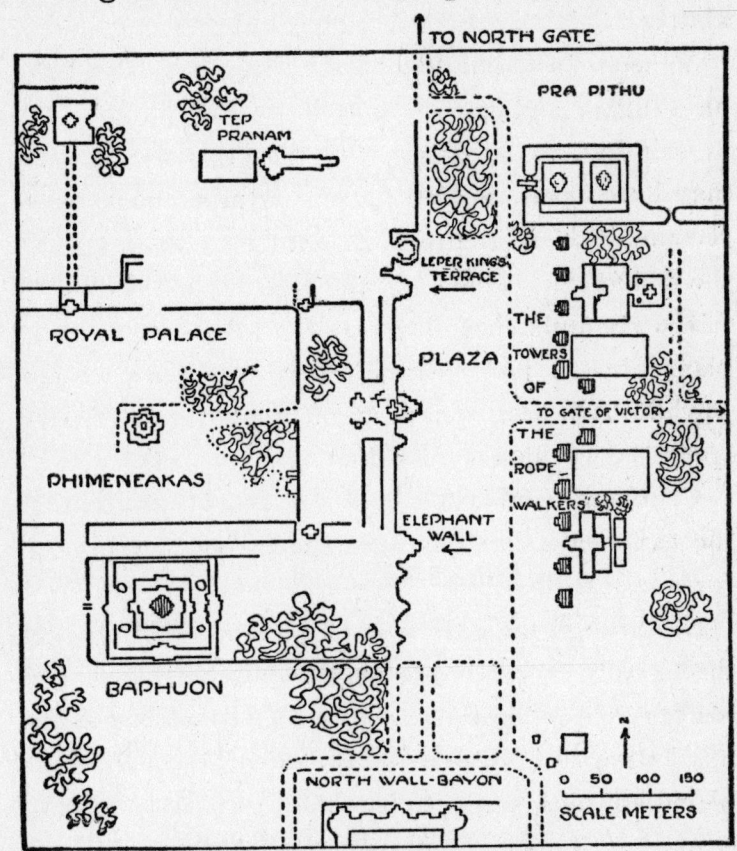

ROYAL TERRACES OF ANGKOR THOM

forgotten the derivation of these stony giants who had watched over the gates since man was young.

"Five great faces of the lord Buddha look out upon

the town," mentioned the visitor. "Four on the faces of the square tower and one of gold on a pinnacle above."

Tcheou-Ta-Quan may have written this after leaving Angkor and memory may have tricked him in the description of the gates. On the other hand, there may have been a golden figure on the pinnacle as he recounts. If so it probably went into the hands of the looters who came when the Khmers had fled.

He recounts that Angkor, for all its wealth and magnificence, had opened the great gates to the world. All who would might pass through them freely save criminals and dogs.

Criminals could not hope to avoid detection at the causeways for they bore the badge of their unfortunate tendencies. Their toes were cut off.

So through the gates passed peoples from all over the great world—merchants and travelers and teachers and ambassadors . . . men-at-arms and the missionaries of strange gods. For Angkor in its placid strength seems to have had an easy-going tolerance of all men and all callings and all creeds.

Along the north and south road these people marched, some to transact business in the marketplaces by the Bayon, some to marvel at the pageantry of the royal terraces, some to prostrate themselves before the Buddhas of gold in the temple whose towers "marked the center of the Kingdom."

The Chinese ambassador never ceased to marvel at the Bayon. He counted over and over its towers "carved with the images of Buddha" and the central spire which rose like a spike of gold over all the city, save the copper tower of the Baphuon pyramid behind the royal palaces.

He describes the frontal terrace of the Bayon as "a bridge of gold" and mentions its sundry carved ornaments including a pair of golden lions. The lions are still to be seen amid the wreckage of the temple and the terrace is still recognizable. But the alchemy of age has transmuted both of them. They are no longer gold. One might gather from the ambassador's account of them that gold leaf played no small part in the ornamentation of the great capital. The temples were probably like those of Siam and Burma to-day, dazzling spears of light against the sun.

The record goes on to tell of minor fanes outside the walls of Angkor Thom, comparing them with the Bayon and recounting their treasures. There is little interest in this part of the chronicle, save where the visitor makes critical remarks about a reclining Buddha whose lotus throne was in the middle of a great fountain that bubbled all the day with clearest of water.

It is in the description of the buildings about the public square that Tcheou-Ta-Quan's contribution toward the reconstruction of the life of Angkor is most valuable. He describes elephant friezes that can be nothing else but the great bas-relief at the south end of the royal terrace, and he mentions that the walls of the great council chamber rose above them.

Archeologists have advanced the theory that the royal terrace was designed to be something more than a reviewing stand for the king and his retinue. Unidentified masses of carved stone found here and there on top of the terraces have led to a belief that at one time the royal palaces occupied this site. Tcheou-Ta-Quan's report supports that theory.

The council chamber, he says, was a vast building whose lofty roof was supported by square pillars ornamented with mirrors. The windows of the great hall had golden frames. The building stood upon a long "bridge" and the term "bridge," as indicated in his description of the Bayon, meant to him a terrace.

"The royal residence and the houses wherein dwell the officers of the court and the dwelling places of the princes all face to the east beyond the great bridge. The great public buildings are made of yellow porcelain. The private quarters of the nobles are tiled with lead.

"Columns of great size support the bridge and are sculptured with many Buddhas (Garoudas?). Long covered galleries run endlessly about the central building of the palaces. They are lavishly designed

ANGKOR THOM—THE GATE OF VICTORY

Here are the last of the Khmers. . . . The frozen figures who sit in the wreckage of a forgotten triumph, clutching the battered body of the Naga

ANGKOR THOM—THE ROYAL TERRACE

Garoudas, loyal to Vishnu their master, uphold the terrace from which the palace of the king has long since vanished

and decorated but show slight attention to architectural design. I have been told that the marvels of the interior of the palaces are almost without number but I have never been able to see for myself as the place is well guarded and the sentries have kept me out."

The sentries kept him out! There is deep irony in that. The king of the Khmers, relying upon boastful inscriptions and pictured records to preserve his name to posterity could not foresee that this inquisitive Chinaman who pestered the guards at the outer gate was the messenger out of an age not yet born, the one person standing between him and oblivion.

But Tcheou-Ta-Quan took these social reverses in good part. He continued to pry into the business of his royal host with the following result:

"The great king has one private wife who lives in quarters adjoining his own apartment, and four others for the points of the compass, North, South, East and West [which indicates that the Khmers in the manner of designating wives at least had plenty of originality]. . . .

"As for the concubines and dancing girls I have no definite information. There are numerous groups of them, each group called by a particular name and placed in a particular status in the household. Altogether I hear that their total is about four thousand but I have never seen them as they are kept in seclusion inside the palace grounds.

"In addition to these girls of the palace are female servants who rank beneath them and number about two thousand. The serving women are not confined to the palace. Many of them are married and have their own homes in various parts of the city. They mark the brow and both temples with crimson and shave the hair above the forehead so that they may be readily recognized as members of the king's household. They have free access to the palace.

"Beneath them are other servants of the king whose work is entirely outside of the palace. These lower servants are strangers and all classes of the people save members of the royal family are not permitted to enter the king's dwelling place.

"The people of Angkor, men and women alike, are very fond of perfumes. They cover their bodies with ointments scented with santal and musk and are careful of their persons.

"The upper classes have many servants—savage men and women who can be purchased for a price and trained to do all manner of things.

"The wealthier families have a hundred or more of these slaves. A household containing ten or twenty slaves is said to be poorly served. The very poor have no slaves at all but that is because they are very poor.

"As a class the slaves are called the Chuang (thieves). They are in poor repute throughout the kingdom and fear to show themselves in the streets. So vile are they that the name Chuang has come to be looked upon as a deadly insult when one man applies it to another even in a quarrel."

The ambassador makes mention of the troubles that had been occupying the warriors in the North. He describes lands laid waste and cities burned, for all that Angkor was still mistress of Cambodia and her wealth still a legend in the courts of China.

The absolute power of the king did not amaze Tcheou-Ta-Quan. In his mention of it he seems to find evidence that these strangers with whom he lived were even more highly cultured than their magnificence would lead one to believe.

"His majesty was the chief of the judiciary and gave a final ruling on points of law. His judgment was invoked even in small matters and could not be questioned.

"At one time the system of punishment was inadequate. Most of the penalties for breaches of the law and social order were fines. In recent years, however, there have been reforms and now a wrong-doer may be flogged. Capital punishment in Angkor is not meted out with ax or rope. Instead the malefactor is taken to a place outside the city walls and buried alive. Habitual criminals have their toes cut off. Thieves have their arms removed and minor infractions are punished by the cutting off of fingers or hands. Gambling and loose morals are not illegal but adultery is frowned upon. A husband is judge of his wife's conduct and he has redress against her lovers. He may take the lover and bind him up and crush his feet between two stakes. If the offender can stand his punishment without murmur he is allowed to go his way. If he makes an outcry he is obliged to turn over to the husband all his property.

"The Khmers have a method for the detection of a thief or a swindler. The suspected person is obliged to plunge his hand into a bowl of boiling oil. If he is guilty his hand is severely burned. If he is innocent his flesh is not affected by the heat and the hand is withdrawn in the same condition as when it was subjected to the test.

"Sometimes there are quarrels between families and it is impossible to judge where justice may lie. So the two families are taken out to the ten towers that stand in the square opposite the palace. They are placed, each family in front of one of the towers and there they sit looking at one another until the gods give judgment.

"The innocent family suffers no ill effects from this vigil. But the members of the guilty family become a prey to skin eruptions or are seized upon by fevers. The gods generally give judgment in such cases in four or five days."

It is worth pointing out here that the chronicle of Tcheou-Ta-Quan is the only definite evidence available concerning the uses of the square towers that line the east side of the square. The Cambodians of Siem Reap refer to them as "towers of the rope walkers" although it is manifestly impossible that any juggler could have reached a rope strung between them. Also they have been called the Houses of the Ambassadors. This designation also seems illogical when one considers that even the king lived in a house of wood and crockery. One must doubt that royal humility had reached such a point that the king would give to visiting envoys a better house than the one he had set aside for himself.

The magic of Tcheou-Ta-Quan has restored for us not only the outlines of the royal terrace but considerable of the royal ceremonial that was enacted there.

KINGS—PRINCES—LITTLE QUEENS 135

"The king of Angkor has recently come to the throne. And he goes about encased in garments of iron so that his body may be protected from arrows and spears. With such garments he does not have to remain hidden inside the palace but may go abroad as he frequently does.

"When he leaves the palace he moves with a troop of horsemen at the head of his column. After the guard of cavalry are standard-bearers with fluttering flags and behind them march the music makers. Next in the procession are hundreds of concubines and girls of the palace with garlands about their heads and candles in their hands. Even in the light of day these candles are burning.

"Next in order are other women of the palace carrying objects of gold and silver—weapons, utensils, and ornaments whose use is sacred to the king. Following them are men at arms bearing lances and shields, the soldiers of the palace guard. In their wake come horse chariots and royal carriages all of gold and drawn by bulls. Behind them are elephants on which ride the nobles and ministers of government and princes of the government. Each rides beneath a red parasol.

"In carriages or in golden chairs or in thrones borne by elephants are the wives and favorite concubines of the king and their parasols are golden.

"The king himself comes last, standing on an elephant and holding in his hand the sacred sword. He is protected by horsemen and soldiers on elephants who crowd closely about him as he proceeds through the city."

All of these things seem to have made a deep impression on the Chinese ambassador. He observes naively that "they surely know how a prince should be treated." He mentions that when his majesty wished to visit places of the court near the palace he was always carried thither in a chair of gold, borne on the shoulders of four girls of the palace.

"The king gives two audiences a day for the disposition of affairs of state. Dignitaries and people alike come and sit on the floor of the council hall and wait for him. Then music is heard inside the palace and men outside the hall begin to make sounds on sea-shell trumpets. Almost at the same moment two women of the royal household step forward and raise a curtain and the king is seen at the gold-framed window with the sacred sword in his hand. All those who have come to the audience clasp their hands together and bow down until their foreheads touch the earth. . . . And so they remain until the trumpeting ceases. Then they are permitted to sit upright again and face the king. If he permits they may come closer to him and as a mark of special dignity may be allowed to sit on a lion skin that is near to him. When he has transacted the day's business he turns about and the girls draw back the curtain again. Then everybody goes away."

So went life in Angkor in those glorious days when the fires were alight in the temples and the elephants marched on the royal causeway.

In some respects its barbarous splendor may seem to conflict with the intellectual progress of the race as shown in its dead monuments. But one who looks back upon it through the eyes of Tcheou-Ta-Quan had better judge it with the mind of Tcheou-Ta-

KINGS—PRINCES—LITTLE QUEENS 137

Quan. The sumptuous show of the court may seem a peacock's parade of savagery to the modern Occidental. But modern Occidentals had nothing at all to do with this culture. A modern Asiatic thoroughly civilized and thoroughly educated would see nothing amiss in it.

It may strike some that the judicial system left something to be desired. The test of the boiling oil might not be considered very good evidence of guilt or innocence in a twentieth-century court even in the Orient. But there is an interesting parallel between these methods in Angkor and the exactly similar methods that prevailed in Europe at the same time.

As for the laws themselves, Tcheou-Ta-Quan's account is sketchy as compared with the ordinances that were engraved on the temple walls. From the time of Yaçovarman there had been a careful classification of sins and a definite and inflexible code providing punishment for them.

Tcheou-Ta-Quan did not know that he was writing his little report for the instruction of Westerners who would not be born for nearly seven hundred years. He wrote merely of the things that had amused him and so, perhaps, he failed to deal as adequately as he might have dealt with a number of those phases of the mystery of the Khmers which are beyond our comprehension.

However, he has enabled us to see the sun tossed

back from the parasols of crimson and gold—the phalanxes of elephants and the warriors and the gleaming chariots—the torches aflame in the public square—and the haughty kings of the Khmers riding down in state from the royal terrace. It is his necromancy that enables us to call back the dead of Angkor Thom on nights when the four faces of Siva are smiling against the disk of the full moon.

CHAPTER XII

Moon Magic

THE RESURRECTION OF THE ENCHANTED APSARAS

For two hours it had been dark. The road outside the bungalow had slipped into blackness as impenetrable as that which enveloped it when fromager roots were pushing through the square blocks of its foundation and tall palms and far-reaching banyans had hidden the sky from Angkor. The lily-strewn moat and the causeway had disappeared, and Angkor Vat itself was back there somewhere in the unplumbed distance alone with its invisible ghosts.

It was unearthly quiet, as jungle country usually is in the dark of the moon. The visitors from the far corners of the earth left the screened porch of the bungalow one by one to lose themselves in the blackness of the lawn and to peer unseeing and unseen into the void where so short a time ago the sun had played at its daily magic with the gray towers

From the night somewhere beyond the moat came the chanting of Buddhist priests in a ritual whose hypnotic tone and rhythm must have seemed familiar to the ancient trees. Even though one knew it at once for what it was, the chant had an eery sound. Nothing seems real in a land of unrealities and the voices of the bonzes might well have been echoes lost in the forest hundreds of years ago and just finding their way back.

Then suddenly out in the black a spot of light and presently another . . . then hundreds of them and a smell of incense. The road that winds about the moat toward the village of Siem Reap has become a comet of wavering flame and the chant of the priests is lost in a murmur of voices that grows constantly louder.

Without warning, there steps into the square of light, that falls from the porch of the bungalow, a figure more weird than the beings with which one's imagination peoples Prah Khan. . . . The figure of a man with hollow eyes—a man dressed in the garments of a king with a crown on his head and a scepter across his breast.

"The King of Angkor," breathes a woman with a laugh that is not entirely convincing.

"Un Roi Fou," comments a French visitor. And there is a moment of hysterical merriment in which more than one startled spectator declines to join. There are enough uncanny mysteries in Angkor without unexplained kings.

This monarch of the shades seems tangible enough

although one's intelligence persists in rejecting the idea. He is clad in a yellow robe something like that affected by the Buddhist bonzes. But resemblance to the priestly costume ceases with the color. This robe is bordered with a strip of red material and festooned with flowers.

The crown which a moment ago looked like one of the carved tiaras of the bas-reliefs now seems to be a frame of wickerwork through which orchids are twined. The scepter, too, loses its illusion to become a rod of bamboo with a poinsettia at the end of it and the myriad rings that shine on his majesty's brown hands have a dubious glitter when one comes close to them.

"The King of Angkor," it appears, is an old familiar figure. There is a story that during the war he was a soldier in France and returned to the great silences of the Cambodian jungle mentally wrecked by this super-service to Siva, the Destroyer.

Now he wanders about the temple, sleeping in its shrines, offering his own insane prayers to its departed gods. Food is given him by attachés of the bungalow or by simple women of Siem Reap who know he is demented but can not be sure that his claims to royal lineage are false. And he acccpts all donations with the detached and dignified air of a monarch receiving taxes.

And so he stood there this night by the edge of the

moat looking off into space and paying no attention to the laughter of the visitors, while the column of flame on the village road came nearer and nearer and a bluish glow, silhouetting the towers of Angkor Vat, heralded the rising of the full moon.

A moment later and the road was filled with torches . . . simple things made of aromatic resins wrapped in dried palm leaves and borne in the hands of bright-eyed little boys, most of whom were naked.

"There is to be a dance to-night," observed the French road engineer, whose practical interpretation of the scene seemed strangely out of place. "The girls come up from Siem Reap to perform in front of Angkor Vat. . . . They are not very good dancers. . . ."

Whether or not they were good dancers meant nothing to these who looked out upon the field of torches. The little boys left the road to take up a semicircular line about the front of the bungalow, spilling over the lawn like the advance of a prairie fire. When halted, they made a hedge of flame through which one was conscious of their wide-open, peering eyes.

A loose-headed drum was beating erratically somewhere in the background and natives were passing up the road out of Siem Reap in groups of three and four, amorphous shadows against the black. The mad King of Angkor stood aloof from the throng taking notice of it only now and then when he shouted an imprecation at one of the torch-bearers. He was treated with a certain deference even by the small boys, perhaps because of the drama that invested him, perhaps because the daft are looked upon as children of the gods by all simple peoples.

The small boys took folding-chairs from a pile at the side of the hotel and presently were on the march again northward, toward the causeway whose cobra balustrades were emerging from the gloom as the rising moon spilled its light into the waters of the moat.

One may walk along behind the escort of the mad king and experience all the strange feeling of being a part of a pagan rite. But there is even more mystery in the proceedings if one goes ahead of the procession—past the wide banyan tree beneath the vast green roof of which chained elephants are stirring restlessly, and over the bridge of the cobra which by a trick of light now seems to float between the white sky and the white water.

The moon is well up now and the lace-work of masonry is detaching itself from the blackness of the wall. Presently a wavering light dances somewhere ahead near the great fate,—a will-o'-the-wisp that flares and fades,—an elusive, uncanny thing that one hesitates to investigate in such a place and on such a night.

But one goes on, albeit a bit faint-heartedly—and discovers it to be a joss-stick swaying in a gentle breeze that fans it to a flame or lulls it to an ember. Some votary from the native village has crept up here to make his little prayer to Vishnu who once owned this house, or to Siva or Buddha who later lived in it, or to the great god Chaos who superseded them all.

Under the coconut palms by the lagoon beyond the main gate is a yellowing glow where the bonzes are chanting their chill monotone.

But one crosses through the vaulted gallery of the gate—an eery place with bats chattering overhead—and one comes out on to the sacred way where the moonlight spills down the hundred steps of the temple pyramid.

And it is easy enough now to reconstruct the people who worshiped here. . . . Their ghosts must pass here always when the moon is full and the long stone road is awash with light . . . elephants plated with silver and gold, dancing-girls in crowns like minarets, priests decked out in bright brocades beneath canopies of peacock feathers, and Asian kings in flashing silks with diadems of gold and rubies, and little queens like the women of the temple bas-reliefs, too pretty to stay in their unmarked graves.

. . . The army of little boys is coming across the causeway, the orange light of the torches mixing oddly with the white. Tomtoms are beating and cymbals crashing. A flute lifts up a thin wavering note and presently one realizes with a shock that girls in incredible costumes are trooping across the stone flags . . . girls with brazen minarets on their heads and silver bracelets on their ankles. To the life, in the last detail, the ladies sculptured on the walls of the temple galleries . . .

It is difficult to realize that they are alive and not one with the visionary kings and priests and elephants that imagination has built out of the moondust. But they are real. . . . The one bit of life in all Angkor that does not seem out of place . . . dancing-girls come to reenact the ancient legends of the Khmers and to relight for one brief hour the altar fires of Angkor Vat.

The flame-bearers set down the chairs in a line across the causeway in front of the first staircase of the pyramid, and then, with much milling and pushing that detracted somewhat from their qualities as reanimated wraiths, they took up their position in a semicircle about the area reserved for the dance.

The five towers of the temple rose gray against the disk of the moon. Never had Angkor seemed more unreal—nor more like what it was, the tomb of a nation's hope. The drums struck a crescendo from a throbbing to thunderous volume and then trailed off amid echoes that seemed to be coming from the top of the empty ziggurat. A tinkling melody of xylophone, bells and a pipe rose out of the ensuing silence, and down between the stone cobras came the dancing-girls.

It turned out to be a hazy, hypnotic thing, this dance . . . in its effect something like the No Plays of Japan except that it was performed without a libretto and all the actors were girls.

The weird lighting effects that made these performers one with the phantoms of the Khmers were furnished partly by the moon and partly by the hundred little boys who played unceasingly with their balsam torches.

The flame of the torches shifted and wavered and queer shadows climbed the walls of Angkor Vat. The resinous smoke, fragrant as incense, made a gauzy background in which the spectators became mere shadows. The xylophone ran trickling scales. The pipes squealed their unearthly melody. And the little ladies of the sculptured galleries came down the temple stairs.

In their odd costuming they seemed to be scarcely larger than the carved Apsaras whose resurrection they were attempting in this bit of necromancy. Their faces glowed corpse white with rice powder and their bare feet glittered with silvery rings. Tall conical crowns surmounted their close-bound hair. Their dress consisted of a long red skirt caught up between the legs and tied at the belt and a blue jacket starred with tinsel. Little upturned epaulets and metallic fangles at the hips designated the dancers who took male rôles. Those who portrayed princesses and queens replaced the jacket with a scarf of silk about the breast and dispensed with the shoulder ornaments.

The dance, as in the No Plays, was the enactment of a legend. It was not a dance at all as Occidentals understand dancing—merely a series of posturings, some of them pretty, some of them not, all of them accomplished only through remarkable muscular control. It was a startling thing to see these girls, their white faces as immobile and expressionless as masks, marching slowly through the drifting smoke and into the light of the torches—arms extended, bodies bent backward and feet advancing and descending with a movement almost imperceptible. Students who have analyzed these dances in Pnom Penh, Angkor, Battambang and the bush towns, say that the march step of the dance is closely patterned after the gait of the elephant. Once this clue is given the effect is obvious. It is by no means the least marvelous feature of the dance that these mites of women should be able to copy so perfectly the ponderous caution of the elephant—the slow motion of his stride and his quick shift of weight.

The chief skill of the dancers, however, lies in the control of the hands. The girls of the Angkor bas-reliefs are shown with an amazing series of hand positions . . . fingers curving back from the palm until they almost touch the wrist . . . arms in an arc that is explainable only on the supposition that the model of the Apsaras had double-jointed elbows. At a first glance the temple sculptures might be classed as caricatures, and a superficial critic might suspect that the artist had exaggerated detail merely to emphasize the Angkorean ideal of grace.

But these living Apsaras from Siem Reap whose only relationship to the sculptures was that of similarity of costume were able to do all these seemingly impossible tricks. Every movement of the friezes was accurately reproduced. . . .

The coryphées went even a bit farther than they might reasonably be required to go in maintaining the traditions of the old Hindu dance plays. They imitated something that was undoubtedly a defect in the bas-reliefs. The carvers of Angkor, like those of Egypt, were efficient in their picturing of all the human body except the feet. They never acquired the technique of showing a foot except in profile and so the ladies of the decoration are all box-ankled or pigeon-toed.

The modern dancers probably know nothing about art and its limitations but they are faithful to their

THE DANCE ON THE TERRACE

Mythic characters of Old Cambodia come down the causeway through the moonlight as the girls of Siem Reap go through their classic posturing

ANGKOR VAT

Were the kings of the Khmers to come back from their ashes they would recognize in this highly conventionalized grouping of princes and princesses and yeacks the same dances that were performed on the temple steps nearly a thousand years ago

models. If the stony ladies are pigeon-toed, then so also must be their sisters in the flesh, and the dance takes on the strange unreality of the puppet show.

. . . Somewhere up on the temple steps old women were crooning. The orchestra sat against the cobra balustrade, hidden by the crowd: a young man with a loose-headed drum—a betel-chewing elder with the xylophone—an ancient with a semicircle of cymbals suspended on a sort of disk—and a half-seen shadow who played the flute.

As the dance went on the little boys rested their torches on bamboo supports and sat back like ebony statuary except when compelled not infrequently to rise, remove their sketchy clothes and stamp out fires started by the resin sparks. Other children were clustered about on the backs of the little stone lions that guard the causeway or on the snaky lengths of the balustrade. Men smoking cigarettes and women down whose chins dripped the red hemorrhage of betel came and went from the shadows of the background as the flames staggered on the torches. And behind all rose the silhouette of Angkor against luminous cirrus clouds and the white face of the moon.

The dance had nothing seductive in it. The themes were all from Hindu mythology portrayed by a series of pictures rather than through any continuous movement. The music was monotonous but carried a melodic theme and was in a syncopated rhythm not at all difficult to follow.

In native theaters where the companies have a large repertoire, performances sometimes start early in the morning and go on and on indefinitely. Any night at any hour in Pnom Penh one may hear the ripple of the xylophones and the muffled sobbing of the drums.

Here the dance starts, as it should, with the dramatic rising of the moon and it continues for about two hours.

The pieces vary in character and number of principals as do the legends they portray. Here is a sample of the scenes produced by the little ladies of Angkor:

The Princess Butsomali obtains permission from the king, her father, to take a walk. She wanders with elephantine step into a garden and there encounters the Prince Prea Somut. The Prince Prea Somut is overcome with love for her—which he indicates by stretching out his arms in the certified gesture for violent passion. She does not seem moved. So he kidnaps her—which is to say, he seizes her by the arm and moves with her slowly out of the circle which is the stage.

Enter a group of terrified servants, searching for the Princess, and the King Kulchak whom they in-form of the kidnaping. The drums indicate his anger as shrill-voiced old women recite a summary of his thoughts. He summons his army,—some eight girls dressed as princes,—and the entire array moves off with a quickened step intended to denote the movement of horsemen.

A new scene unfolds. Prea Smut comes in with the stolen lady and the audience is informed in Cambodian that the pair now have reached a mountaintop where lives Vekean, an amorous giant.

As if to prove this advance information Vekean arrives. He is instantly recognizable as a giant inasmuch as he wears the mask of the Yeacks—a blue false face with protruding eyes and teeth. He casts Prea Somut into a deep sleep and makes the gesture of violent passion toward the Princess Butsomali. She realizes for the first time that she is in love with her kidnaper and she makes vain efforts to arouse him. Love is such a funny little thing even in the classic dances of the Hindus! She fails to get any response from her beloved, but she finds in his hand a magic wand and with this she calls several other Yeacks who kill Vekean, the Amorous, before he has got well started with his wooing.

Prea Somut awakens. The Princess tells him of her love although she stands about two feet away to do it. . . . The flight from the irate father Kulchak continues.

In the next scene Prea Somut meets his own father the King Kanurat and informs him that Kulchak is seeking to recover his daughter with an army.

As a climax the armies of Kanurat and Kulchak meet in battle and Prea Somut enters his capital with his bride in triumph. . . .

Most of the dances are like that: kidnapings, chaste love scenes, fights with Yeacks, battles with bereft fathers, rescues of stolen maidens and triumphant entries. . . .

The dance of Angkor came to an end as weird as its beginning. Fifteen girls who had been moving slowly but perceptibly suddenly stood like statues with their arms outstretched and their fingers turned back as if the charm of the moon that had taken them out of their niches in the galleries had lost its potency. And before one could make sure that they were not actually going back to their place in the friezes, the little boys scrambled to their feet, the torches were lifted up and the flaming procession started back through the black slot in the gate and across the moat.

CHAPTER XIII

The Dancing-Girls

ECHOING FOOTSTEPS OUT OF THE PAST

As if more mystery were needed to complicate the story of Angkor, archeologists have been startled to discover evidence that the magic of the dance which now and then stirs the wraiths of the Khmers out of their ancient dust heaps is older than the city of Yaçovarman, older even than the shrines of carved brick which were the nurseries of this old civilization. Sappho Marchal, who made a considerable study of Cambodian theatricals, traces the entire ritual back to the India of a day before any Aryan movement took its way toward Indo-China.

Some authorities have been surprised to find in jungle towns far north of Angkor troupes of dancers wearing the same costumes, portraying the same characters, and observing the same tricks of motion and posturing that one finds at Pnom Penh or Siem Reap. When first the French were permitted to look upon the royal Cambodian dances in the capital they concluded with plenty of reason that the scenes were merely copies of the carvings of Angkor Vat and the Bayon, and ascribed to them an antiquity no earlier in its origins than the rediscovery of the Khmer cities. The problem seemed less easily solvable when the same performances were seen in regions entirely out of touch with both the Cambodian capital and the region of Angkor. It became plain then that the dances were following an ancient tradition and that instead of being models for a new art the Apsaras were merely representations of a very old one.

Monsieur Groslier proved a connection between the coryphées of the Khmers and those of old India by checking back, piece by piece, the costumes of the Cambodian troupes against those of friezes in temples of Madras and Bengal: double belts about the hips, the method of hinging double bracelets, the filigree work on the bracelets themselves.

Marchal, after a study of the evidence presented by inscriptions and carvings in Angkor, says:

"The dance was greatly honored during the Angkorean epoch. There were two varieties. One inscription tells us that the daughters of the nobles of the realm—even the royal princesses—took part in the dance. They played before many personages. On the other hand the coryphées attached to the temple had a sacred character and their dance was not that of the theater. Moreover, their costume was always the same. The bust was nude and covered with a wealth of jewels and the sarong whose panels

ANGKOR VAT

The little Apsaras maintain their vigil after centuries of loneliness

hung down on either side was caught up at the rear to allow greater freedom to the legs.

". . . There were then two sorts of dancers, the sacred coryphées of the temple and the actresses of the court—the women of the king and of the nobles.

"Something of the same sort is found in our day in India where there are to be found the devadasis and the nautehyn, these latter being the dancers of the rajahs.

"The inscriptions indicate that the dancing-girls chosen for the sacred service were recruited as in our times royal entertainers are recruited from among the most beautiful women of the realm, and proficient in singing and dancing. The earliest representations of them which have been found date from the eighth century.

"The modern actresses, then, are the descendants of the temple girls. They inherit from the profane dancers nothing except a talent for playing the classic pieces.

"The Siamese after they had shaken off the yoke of the Khmer domination and as a result of conflicts which resulted from the sacking of Angkor, took over in part the civilization of the people they had conquered. The dancing-girls were subjected as a result of this to certain modifications. The cone of the ancient Khmer crown was heavy and low. At Angkor among the coiffures of the women which were so numerous, we find only two or three wearing a diadem with a single point. The ornament which fell from the middle of the cincture of the girls of the bas-reliefs is to be found today in the costume of bird-women.

"M. Groslier informs us that 'the velvet fringes and little disks of metal,' which have been introduced into the costume, were brought to Siam by the Portuguese.

"The same author tells us also that the mantle of the dancing girls is of Khmer origin. It is the conventionalized form of the wrap which Cambodian women still wear about the breast and whose panel, lightly thrown, hangs over the back from one shoulder, the other shoulder remaining nude. It is to be regretted that this graceful fashion of wearing the shawl is tending more and more to lose favor.

"These dances, the only living and breathing splendor of the Angkorean period which Cambodia has preserved, are unique. They are the most beautiful conception of an ancient art. They have all the soul, all the ideal, of the Cambodian people. They are exciting the admiration of artists who after having known and understood them for some time have all at once come to know the sum of beauty that is in them."

The most important troupe of Cambodian dancers is in Pnom Penh and until a few months ago was an integral part of the royal ménage. Travelers for generations have written about them and have agreed in classifying them as the living survivals of that civilization which expired hundreds of years ago on the banks of the Tonle Sap. Recently however, these custodians of the culture of the ancient Khmers became sufficiently modern to protest about their working conditions. They went on a strike and appealed to the French resident for a readjustment of their status. As a result they are no longer the dancers of the palace but a sort of state troupe whose performances are under the direction of the protectorate.

The girls of the Pnom Penh Company were recruited from all parts of the realm. It was considered a high honor to a family when one of its daughters was chosen to dance before the king. Socially it was an accomplishment, as an act of religion it was very meritorious, and financially it was profitable to an extent that depended more or less on the beauty and accomplishment of the girl.

Training of the coryphées for the royal ballet was started with gymnastics at the age of eight years. But it is likely that little girls brought down to the school at Pnom Penh had been undergoing treatment for promoting the flexibility of the fingers and elbows since they were able to walk. About Siem Reap today one sees mothers patiently bending back the fingers of their girl babies, massaging elbow joints and muscles in the hope that some day these children may be found worthy of a place in the ballet. Without flexibility and perfect muscular control it is impossible for the girls to make any headway with the intricate movements of the dance.

The royal dancers lived at the palace under the direction of the principal wife of the king. They were kept in seclusion although allowed to receive female visitors, and were considered a part of the harem. They were paid small sums for their performances but had as their chief reward the hope that one day they might become wives of the king. They knew that in old age they would find employment as dancing teachers or wardrobe mistresses.

The Pnom Penh Company, however, is only one of a number in Cambodia. Auguste Pavie found theatrical troupes even in villages far back in the jungles.

Marchal says that these troupes are generally made up of girls of the immediate neighborhood educated for their work more or less haphazard by some former member of the royal ballet. The form of the dance is rigidly adhered to. The costuming, while not so beautiful as that of the king's company, is the same in design. She says:

"The more the girls have occasion to dance, the more proficient they become in their art. This is doubtless the reason why the troupe of Siem Reap, so often called to give performances for visitors to Angkor, is one of the best.

"The life of these young women, accustomed to their work from infancy, is not entirely analogous to that of the girls of the palace at Pnom Penh. They live in the villages and are entirely free from the demands of the customary occupation of Cambodian women. Many of them are married.

"They have all the repertoire of the royal actresses with, often, more liberty of interpretation.

"There are also itinerant troupes which give performances in the larger villages for periods the length of which depends entirely on the enthusiasm with which they are received. These companies are no different from the regional troupes."

ANGKOR VAT

Little ladies of the dance trip down the terraces restoring life to
the cold nymphs of the bas-reliefs . . .

One might find a thought that here in Asia where woman has always been a creature of no consequence she appears as the sole preserver of the spirit of a mighty empire.

For, when they drift through the moonlight and smoke on the terrace at Angkor, these girls are not women of Cambodia but the daughters of the Khmers. Angkor stirs in its grave and revives at their summons. The scenes as Prea Somut seizes his bride, and Piphok-Neak, King of the Nagas, rescues the child of the Princess Chantea, are not of to-day but of the time when the gilded elephants marched over the causeway and the ladies of the court rode to their devotions under scarlet umbrellas. The girls of Siem Reap and the vestals of the temples are sisters. . . . And only the negligible calendar lies between them.

CHAPTER XIV

The Old Crone, the Four Hens and the Unfortunate Thief

WHISPERS OUT OF THE OLD MARKET-PLACE

Sun in the market-place . . . A water-buffalo stands knee deep in the mire left by the recent rains, and white paddy birds roost on his back searching for the animalculæ which he may have accumulated in his wallowing. . . . Monkeys play about in the white road. . . . A coffin-bird, unseen in the greenery, goes on appropriately driving his nails. . . . And the loneliness of Angkor Thom is inconceivable.

Here were a million people, proudest of a proud race. Now there is empty desolation. Here came merchants with silks out of the North and rubies and sapphires from the western coast, plodding along from the North Gate with long trains of sleepy camels and dark-skinned bearers. Here came sellers of rice and salt and fruit and vegetables with their wares piled in heaps in wicker baskets suspended balance-like from bamboo staves over their shoulders. Here came the housewives of the poor and the servants of the rich to drive a bargain for their dinner. Here was the center of the great kingdom and, for that matter, the center of the Eastern world. . . . A breeze stirs the long grasses and makes little whirls of dust in the white road. . . . The coffin-bird drives his interminable nails.

Yin looked out toward the shimmering distance, the odd light of his uncanny second-sight in his half-closed eyes.

"All the people out of the old stories are here," he said. "I knew them all before I ever saw Angkor and now they seem like old familiars. The legends have kept my people alive."

And there seemed to be some truth in that.

Dorgeles, the French author who passed through here some years ago, voiced the regret that Angkor was a place of death without ghosts. Any one with imagination, he said, could repopulate the arena of the Colosseum at Rome with the glorious figures of an antiquity that tradition has kept alive for us, whereas imagination stood balked before the silent halls of the Khmers. Ruins are fascinating only inasmuch as they are the work of man and intertwined with his destiny. Without legend the great square of Angkor Thom is merely a sun-swept open space among the trees and man has no part nor interest in it.

"There lived here once an old woman who had four

fine hens," observed Yin with the manner of a savant who has just translated a difficult inscription. "I do not remember her name but it probably is of no consequence. She lived here and she owned the four chickens—the legend is quite definite on that point.

"Of the four only one possessed the talent for the laying of eggs."

One might marvel at the manner in which this sprightly bit of information had been preserved to posterity when so many other things concerning the Khmers and their life and works remained in obscurity. But legend is like that.

It is concerned not so much with the glories of kings as with the qualities of inglorious hens. Kings might chisel their well-edited records on the massive walls of temples, whereas barnyard fowl and the poor old women who owned them must live and die unknown and unsung save for the kindly interest of the tellers of tales.

"The old woman took great care of the egg-laying hen," went on Yin. "She carried grains of rice to its nest and drove away the other chickens which would have stolen its food. She loved the other chickens, no doubt. But most of all she had affection for this one that laid the eggs. And who can say that her attitude was anything out of the ordinary?

"Then one night came a thief, for they had thieves even in those days, Monsieur. Some of these thieves

OLD CRONE, FOUR HENS AND THIEF 163

were caught and their toes cut off for the guidance of others. But many got away undetected. And so it was with this thief who came to the house of the old woman with the four hens. He stole one chicken and went his way and in the morning when she came to give the rice for their petit dejeuner she found that her beloved hen that laid the eggs was not there.

"She wept bitterly and was consoled by her neighbors who knew how she had cherished this chicken.

" 'The thief couldn't have stolen one of the non-laying chickens,' she said. 'He had to take the one that gave me the delicious eggs and now I have only three chickens that eat the rice and produce no profit. I shall make this thief pay dearly for what he has done to me.'

"Now no one paid much attention to this threat. Every one thought that the old woman was maddened because of her losses. For how could she take revenge on the thief when she had no way to tell who the thief might be? But she had a plan because she was a wise old lady.

"That morning she came here to the market-place. It was not the same sort of market-place that we have in Saigon, Monsieur, a street of booths and shops. It was more like the market along the river in Pnom Penh. Each day the merchants brought their goods here to the public square and sat about until they had done their selling. If the elephants were drilling in the square they moved their market-place somewhere else—perhaps on the side of the Bayon—perhaps even to the terraces of the temple itself. But wherever it was at that time the old woman came to it and she stood among the baskets of the merchants and began to cry out in a loud voice that she had been very unlucky.

" 'I had only one chicken that was fit to eat,' she said. 'And that is the one that has been stolen from me. For many days I have fed that chicken with grains and herbs that I gathered with my own hands. I fed the chicken carefully after a secret recipe of my own and I had intended to kill it and cook it with a stuffing of datura leaves.'

"When she spoke of the datura leaves every one looked at her for the datura then as now was very poisonous. But she explained at once.

" 'It was my private secret,' she smiled. 'The herbs I fed the chicken made it strong against the poison that sometimes is thought to lie in the leaves of the datura. When a chicken is so fed only the piquancy of the datura is absorbed in the cooking and there is no such delicious dish in all the realm. And now somebody has stolen my chicken and I shall never know the loveliness of its flavor.'

"And she repeated this story several times, Monsieur, so that all who came and went that morning—and there were hundreds of buyers and sellers—heard her explain precisely how she would have cooked the lost chicken with a stuffing of deadly leaves.

"And it happened that the thief who had taken the hen that laid the eggs was one of those who heard. He listened attentively and then he went up to the old woman and asked for more details. She knew at once that he was the thief because she had made it clear that only a specially dieted chicken could be cooked in such a fashion.

" 'Some day I must try that dish,' said the thief.

" 'The recipe is good only when the chicken is prepared in my secret way by the feeding with the cooked rice and special herbs,' she told him.

" 'I shall be very careful to use only one of your hens when I get around to trying it,' the thief assured her.

"And that night he went home from the market, killed the hen he had stolen, and cooked it with a stuffing of poisonous leaves. He ate it and told his wives that the flavor was not so good as he had been led to expect and he chided them for having bungled the directions.

"But he did not continue his criticism very long. Before he could chastise any of the wives he was taken with violent pains and he died before the morning. As for the old woman it is not said what became of her."

As Yin spoke one felt the shock of discovery that

human beings had lived in this town . . . human beings who, for all their godlike qualities as engineers and temple-builders, still found time to worry about the theft of egg-laying hens and to deal with such matters forcefully and relentlessly.

"And there were other strange things done in this city," went on the voice of the Khmers. "Have you heard the story of the youth with four wives and the king's peacock? Very well then. This is it. . . ."

As Yin remembered the matter—and he spoke of it almost as if he might have had a share in it during a previous incarnation—there lived in the reign of Yaçovarman, a Hindu scholar, renowned throughout the kingdom for his wisdom and his insight into practical psychology.

"As a result of his gifts he was followed wherever he went by a retinue of youths who sought to share his learning. He was probably the most successful teacher who ever conducted a school on the steps of the Bayon.

"One of his sayings was widely circulated throughout the land because of its obvious truth: 'If you would marry,' he said, 'take as your wife a young maiden or a widow for then you will have gratitude as a goddess in your house. And do not take to wife an aged crone or a divorced woman. If you do you will live with spitefulness and trouble.'

"Now there was among the pupils of this learned

philosopher a youth who had a doubting disposition.

"'There is too much of this loose talk going around,' he said. 'Here is this graybeard who never has been married to any woman, young or old, widowed or divorced. What does he know about marriage? I intend to make a test case of this.'

"So the youth went out into the town and visited all the women of his acquaintance, making no secret of the fact that he had recently inherited a large fortune. And after some search he found four women willing to marry him. One was young; one was old; one widowed and one divorced.

"'Now we shall see how much of this philosophy is the buncombe,' he observed, and he set out with rare skill to make an experiment.

"The king's palace stood then over on the terrace of Garoudas beyond the Terrace of Elephants. It was a long broad building made of polished wood and tiles of crockery and lead. And it was closely guarded.

"The king had many wives, and the attendants of the palace numbered more than a thousand. But of all these splendors his majesty was proudest of a golden peacock that voyagers had brought to him from the far land of India. He was so fond of this peacock that he kept it in his own apartment and fed it with his own hand.

"The youth in making his plans decided that he

would have to steal this peacock. He knew there would be difficulty in the way of the theft because the palace was closely guarded day and night. Only nobles were admitted to the broad verandas and outer galleries. Into the royal apartment no men were admitted at all.

" 'This is a serious problem,' the youth confessed to himself. 'If I try any of the ordinary methods of housebreaking, such as crawling in through a back window, I shall probably be detected and drawn and quartered. I shall be successful only if I get past the guards some place where they are not looking for trouble. And that seems to be the front door.'

"Next afternoon his majesty rode forth with his escort of soldiers, dancing-girls, concubines and elephants to visit the golden temple. And as soon as he had departed the youth presented himself at the palace gate.

" 'I am a peacock doctor recently arrived from India,' he announced. 'His majesty just met me and told me to come here and see what is the matter with his golden peacock. Or at least I thought he said he had a golden peacock. Am I right?'

" 'You are certainly right,' replied the guard. 'I didn't know anything was the matter with it because I am not allowed to look at it and for that matter I don't think you are.'

"The youth shrugged his shoulders.

" 'It's a matter of no moment to me,' he said pleasantly. 'His majesty asked me to look at the bird and I have come here. If you won't let me in no harm is done although probably you will be boiled in oil in case the peacock dies.'

" 'On second thought,' said the guard, 'I feel sure that the peacock should have attention and a lot of it.' So he led the youth through glittering hallways to the royal apartments.

"The youth looked at the golden peacock, strutting against a screen of black silk, and he gasped convincingly.

" 'I am just in time,' he said. 'The bird is in danger of death. I must take him with me at once to my lodgings where I have the proper methods for his treatment. If I leave him here while I run there and back it will be too late.'

"The guard demurred but speedily remembered the prospect of boiling oil and eventually gave in. The youth wrapped the peacock in a sarong and left the palace.

"That night he took the bird to the house where his four wives were busying themselves in preparations for dinner.

" 'I have stolen the king's golden peacock,' he said. 'It will give some needed variety to our menu. But of course I can not kill it here where the feathers and such would betray me to the watch. I shall take it out into the gardens behind the twelve towers and fix it up for cooking. Have the pots and condiments ready for I shall return in a short time.'

"Then he took the peacock to the house of a friend and placed it in a box where it would be well cared for. On his way home he stopped at a poulterer's and bought a large fat capon already prepared for cooking. This capon he brought to the four wives.

"'Here is the peacock, my loves,' he greeted them happily. 'I can't promise you such delicacies every night. But this night, at least, we shall have a feast worthy of our unbounded domestic happiness.'

"So the four wives dutifully fanned the fire and roasted the fowl on a spit. All of them pronounced it excellent food.

"The next day the king discovered that his peacock was not in the palace. There was considerable mystery attaching to the case. Only the guard at the outer gate could have told what had happened and he wisely refrained from comment. Criers were sent abroad through Angkor Thom announcing the terrible fate that awaited the thief when he should be caught and there was no other subject of conversation in the market-place.

"The youth noticed that his wives were exceedingly nervous. Worry seemed to affect them differently. The young woman and the widow retired to their corners and wove mats without speaking. The old woman and the divorcee made hasty excuses to leave their usual tasks and go into the market. The young husband then hired a friend to watch his house and he himself went into the market to take up his station near his two gadding wives and under the cover of a pile of pottery to hear what they had to say.

" 'You wonder what happened to the golden peacock,' the aged crone said to the nearest rice pedler. 'Well I know a secret that I could tell if I wanted to. I could tell just how you cook golden peacocks if your husband steals them from the king and brings them home. I know from experience.'

"And the divorced woman meantime was whispering something of the same sort to the woman who sold sarongs.

" 'But don't tell a soul,' cautioned the divorced woman. 'If this got out it would make all sorts of trouble.'

" 'I wouldn't think of telling anybody,' protested the sarong seller.

"The youth went home and was told by the friend he had left on watch that the young woman and the widow had not ventured out all morning nor had they received any visitors. Presently the old woman and the divorced woman came home and soon after them came the police. The youth was manacled and dragged across the great square to the Hall of Council where the king came to pronounce judgment.

" 'What is this I hear about your killing my peacock?' roared his majesty.

" 'I didn't kill the peacock,' replied the youth. 'I borrowed him. I'll admit that. But I treated him very kindly and it was all in the interest of science. The peacock is just as good as new and is at present carefully sheltered in a box in the home of my friend Chan.'

" 'I doubt that very much,' replied the king. 'But we shall see. If anything has happened to the peacock I shall tend to your execution with my own fair hands.'

"Guards went to the house of Chan, and, greatly to the surprise of everybody but the youth with the four wives, returned with the golden peacock alive. His majesty looked puzzled.

" 'Now tell me,' he suggested, 'just what all this is about. I was told that you had killed and cooked this peacock and here he is alive and well.'

" 'It is my fault, O king,' replied the youth with the four wives, 'that I am something of a skeptic. I have been the pupil of the great teacher who dispenses wisdom from the terrace of the Bayon and I have believed many of the things he has taught. But I ventured to doubt him when he began to speak learnedly of women.'

" 'No man should do that,' admitted the king.

" 'Very well then, your majesty gets my point. I

heard him discourse on the relative merits of young women, old women, divorced women and widows as wives and I decided to test his theory. I borrowed your peacock, told my wives that I had stolen it, gave them a dressed capon to cook and waited for results. The divorcee and the old woman went out and talked and so betrayed me and I pray your majesty's gracious mercy.'

"'It would be silly to sacrifice an empirical philosopher such as yourself,' replied the king. 'We shall call in your talkative wives and have their heads removed. At the same time I shall make something of a holiday by issuing a similar order in behalf of a dozen old women and thirteen divorced princesses out of my own harem.' And so it was done.

"That night the king and the youth with the formerly four and now two wives sat on one of the balconies of the palace discussing the complications of life in Angkor.

"'Man has lived with woman for thousands of years and knows nothing about her,' mused the king.

"'I should hardly go so far as to say that, your majesty,' objected the youth. 'I can cite my own case to show that occasionally a man is born with intellect enough to circumvent these females and strategy enough to learn their tricks. I have proved, for instance, the danger of wedding old women and divorcees.'

"'You are a bright youth,' the king admitted. 'And for that reason you will make a useful addition to the palace staff. But you will pardon me if I doubt that you are the fine flower of the wisdom of the ages. . . . Most men would refrain from marrying old women just out of an artistic sense, and as for divorcees, they somehow have the knack of marrying whom they will whatever he may think about it. . . . I was certainly glad to find an excuse to get rid of my quota in these two classes whether or not they are, as you maintain, a source of gossip and trouble.'

"'As I maintain,' repeated the youth. 'But I proved the point. The old woman and the divorced woman betrayed me.'

"The king shook his head.

"'No,' he replied, 'that's just the point. . . . I knew you must be thinking something like that. But they didn't betray you. We got it out of the guard with a pair of thumb screws and a Chinese sword.'

"And then they both looked out across the great square toward the smoke drifts that wreathed the dozen towers, the while they pondered on the difficulty of learning anything about womankind."

CHAPTER XV

Pnom Bak Kheng and the Dozen Daughters of Angkor

VOICES IN THE HORROR CHAMBER

About midway between Angkor Vat and the South Gate of Angkor Thom a secretive path leads off to the west of the white road between the battered carcasses of stone lions and shapeless masses of carved rock that once may have been part of a balustrade. The fromager trees clutch at the path from the jungle that adjoins the road, and in passing one must be on the alert or he will not see this area-way through the veils of green. If one discards the impulse to remain on the highway, aloof from the bugaboos of the dark, he follows this path on level ground for only a few feet through the forest verdure and then sees it vault skyward like a flattened ramp on the face of a pyramid. And, climbing breathlessly, he comes to the summit of Pnom Bak Kheng.

There is no reason, of course, why in this region of riddles Pnom Bak Kheng should not have a private puzzle of its own. Every haunted corner of Angkor shares in the general mystery of the Khmers. And here the shadows seem to lie a little deeper, for this hill is like nothing else in the district.

In the first place, it is a natural hill, a butte which steps abruptly out of the flat plain of Cambodia to a climax in the pinnacles of a forgotten shrine.

One would think that this should have been the site of the great temple, furnishing as it does not only the core for a ziggurat but a source of building material. Odd that the Khmers should have preferred to make a butte of their own for Angkor Vat when here was the nucleus of a pyramid already formed. The explanation seems to be that there was a shrine on top of the Pnom Bak Kheng when the architects laid out Angkor Vat, and the inference is logical that the shrine was held too sacred to permit its being torn down.

Some writers have held that possibly Pnom Bak Kheng furnished much of the stone with which Angkor Thom was constructed—that at one time it was much larger than at present and was trimmed down to its present symmetry by ages of quarrying. Others have gone so far as to assert that its presence more than any other factor in the region determined the choice of a site for the capital. The theory is not without its merits. For despite their assets in slaves the early Khmers would logically have sought to place their city near a supply of stone.

Whatever its uses, Pnom Bak Kheng is here, swaggering and dominant even in decay, looking out over the jungle and the gray masses of the lowland temples as a graybeard baron might peer down upon well-dressed upstarts of a younger generation.

The inevitable step pyramid crowns the slope. But the retaining-walls are mostly hidden in forest growth, the stairways are sagged and crumbling, and the sanctuary of the top stage has almost entirely disappeared.

Buddhist ambition rather than time and weather and the strangling forest seems to have served as the instrument of Siva, the Destroyer, in the fate of Pnom Bak Kheng. There are evidences of repair work on the shrine—a motley rearrangement of carved friezes that were dedicated to the Brahman gods—and an attempt to replace the old figures with those of Buddha. If Pnom Bak Kheng is to be taken as evidence, the art of the Khmers had reached its ebb when Buddhism became the dominant religion.

Buddhism is still in active possession of the hill. About midway between base and summit is a little hut obviously of recent origin—and inside the hut is a copper depression some three yards long and two wide representing a footprint of Gautama himself. The footprint is interesting to archeologist and chiropodist alike inasmuch as all the toes are represented as being the same size and the same length. Bonzes who give no thought to these minor realities come here daily to light joss-sticks at the entrance of the shed and to sing their offices as they sing in the heights of Angkor Vat.

One may ride from the white road to the steps of the ziggurat on one of the elephants from Angkor, or he may take the more difficult path squarely up the hill afoot. In either case he will become aware after a very few feet that he seems to be progressing over a vast drum. Pnom Bak Kheng is echoing—resonant—over a great portion of its area. And this is not the least of its mysteries. Whether the bowels of the hill are hollow because of natural caves or because of unplumbed subterranean works of man no one as yet can venture a guess.

On top of the slope remains one lone sample of the high towers that were a part of the central shrine. One enters it to discover that he is standing on the brink of a square crypt that drops away sharply into blackness. And this, too, is unexplained save by the legend, *The Twelve Young Women of Angkor,* a story that any of the Cambodian guides will relate in more or less fragmentary state. However it came to be placed there, the square well is proof enough that the Khmers could have tunneled the hill had they cared to do it.

Auguste Pavie, who made a study of ancient Cambodian literature, relates that when he came to

ENVIRONS OF ANGKOR THOM—PNOM BAK KHENG
One of the sandstone lions decorating the stairs

PNOM BAK KHENG

Pnom Bak Kheng, years ago, the connection of the story with the shrine was fully believed by the natives although few of the details of the affair were known to them. He says:

"I heard mention of the story for the first time when the guide was showing me the cistern under the tower on top of the butte. In pointing it out he told me:
"'Rothisen, the Buddha, our master, was born there. His mother and his eleven aunts were thrown into that well after their eyes had been put out.'
"And that was all of the tale he had ever heard."

Later, in villages well up beyond the head of the great lake where the name of Angkor was hardly known, he heard in all its nuances this bit of magical history of Pnom Bak Kheng which Angkor itself had forgotten. And this is the story:

In the days when three captive nations were marching down the long road from Kok Kher with the carved stone for Angkor Vat, there dwelt in this broad land of the Khmers a poor wood-cutter. The wood-cutting business had been very bad—partly because there wasn't so much wood to cut and partly because nobody could think up any good reasons for using wood.

Transportation was the chief difficulty. The wood-cutter had heard that at Angkor Thom one could get a fair price for wood cut in lengths suitable for fires. But the roads were filled with sweating savages carrying lumps of rock suspended on bamboo poles which they balanced on their shoulders. He couldn't find porters willing to carry his faggots nor enough road space to carry them himself.

"This temple building is going to cause a lot of trouble in this country," he told his wife. "Once people made things out of the trees but now they'll have nothing but stone. You can't eat stone."

"For that matter you can't eat wood either," replied his wife. "And anyway all this talk about eating anything is largely academic. I haven't had any practise for the past week."

The wood-cutter was saddened for people starved to death in those days quite as readily as they do now.

He looked about for the hundredth time to discover some manner in which expenses might be reduced and he noticed as he always did that his calculations began and ended with the daughters of the household. There were twelve of them—all of them good strong healthy girls who seemed to have been born hungry.

"There is only one way out of this," he said to his wife. "We have too many daughters and we'll have to get rid of them. The gods have certainly been kind to us in that we have not been saddled with sons. Sons we might have had to keep. But daughters are something else again."

So he took the twelve children out into the forest where in more prosperous days he had cut wood for the Angkor market and he left them there to shift for themselves.

The story thus far is remarkable only in its resemblance to the tale of *Petit Poucet* by Perrault, and the numerous versions of the Babes in the Wood. Monsieur Pavie points out that the appearance of the story in France followed the homecoming of French emissaries sent by Louis XIV to Siam in 1686. But the same tale with different casts of characters had been in circulation in Europe before that. It is amazing to discover even this fragile link between the empty shrines of Angkor and the nurseries of the Occident.

Neang-Pou, the youngest of the wood-cutter's daughters, led her sisters out of the forest and home again and the distressed father was forced to lose them a second time. The second effort was more successful. The girls were dying of hunger when discovered some time later by Santhomea, the Queen of the Yeacks or Ogres who took them to her castle, and for some reason, known only to herself, watched over them as they grew to womanhood.

The young women were not entirely satisfied with their lot. For all that she had rescued them the ogre queen left something to be desired as a companion, and so one morning they ran away.

Apparently they had profited by their earlier lessons in forestry, for this time they were in no peril of death from starvation. They spent their days looking for edible fruits and berries and their nights sleeping in tall trees.

One morning they overslept and a captain of the guard of the King of Angkor discovered them nesting in the branches of a banyan. He took them with him and they journeyed through forest and rice field to the great city of Angkor Thom.

The world was moving into Angkor Thom that morning, for there was to be a contest of bullock racing in the great square and after that a bit of elephant fighting and some polo. The road north of the four-faced tower of Siva was trembling with vehicles and marching men and women come hither to make holiday. The twelve sisters, who had lived so long in the seclusion of the forest and after that in the corridors of Queen Santhomea, were amazed to see so many people. To them it seemed that there could be no living creature left between Angkor and the four corners of the earth. And the captain smiled at this conceit because he knew that there were many, many more.

Men and women alike were garbed in gaily colored sarongs. They rode in carts painted with red lacquer and pulled by water-buffalo whose horns and hoofs were gilded. Sentries encased in iron that shone bright as the pools in the garden of Santhomea leaned on tall spears at the gate of the god and looked with pleased eyes on the wood-cutter's twelve daughters.

So, eventually, they came before the king. He listened to their story with interest and considered long concerning a proper adjustment of their case.

"You are all wonderfully fair," he told them. "The ordinary rules of judgment do not seem to apply here. It would be impossible for me to choose one from among your number to be my wife. So I shall marry the entire dozen of you." Which he did.

So they lived for many happy months in the apartment of the king, while Santhomea, still anxious for their company although the chronicler gives no good reason for her anxiety, searched the broad land of the Khmers from Battambang to the delta of the Mekong and found no trace of them. They might have gone on indefinitely, living as did all the other little queens of Angkor and after a while dying as the others did to leave no hint to posterity that they had ever existed, but Santhomea was resourceful. And one night up near the head of the great lake the Queen of the Yeacks tried out a new magic that showed her exactly what had happened.

From that time on her only thought in the search for the twelve sisters was one of revenge. She was determined to make them pay, not entirely because they had run away from her but because they had profited by running away,—which would seem to indicate that human nature in Angkor was much the same as human nature elsewhere.

She went back to her castle and tried some new magic as a result of which she was able to take the form of a beautiful woman and have herself transported to Angkor Thom. She presented herself before the king and announced that she was a queen come from afar merely to prove to herself that all the stories she had heard of his grandeur and power were true. He invited her to remain in the palace as his favorite wife and Santhomea languidly assented.

The king became bewitched. It was to be expected that Santhomea in picking out the human form suitable to her undertaking would make herself the most beautiful woman in the world. It was natural enough that her superior powers should have merited her a place as favorite wife. But it was proof of unfair influence that the king should have forgotten entirely the twelve girl wives whom he had recently loved to distraction.

Santhomea remembered them. One day she demanded that they be put away and announced that she would give personal supervision to the removal of their eyes. When you want a thing done right do it yourself.

Santhomea appears to have been like so many

female mathematicians of her period. She had only twenty-three eyes as trophies of her work when the sentence had been executed. But she failed to notice that the count was wrong. The wood-chopper's daughters were taken up to the cave on Pnom Bak Kheng and left there to starve.

They did not starve. Food came to them in meager quantities from one source or another. But they suffered continuously. Sons were born to the unhappy wives one after another. But they all died save that of Neang-Pou, the youngest and most fortunate of the group. It was she who had managed to conceal one eye during the encounter with Santhomea, and because of her sight she was able to get her baby more than his share of food.

The boy, who was called Rothisen, found a way out of the cave and wandered freely about Angkor where his resemblance to his mother eventually caught the eye of the king. Simultaneously it caught the eye of Santhomea. She became aware that she had been a bit too sure of herself in believing all the children of the twelve sisters to have died. And to remedy the oversight she gave Rothisen a note to carry to her castle in the North. The note which was addressed to her daughter gave instructions that the youth was to be executed immediately upon arrival.

Rothisen set out, dressed as a prince and riding a

princely horse. En route he was kind to a hermit. That night as he lay asleep the hermit read the letter he carried to the daughter of Santhomea. And he substituted for it another letter suggesting to the girl that she marry Rothisen at once.

So Rothisen came eventually to the end of his journey and found marriage waiting for him instead of the death that had been planned.

... Rothisen was very happy with Neang Kangrey, his wife. In the lotus atmosphere of the palace of the Yeacks he lived for many months, forgetting his old home in the cave of Pnom Bak Kheng and the women with whom he had spent his childhood. Then one day he opened a door which had been sealed with many dooms by Santhomea and he saw looking at him reproachfully twenty-three eyes. One eye seemed more reproachful than the rest. He realized now for the first time what had happened to his mother and his aunts.

So he took the eyes and with some magic borrowed from Neang Kangrey went back to Angkor where he unmasked Santhomea and restored sight and youthful beauty to the twelve sisters. It is said that the wood-cutter's daughters, who came back to the palace as young as they had been when they were imprisoned, found their husband somewhat aged and crochety. But then everything can not work out as it ought to even in the best of stories.

One can not but wonder just how much historical basis there may be to these stories that are still circulating in Cambodia, echoes of the voice of some minstrel who started them centuries ago. Perhaps one skilled in folk-lore might reconstruct from the affairs of Rothisen and Santhomea and Neang Kangrey some explanation for the hollow sounds in the hill below the crowning shrine.

The sun is dropping into the Tonle Sap whose glint is visible through the thinning trees beyond the old Western Baray and Pnom Bak Kheng stands against a halo . . . mysterious gate to a whole procession of mysteries.

From the battered tower on the summit one may look across the surf of green to the gray-white atoll which is Angkor Vat. Nowhere else in all this district does one realize so poignantly the vastness of this desolation nor the eagerness of the jungle. One comprehends for the first time the grandiose plan of the great temple, its symmetry and its size. It dominates the forest just as it dominates Angkor Thom, a mountain of grandeur yet somehow as unsubstantial as a mirage.

Pnom Bak Kheng's natural shape may have led to its use as a giant "linga" in the service of the Destroyer. It may have witnessed the obscene rites of many a witches' Sabbath in that far day when so many demons of the air and earth and sea were abroad in the land. It may have reddened with human sacrifice or smoked with suttee. And it is in the realization of its past that one is aware of its hoary age.

It belongs to the horror-chamber period of Angkor and it is fitting that its ghosts should be the little blind ladies of the legend, the dark wraith of the ogre queen and the wailing phantom of the child murderer. For all of which, even in its crumbling desolation, it is Angkor's principal monument to Beauty. If only for the panorama of the old Khmer kingdom that spreads out before it, the vision of the temple towers freed at last from the embrace of the trees, and the closely massed ranks of the jungle marching off to the horizon, Pnom Bak Kheng is worthy of its shrines.

CHAPTER XVI

Four Faces of Siva

OLD GODS HOLD THEIR TONGUES

A MOAT, green with algæ and strewn with waterlilies trails a snake-backed expanse to the right and left. Beyond it a wall, dusty and swaggering as the ramparts of Babylon and as dead, pushes up out of entangling lianas and fromager roots and gives the jungle a long straight face of red and greenish gray. A causeway cuts out of the forest to the south and over the water between the wreckage of stone cobras and squat giants who once held them in place as a balustrade. Directly ahead rises the square tower of a city gate and from its eminences four faces of Siva, the Destroyer, leer appraisingly and with obvious satisfaction on the whispering ruin that was Angkor Thom.

It is an arresting thing this gate—typical not only of the Khmer architecture but of the spirit of the nation. "They that live by the sword . . ." Siva rode with the legions of the Khmers when they were the scourge of the North. He was well served in the armies that marched with sword and torch and elephant against the Chams of the East. And he found these people faithful to the end for they made a godlike sacrifice of themselves when at last they walked out to leave the Destroyer here, alone and victorious, in his empty temples.

The exterior faces that gaze so placidly on the visitor from beyond the jungle are as inscrutable as that of the Sphinx. They are neither smiling nor leering. Not even the glaring sun gives them warmth.

But as one looks at them, fascinated, he discerns a certain quality aside from their gigantic size. The face turned to the south—to the ancient road over which voyagers must come to the city gates from the lower reaches of the Mekong—is terrifying in its effect. The east and west faces seem to be dozing or lost in the contemplation of the Infinite. The north face, which looks down upon the town, conveys an impression of tolerance, almost kindliness, and this through no perceptible trickery on the part of the sculptor.

One of the temple inscriptions quotes a king as referring to this capital as "Yacodhapura, the mighty and terrifying city." And one senses a definite plan in the shades of mood expressed in the images of the municipal god. A hostile visage was turned toward those who dwelt outside the favored enclosure of the capital. A hint of friendship was

ANGKOR THOM

Desolation now marches through the east wall of Yaçovarman's capital, where once came the victorious armies with hundreds of thousands of slaves

given to the faithful who looked at the tower from the inside.

At one time these four-faced towers, which are found repeated almost endlessly wherever the Khmers erected a temple, were a source of much puzzlement to the archeologists. At first it was supposed that the god so lavishly honored must be Brahma the Creator but recent study has proved otherwise. The towers which are square, rising to a conical summit, now are known to have been designed as representations of the linga, the phallic symbol under which Siva is still worshiped in parts of India. The faces, therefore, are undoubtedly those of the god whose device they adorn.

Siva was looked upon not only as the deity of death but as the spirit of rebirth. Nature withered at the fall of the year and that was obviously the work of the Destroyer. But almost immediately the grain fields sprouted once more and the lost fertility of the world returned. And this was not the gift of Brahma who had created things in the first place, nor of Vishnu who preserved them. Hence, in the person of Siva were linked the twin mysteries of life and death, and the god was petitioned alike by warriors bent on slaughter and by timid wives who wished for sons.

So it is Siva, all things to all men among the Khmers, who stands guard at the gates of Angkor

Thom, and his aura—intangible and thin inasmuch as the auras of dead myths are exceptionally wraith-like—that flickers in one's path to the North.

Angkor Thom in its day was probably the largest city in the world. In the early ninth century when Yaçovarman was supervising the completion of its walls there was no community in Europe to compare with it. Rome had collapsed and stupid barbarians were still wandering over the western frontiers. There was no London as we understand the city of to-day. Paris was a straggling community still comfortable within a narrow enceinte. France had not yet decided to be a nation. Germany was still a stamping-ground for nomadic tribes.

Angkor Thom in extent and population was the size of Carthage at the time of its fall. It was as large as Rome at the beginning of the Christian era. It had something of the intellectual status of Athens and the might of Babylon.

Its walls which still rise intact out of the moat are twelve kilometers in length and from ten to twenty feet high. Four gates, placed at the cardinal points of the compass, gave access to the town, each in the middle of the wall it pierced. A fifth arch broke the enceinte on the east side a few hundred yards north of the main gate, a triumphal entryway for kings. The city was square and two boulevards connecting the principal gates divided it into quarters.

Angkor Thom gives testimony to the restless spirit of the Asian monarchs in that it is geometrical in plan. It did not grow, as European capitals have grown, out of some haphazard community that acquired population and territory in long periods of undirected growth. This capital was carefully thought out before it was definitely located. Its streets were straight and crossed each other at right angles. Its royal buildings were grouped in a sort of civic center at a point equidistant from its gates. It has none of the crooked corners and slipshod additions of old Occidental towns where cow-trails became boulevards. One does not have to translate its inscriptions to read its history:

"A king came here with an army of subjects and a limitless host of slaves and he built this capital on a site where no city had stood before."

The king was Yaçovarman and this city, before the Sanskrit "Nagara" (capital) had been corrupted by the Cambodian tongue to Nokor and then to Angkor, was called for its founder Yacodhapura. Yaçovarman was by no means the first of his line. As a matter of fact, he was the thirteenth of those monarchs whose names appear in the chronology of the Khmer civilization in the valley of the great river. But he was the first great builder, perhaps the greatest of the great builders. It was he who gave to the

Khmers their incentive for erecting vast pyramids of stone and so, indirectly at least, it is to Yaçovarman that the world owes to-day what little it does know about the culture of his people.

To the five ornamental gates of the city of Yaçovarman, five sculptured causeways fifty feet wide and three hundred feet long stepped across the moat. And here the art of the Khmers took its first great leap from the traditions of the Hindu teachers. The balustrades were unlike anything that the world has seen before or since. The rails were the multi-headed cobras previously mentioned, and the upright supports were squatting giants who held the body of the carved snakes crooked in their arms and resting on their knees. To-day many of these giants have grown tired of their work and have slipped off into the moat. But an army of them remains. Originally there were fifty-four on each parapet, one hundred and eight to a causeway—a total of five hundred and forty on constant duty about the five gates of the city. Their average height—measured from the pavement to the top of the head in their crouching position—is something over eight feet. So in their stone bodies one finds a representation of men who in an upright position would have been about twelve feet tall. These statues are anatomically correct and well proportioned.

Archeologists identify the giants as demigods of

Hindu legend, but their faces, save on the west side of the town, are remarkably human and quite pleasant. They seem to be reassuring the visitor against the dubious welcome of Siva on the gate behind them. On the west side, however, it appears that few friends were expected. Possibly Yaçovarman expected in that quarter the attacks that later came down upon the city along the great lake. At any rate, the western giants are hideous and threatening, poised on their toes as if prepared to leap forward at a given signal and toss their serpent into the faces of the foe.

The towering portals had as decoration, in addition to the heads of Siva, sculptured wings on either side representing triple-headed elephants in deep bas-relief, their forelegs serving as columns, their trunks gripped about sprigs of lotus. The vaulted entryways are about twenty feet high, and markings in their masonry show where once were set the hinges of the gates. The gates themselves were made either of bronze or of wood and have disappeared as the result of looting or decay.

From each of the five towers the straight roads cut into the city to reach a fitting terminus in the group of temples and royal buildings on the central plaza. French artistry has rebuilt these highways without departing perceptibly from their original plan. It was easy enough to locate them, for traces of their curbs were found even among the trees, and hundreds of years of disuse had not entirely obliterated their gradients. The roads were very nearly a mile long and ninety feet wide. Debris of household pottery, building tile and fountain conduits, unearthed along these axes, would indicate that the journey from the walls to the heart of the city was through a region of gardens in the midst of which stood the palaces of the nobles.

The East Gate to-day bears the traditional name "Door of the Dead," and the road that pierces it is believed to have been a sort of via sacra consecrated to religious pageantry. At any rate, the East Gate gives the best view of the Bayon temple rising from its dragon-guarded terraces to its dominating central tower.

Etienne Aymonier, historian of the Khmers, points out that although the objective mass of the civic center is the same no matter what one's point of view, the perspective varies and the terrific ruin of the Bayon as seen from the west is an entirely different thing than it appears to be from the east.

The South Gate, through which one enters Angkor Thom as he comes up from Angkor Vat, is believed to have been the portal of the merchants, and it is probable that the markets were somewhere near the point where it approaches the gray shade of the central temple. It, too, presents an instant view of the Bayon and a perspective that sweeps upward majestically from the feet of the giants to the "stone tiaras of the pyramid."

The north highway comes southward through a region of minor temples and along the public square, an open space half a mile long and one hundred and fifty yards wide, where the Khmer culture held its fêtes, drilled its elephants, massed in pageants to its gods and girt itself for war. This road is by far the most interesting of the four in that it leads past the royal terrace amid traces of kingly palaces, public buildings and the fanes of conflicting religions. But like the others it comes to the same climax in the shrine of the Bayon, "the temple to the great lord Siva, supreme ruler of the world."

Other streets led off at right angles from these principal thoroughfares. One can envision them lined with shops and the homes of the wealthy in the immediate vicinity of the palace and plunging into squalor and slum as they took their course toward the walls. Virtually nothing of this civic life of Angkor Thom has been recorded either in the inscriptions or in the no less easily translated evidence of ruins.

The Khmers, who have left the world some of the most remarkable buildings ever constructed of stone, were primarily a race of woodworkers. Much of their engineering and no small amount of their ornament seem to have been derived from principles that they established when carpentry was their foremost art. And so, even in the days of their glory, the forests gave them the material for their homes. Their temple pyramids were mountains of rock but their private dwellings—even their palaces—were constructed after a plan that went far back into the traditions of the race. They were wooden structures with occasional embellishments in the way of tiled roofs and lead-plated walls.

So the city that was the real city—the city of the people of Angkor—was blotted out by fire or weather or the hungry white ants almost as soon as it was deserted. Only through their piety and the immodesty of their kings did these mysterious millions escape the oblivion that pressed so closely upon them.

Yaçovarman, called with some logic the "King of Glory," reigned over the Khmers from 889 to 909 of our era. He was the son of Indravarman and the queen Indradevi which means little or nothing to one who can not mold personalities to fit the echoing names of Angkor. He was educated by Vamaciva, a Brahman of princely lineage, and that means much. He was less than twenty years old when he took the throne of what was even then the most thriving country of the Orient. The inscriptions tend to show that the first years of his administration were under the tutelage of this Vamaciva who had been spiritual adviser to the late king. One may gather that the Brahman had no small part in the development of the aspirations that led to the building of the capital.

The royal city at that period is believed to have been in the neighborhood of Pra Khan of Angkor which lies ruined beyond the north wall of Angkor Thom. If so the arts of the Khmers had come a long way toward perfection. They were receiving stimulus from Java through an influx of missionaries and teachers.

Yaçovarman was probably the most free-handed letter writer in all the royal line of Angkor. He was duly appreciative of his own works and with considerable foresight he put up enough great walls to permit the carving of his eulogies in suitable array. Thanks to him the dates of the early history of Angkor Thom are well fixed. But for all of that the man himself is an enigma not easily detached from the shadows of his temples.

In the first place he had most of his inscriptions written in a new alphabet that does not seem to have survived long after his death ... an alphabet which shows distinct evidence of Javanese influence. For the rest he submerged himself in his works and it is only through a few bas-reliefs and isolated chronicles that one finds him to have been human and not a stone figure such as his lord Siva.

He was a man of gigantic stature, if we may believe the fragmentary evidence of the inscriptions, a man capable of fighting a tiger with his bare hands. And he brought to his program of public works all the energy that one might expect to find in a person of exceptional physical strength. He was a dreamer with great hopes for the future of his race. A religious enthusiast whose belief in his lord Siva was vivid enough to make the god an active partner in his works. And he was a king of kings with proper pride in his calling.

Early in his reign he sent to the widely scattered communities of his realm steles engraved in Sanskrit and his new alphabet announcing to all and sundry that he intended to give to Siva "a noble monastery as a fitting tribute to his glory." This monastery was undoubtedly the Bayon which Yaçovarman rushed to completion with a speed that might be considered incredible even in these days of mechanical building devices and easy transport.

When the armies of slaves were brought to the site of Angkor Thom and the first basketful of earth was taken out of the ditch that was to be its moat is not known. But it is historic that eleven years after the son of Indravarman took the throne he came through the North Gate into a completed city. The tower of the Bayon stood against the sky like nothing else in the world, the finest expression of a people aware for the first time of their own magnificence. And into the town came the rejoicing thousands to gaze, awe-stricken, at this reincarnation of Babylon and to hope, as Yaçovarman must have hoped, that the destroyer god would appreciate the signal honor that had been conferred on him.

CHAPTER XVII

The Capital of the King of Glory

THE PUZZLING WORKS OF YAÇOVARMAN

Lord Siva seems to have been eminently impartial in his gifts of destruction. Before Angkor Thom was a year old Yaçovarman, the King of Glory, was fighting for its preservation and his own. A prince named Bharata Rahou Sambouddhi organized a rebellion for grievances that unfortunately have not been recorded, and one calm evening, when the moon had gone down behind the Bayon, made a successful raid on the royal terrace.

The outer sentries of the palace were killed. The inner guards, when they suddenly became aware of armed men bursting through the gates and coursing along the galleries, fled into the gardens and never came back. Yaçovarman was aroused from his sleep by the noise of the attack and dashed out into a corridor to engage in what was virtually single-handed battle against the rebels.

The inscriptions give only a brief record of what happened. They take the prowess of the king for granted and mention only that he "fought in person and was exposed to many grave dangers," and that "two nobles, loyal to him, sacrificed their lives to save him."

But one can reconstruct the scene easily enough in view of the outcome. Yaçovarman had the advantage of a front restricted by the width of the corridor. Despite the number of rebels only two or three could reach him at once and these were silhouetted against the light of torches borne by the men behind them. Back to wall this giant who could kill tigers with his bare hands battered down rank on rank of his foes until presently he split the skull of Bharata Rahou Sambouddhi and the revolt was finished.

Many have read in the incident an augury of the fate that was one day to overtake the Khmers. Where cities capable of housing a million souls could be built in a decade it seems more than likely that there was fecund soil for revolt. Subject races did this building—bitter savages waiting despairingly for a chance to free themselves. What odds to them if a civilization should go into chaos as a result of their rebellion? Civilization meant nothing to them but the privilege of hauling cut rock for incredible miles over scorching roads. They got nothing out of culture except bad food and welts from a rawhide whip. Angkor seems to have had within it the elements of its own destruction from the day when Yaçovarman first stood before the Bayon and marveled at his handiwork.

One who looks upon Angkor Thom through modern eyes may see in it plenty that smacks of vulgarity. In the year 900 it must have seemed a jumble of architectural monstrosities had there been any standards for a judgment of such matters. Its designers apparently had no idea of restraint. Its carved elephants are all life size. Its Brahmanic symbols are repeated endlessly until the eye is bewildered in the contemplation of them. Its temple was intended to be the largest building in the Orient and probably was. The faces of Siva which scanned the town from every wall of every pinnacle were gigantic and amazing rather than masterpieces of art.

And yet it is probable that no race as young culturally as these works indicate the Khmers to have been ever produced anything to compare with Angkor Thom for the sheer boldness of its conception and the sheer energy of its execution. The Khmers were still little more than experimenters in the fields of engineering and architecture. They had not yet arrived at an idea of Art. That was to come more than a hundred years afterward in the erection of Angkor Vat. But there is something superb in the picture of them as youthful Titans playing with

THE BAYON

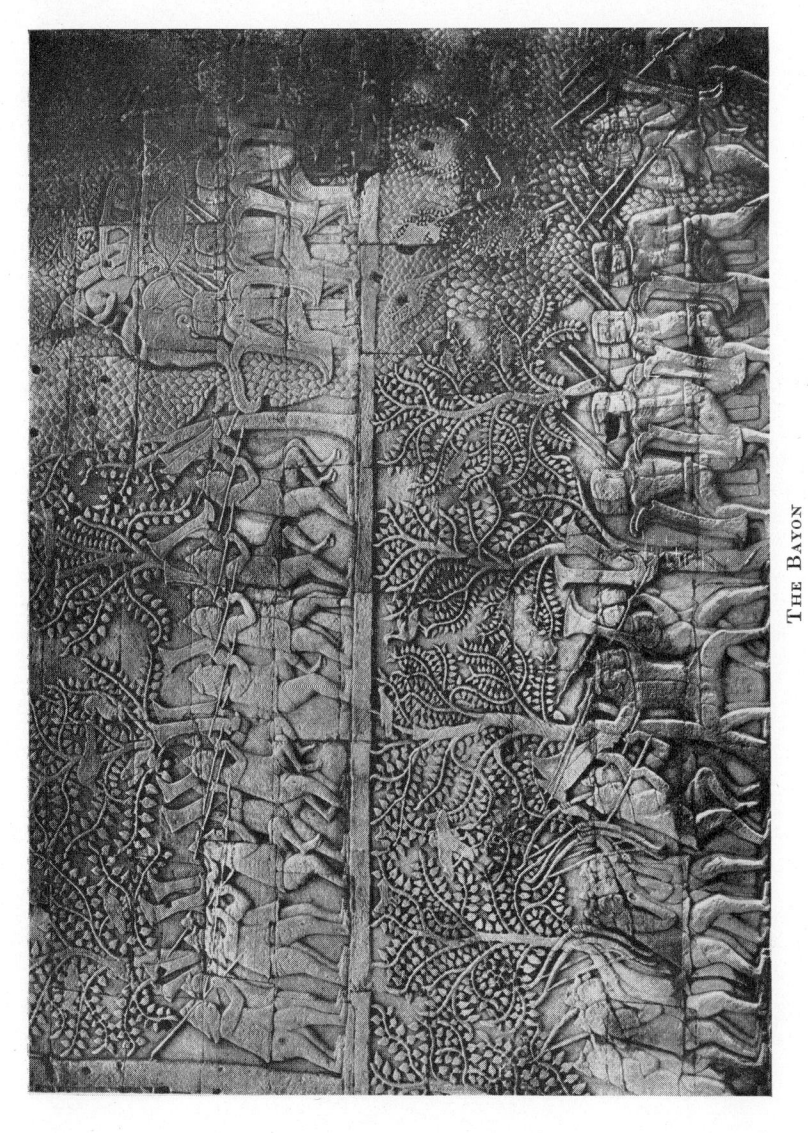

In a mile of friezes such as this the history of the Khmers appears to have been one long scroll of war

mountains of rock and tossing up mighty, if over-decorated, cities as a sort of casual gesture.

The Bayon, dim and gray and on the verge of total ruin, is beautiful enough in its decay. The never-ending faces of its tower-cragged summits have been weathered to mere shadows. The lions and dragons and nagas that gave a rococo outline to its terraces are dust or unidentified heaps in the marsh ground of the temple area. And in its ensemble it is now a fitting shrine to the god of desolation, more nearly than it was when the priests of the Khmers sang their chants in its narrow galleries.

Shiny new with its dragon terraces intact and its white walls rising up to pinnacles flaming with gold leaf it was hardly beautiful. It was awesome rather than esthetic. It lacked the definite plan that was later to distinguish Angkor Vat. Its galleries were narrow and dark, and tangled themselves into labyrinths. Its central tower was misshapen and some of its lesser spires were out of line with the mass they decorated and out of plumb. But even so it was the greatest work that man had yet produced in the Far East . . . monument to a nation that had almost found a soul while groping in the dark.

The name "Bayon" is not translatable. Aymonier supposes it to have been a term designating a reliquary for the ashes of kings and princes. That it had a close connection with the royal line is manifest when one considers that it was the point of departure from which the entire plan of the regal capital was derived. It had no temple area as earlier temples of the Khmers had had. The entire city of Angkor Thom was its temple area.

The best face of the shrine was turned toward the east and the road from the East Gate came to an end in the dragon terrace at what was virtually the sacred portico. The terrace, portions of which are still to be seen, was one hundred and fifty feet long and seventy-five feet wide. Multiheaded serpents were its balustrades.

From the terrace a staircase of stone rose toward the first stage of the pyramid.

Four lateral stairways dipped down to the square ponds that flanked the ascent. These approaches were decorated with scores of little stone lions.

The platform at the head of the rising stairs led to an ornamental portal surmounted by towers of Siva.

Beyond the high arch one came to the first galleries. These galleries were continuous about the edge of the first stage of the ziggurat. They had a total length of some six hundred and sixty-six yards—east and west galleries one hundred and seventy-seven yards each and north and south galleries one hundred and fifty-six yards each.

Steeper stairways led to the second stage which measured two hundred and eighty-five feet on its long side and was nearly square. Here the galleries intermingled in an architectural riot. One sees the remains of an outer enceinte and a double inner gallery with a bewildering array of cross members. Each crossing was surmounted by one of the four-faced towers, and this stage of the temple was made a great forest of spires through which the complacent leer of Siva was multiplied as in a hall of mirrors.

The third stage, whose roots went down to the very base of the pyramid, was two hundred and ten feet on the east and west side and one hundred and seventy-four feet along its other face. Here also was a maze of side chapels and communicating galleries. A dozen little shrines stood about the edge of this stage reached by colonnades and corridors that were a lace-work of sculpturing. The sanctuary of the god was in the exact center, a dark and dismal chamber, unornamented and virtually inaccessible.

It stands there to-day—doubly pathetic as the rain sluices down from the chipped roofs, doubly silent when the sun is on the temple and the monkeys are chattering outside. It is no more empty now than it ever was perhaps. That deity no longer fills its throne is no surprise. The tragedy is not in the gods who have gone out into the twilight but in the human hope that was enshrined here with them and now has vanished.

Up above rises the central tiara to an apex one

hundred and forty feet above the ground level, lifting to the greatest eminence it ever attained in Angkor the silent mask of the tight-lipped, deaf-eared Destroyer. There were forty lesser towers similarly decorated. Their wreckage spills down into the deserted courts.

Aymonier has this to say of the Bayon:

"This great temple of the new capital—this vast step pyramid with its dominating tower—was perhaps the masterpiece of pure Cambodian architecture; remarkable among other things for the power and extreme originality of its architectural idea, expression of an art heavy enough, perhaps, but young, vigorous, and achieving so nearly its apogee. Its architects were able to assemble galleries, domes and sanctuaries in a grandiose aspect that could be envisioned in a single glance and we can see that the surroundings of the temple contributed admirably to this magic spectacle."

What remains of the magic of the Bayon to-day is to be found principally in the bas-reliefs along the inner walls of its galleries. There one steps out of the depressing atmosphere of decay and death and comes suddenly face to face with the Kingdom of the Khmers marching in all its ancient grandeur . . . through the heaven of Indra and through the marketplaces of Angkor Thom . . . over fields of battle and under enchanted seas. Miracle and commonplace mingle here in this chiseled cinema as one would

The Bayon

Still defiant, as if unaware of the ruin that lies behind them, the little lions peer haughtily at the world from the eastern porch

The Bayon

Little lions with short wheel-bases and no tails keep their endless vigil at the east portal of the crumbling shrine

expect them to mingle. Here, if nowhere else in the meager records of their existence, the Khmers are as they ought to be, creatures that once were demigods.

There must be nearly a mile of these bas-reliefs—a mile of charging elephants and parading kings and battling warriors intermingling with gods who ride on strange beasts and common folks who carry on their simple domestic pursuits in a manner that shows them to be unaware of their distinguished company. In this almost endless panorama are unfolded the scenes of the Râmâyana, the *Iliad* of India, the legend of the young Prince Kambu who married the daughter of the monarch of the Nagas, and the deeds of Yaçovarman who "killed an elephant with one hand and strangled a tiger." Princely nobles ride to the chase or lean from their horses in a game that must have been something like polo. Animals rove through dense forests. Schools of fish move about in a stony sea. War-craft meet in naval battles. Acrobats, hand balancers and jugglers try to complete their difficult tricks as they have been trying since they were frozen in stone here a thousand years ago. Women nurse their babies or prepare their meals in pots of familiar shape over open fires. Merchants dispense their wares from wicker baskets.

Brahmans and dancing-girls and pilgrims and princesses and concubines and slaves come out of the mists only to return again. And in the background move the elephants—hundreds and thousands of elephants with unbrellas spread over them in token of a state procession or with archers leaning out of the palanquins tossing death to the Chams.

It is natural that one should marvel less at the monstrous bulk of the pyramid than at this whispering gallery of antiquity. Out in the sunny courts the twentieth century stands looking at a temple and noticing only its decay. Here one loiters in the year 900 and sees the Khmers setting out on the road to their power and glory. True the action has ceased; the bows are bent but the arrows never fly. The babes at their mothers' breasts are doomed never to attain manhood. The elephants lean forward holding in midair the feet that they can not set down again. The marching warriors will reach no objective. The petitioners who sit endlessly in the Hall of Audience must for ever fail to obtain a judgment from the king to whom they speak. But even so the enchantment that arrested the life of the nation in the cloisters of the Bayon is whiter magic than that which obliterated it from the cities beyond the threshold.

North of the Bayon is the plaza where in Yaçovarman's day the social life of the capital was centered. It corresponded, probably, to the arenas of Rome as the scene of races and games and spectacles and as a drill field for soldiery about to embark on one of the interminable expeditions against the Chams or the Thais.

Little enough is known of the ceremonials and pageants that were held here, but civilizations after all do not differ from one another in any great degree. . . . And so we can see the Khmers massed in the square, tense at a declaration of war or delirious with victory, taking up arms for battle or witnessing the more peaceful amusements of gladiatorial combat or elephant fighting.

"Their contests and games probably were very brutal," comments Aymonier. "It is likely that the climax of the most popular of them was reached with the death of one of the participants if one may judge from what we know of the customs of the Cambodians, softened probably by time, and from the struggles of bleeding pugilists that even now hold a particular place in the festive program of New Year's Day at the royal palace beneath the interested eyes of the sovereign and his court."

Along the east side of the public square were ranged groups of small temples in front of which, close to the road that edged the field, stood ten square towers with pyramidal tops.

The little temples on this side of the town nestle deep in the clutches of the jungle. The work of clearing has been less complete here than elsewhere in Angkor Thom—although one may reach all portions of all the shrines without difficulty. The fromagers seem to have retired a step or two, undefeated, confident that one day the Pale Ones will go away, and the Cambodian and Annamite axmen who are continually burning up the underbrush will lie down to sleep as nature apparently intended them to do. Then the forest can come back again to take over the property that it labored so diligently to obtain.

The north corner of the eastern temple area is given over to the five shrines of Pra Pithu, manifestly a Brahman center and possibly a theological seminary. Even in Yaçovarman's day religious thought among the Khmers had undergone considerable agitation and new gods were daily being added to the pantheon which acknowledged Siva as its ruler. One is surprised to find evidences of tolerance among a people in whose lives the state religion was so vital a factor. But there are such evidences. Vishnu had his shrines among these little temples just as he had his emblems on the royal terrace across the square. Brahma dwelt in Pra Pithu and farther along the highway that led to the North Gate, Buddha was honored with a shrine and monastery.

Yaçovarman was probably the most notable zealot in all the chronology of the Khmers. He made his prayers to Siva out of masses of rock and the sweat

THE BAYON

Through this northern portal walked the kings, proud of a work which they boasted would live for ever

and blood of hundreds of thousands of slaves. His pious aspirations are better known than his deeds. But for all that he seems to have been a cautious king. The lesser gods were after all the lesser gods but there was no telling what annoyance they might put one to in a future existence. . . . Better to placate them here than hereafter, and really it took so little to keep them contented.

CHAPTER XVIII

A Cinema in Stone

THE LEGEND OF THE LEPER KING

On the west side of the public square the stone elephants walk in endless array—the final and most enduring pageantry of the King of Glory. There are scores of these elephants carved in the rock of a terrace that lifts this portion of the town some ten feet above the road level. They come out of the shaking heat near the gray skeleton of the Bayon and proceed northward trunk to tail for hundreds of yards.

Their procession ceases at a staircase where they step out of the bas-relief far enough to permit their trunks to serve as a decorative balustrade. Down these stairs, perhaps, came the regal processions described by Tcheou-Ta-Quan, the Chinese chronicler, to spread out over the square a tapestry of brass and gold and iron and crimson—live elephants ranging alongside their stony images and destroying none of the magic of the bas-reliefs by contrast.

Beyond the stairs the terrace proceeds again, this time with an elaborate decoration of gryphon-like figures that archeologists have identified as Garoudas, the creatures half men, half eagle who bore the god Vishnu on his journeyings. Another stairway breaks through the convention of the Garoudas and steps down to an east and west road that plunges across the square and through the jungle verdure of Pra Pithu to the portal which legend has identified as the Gate of Victory.

It is probable that somewhere near this portion of the wall was the royal palace. The position of the Garoudas, standing with uplifted arms like caryatids, has supported the belief that at one time buildings stood on top of the terrace. Tcheou-Ta-Quan's description of the royal audience hall and of the close-guarded mystery that was the king's dwelling-place is further evidence in the same direction. Cambodian legend had it that in "the ancient capital of the Khmers was a wall of stone elephants who bore on their backs the house of the king." And archeology has ratified the story sufficiently to mark the site where the palace probably stood.

Beyond the wall of the Garoudas is still another extension of the terrace and a more elaborate collection of carvings. The sculpture here is made up of three tiers of small human figures, most of them suppliant, none of them betraying any connection with the legend which gives this portion of the wall its identity as the Terrace of the Leper King.

About the Leper King and his terrace, more later. Seen purely as an architectural feature this group of carvings seems to support the theory that the plan of Yaçovarman was altered by succeeding monarchs to meet the need for more administrative buildings.

The depth of the terrace was something more than six hundred yards, and the royal park was protected on the west and north and south by a moat and a double enceinte, traces of which are still to be found. There is evidence, moreover, that the dubious protection of the terrace wall was not taken at more than its face value by monarchs who probably knew only too well the volatile nature of their constituents. Set back from the face of the terrace, archeologists have discovered the remains of a gateway, unarched and unornamented but a beautiful architectural specimen which they believe to have been a part of a rampart which vanished before the Khmers left Angkor. This was probably the principal gate of the palace grounds. There were four secondary gates, two to the north and two to the south.

As for the palace itself, nothing has been found to give indication concerning the shape of it or the material with which it was constructed. The testimony of Tcheou-Ta-Quan that it was tiled with lead and decorated with porcelain remains uncontrovertible.

Early archeologists identified the little temple of Phimeneakas, "Shrine of the Air," at the rear of the

THE BAYON

The four faces of Siva peer from every crumbling tower

terrace enclosure, as a probable royal residence. The temple, in view of what is now known about Khmer architecture, could not be mistaken for anything but the sacred ziggurat that it was. It is obviously—even in its ruins—a three-stage pyramid. It is not quite a hundred meters square at the base and is less than fifty feet high.

Authorities now believe it to have been a sort of chapel of the royal house, probably connected with the ceremonials of investiture. Legend gives it an even more intimate connection with affairs of State as the home of a highly important ghost.

Here once more speaks Yin:

"The daughter of the monarch of the Nagas lived in that place when the Khmers ruled the world from Angkor," he said modestly, as he tore his attention from the scurrying monkeys.

"You may remember the legend. She was not a mortal. Her father was a demigod and her natural shape was that of the cobra with the seven heads. It was only to marry the Prince Kambu of the Arya Deca that she took the form of a beautiful woman. He objected to wedding a serpent.

"The result of that marriage was just what might have been expected. Kambu grew old and died. But the Princess of the Nagas did not die. She was immortal. She could not go back to her people because she had lived so long in the land of the Kambujas that she did not know the way to the cave where her father ruled.

"So she followed the Khmers through the valley of the great river until they came to Angkor and then she appeared to the king who built this town. She told him that he was to construct a temple near the royal palace. That is how the Phimeneakas came to be built.

"But that was not the only demand of this snake woman. By day the magic was all right and she could be a seven-headed cobra and sun herself in the top gallery of her temple. But when the sun went down the magic collapsed and she became a woman once more.

"She did not wish it so. Her husband was dead. Her sons too were dead. Her descendants she scarcely knew. And she wanted to be just a simple immortal once more. But she had been away too long from magic and such things. She had forgotten the charms that would make her as she had been before she became a woman.

"Then she decided upon a very important course. She figured that the lord Siva to whom her father had vowed allegiance must have some purpose in keeping her among the Khmers. She decided that she would be the permanent first wife of all the Kings of Cambodia.

"So it became the rule that each king as soon as he

took the throne must be wed to the Princess of the Nagas. Each evening he must pay her a visit of state in the temple of Phimeneakas and that before he saw any of his other wives or concubines, for the Princess of the Nagas was very jealous. And she would not be deceived because she was wise as a serpent.

"And that's the way it went on for hundreds of years. The kings did not find the arrangement much of a hardship. She was the most beautiful woman in the world and she had learned a lot during the time she was compelled to live as a mortal. She had a very nice disposition and was able to tell the kings many things about running the kingdom and handling the royal household.

"But there was one stipulation: The Naga Princess demanded constancy. At each wedding she told her new husband that should he fail just once to make the evening visit great woe would come upon the land of the Khmers. . . . And in the end that is just what happened. One has only to look upon the ruined temples to see that this story must be true."

. . . A beautiful queen half serpent, half woman, with the destiny of a nation dependent upon her whim! One does not have to look deeply into this matter to see the resemblance to the Melusine legend of Europe. Three or four important principalities came to a spectacular and appropriate finish because of the fish-tailed Melusine whose ubiquity has been one of the most charming features of her story. Why then begrudge the Khmers the solace of her company—and her vengeance—in another guise?

South of the Phimeneakas, and set well back from the eastern edge of the terrace, is the Baphuon Temple which Tcheou-Ta-Quan designated as the tower of copper. There is nothing about it now to identify it as a tower of copper. A garden of jungle growth is sprouting from its summit and even the constant attention of archeologists has failed to keep the vines from strangling its galleries.

It was erected at some time subsequent to the era of Yaçovarman and probably was intended to replace the temple of Phimeneakas. Its base is about six hundred feet square and it was close to one hundred feet high.

In construction it approaches more nearly the Egyptian type of pyramid than the other temples of Angkor Thom. It rises in seven stages, three of which are encircled by narrow galleries, and so its rise from base to pinnacle is more rapid and its pyramidal shape more apparent than in ziggurats such as the Bayon.

The Baphuon excited the imagination of others than the impressionable Chinaman who wrote of its copper spire (which probably it never had.) Some of the inscriptions on contemporary shrines refer to it as the "Mountain of the Golden Horn," and others give it a still more improbable designation as the "Mountain of Gold."

Judging from Sanskrit texts translated by Aymonier one might hazard a guess that it was named after the "Mountain of Gold" which stood in Djamboudvipa, the dwelling-place of the gods. At any rate, it was dedicated to the "Lord of the Mountain of Gold" who may have been Siva or Vishnu. It was served by priests of the royal household.

So much for the minor mysteries of the royal terrace. The most interesting puzzle of this ancient haunt of the kings is to be found in the Terrace of the Leper King already mentioned. The figures engraved on this end of the wall have been identified as lords and ladies. Certainly they are human figures and there are hundreds of them.

The terrace at the point where they join the panorama juts out in the form of a Latin cross, and prosaic judgment has conceded that at one time it served as a sort of reviewing stand, connected to the royal palace by a gallery, for the convenience of his majesty in watching the spectacles in the public square.

However, one of the Cambodian legends that took on new life, after the rediscovery of Angkor, had it that the city of Yaçovarman was founded by a leper king and without need for further evidence the natives of the region connected the story with this northern terrace.

The adaptibility of the Cambodian mind is evidenced in some recent archeological developments in the neighborhood. One of the curators noticed after a heavy rain that a bit of carving stuck out of the wall some distance behind its eastern face. He assigned a workman to do some excavating and within a few hours had made the astounding discovery that there were two façades, each intricately sculptured and separated from each other by a passage about a foot and a half wide. The puzzling feature of the case was that the carving on the inner wall was exactly the same as that on the outer, thus obviating at once the theory that the false front had been designed merely to conceal a passageway by which the king could reach the terrace unseen.

One plausible explanation advanced by the archeologists is that the original terrace was too small and that the outer wall was added merely to give it size and shape symmetrical with the rest of the wall. Such a thing might well have happened inasmuch as time, labor and material meant nothing to the Kings of Angkor. The theory does not explain, of course, why there should have been a stairway leading out of the slot between the walls to the top of the ter-

THE BAPHUON

Whose vaulting stages gave to the Khmers the promise of the great temple of Angkor

race. But scientific conjecture and the positivism of legend have many points in common, one of them being that they ignore what they do not care to make clear.

As for the folk-lore that has to do with this corner of Angkor it has the advantage of considerably more romance than is to be found in the debates of the experts over the building problems of the Khmers. In brief this is it:

The story has to do with the brave monarch, cherished of the gods, who founded Angkor.

He was not a popular king, this city builder. The people who had carved the rock and carried it for long miles on their shoulders to construct walls and terraces and temples and palaces, were just a little put out with the prince who had ordered them to do it.

In his harem, however, the king continued to enjoy popularity, for, in a fashion that seems to lift him apart from his Asiatic contemporaries, he was thoughtful of women and he was never harsh with them, despite the fact that he had four wives. The wives loved him although his subjects did not, and he tried to derive therefrom whatever consolation there may have been in his heritage as a king.

One day the wives overheard a plot against him and advised him to flee from Angkor. He considered the plan carefully.

"I have been thinking of some such plan," he admitted. "Angkor has been getting hotter day by day and while I shall not exercise much sovereignty over the jungle I shall probably live a long time there—which is more than I can say about the situation here."

So in the morning he set out secretly through the North Gate with his four wives and wandered far afield, while two of his generals, Vayvonksa and Thonnit, mustered the men of their commands and fought for his crown.

The king and his several queens had been gone a long time before they found out anything about this and then information came to them quite by accident.

They chanced to visit a holy hermit who possessed a heart of gold beneath a soiled exterior. Almost immediately he knew that he was looking at a king. Whereupon he whetted his second sight and discovered all that was going on in Angkor.

"You will conquer both rebels," he forecast. "And in triumph you will find only mire. But do not lose heart for in the mud are unsuspected jewels."

Neither the king nor the wives could make much out of this . . . but no matter, it was obvious that they had business in Angkor so they started out at once southward through the jungle. And before many days they came upon the army of Vayvonksa. The king, unrecognized, enlisted with his former general as a mercenary.

Vayvonksa marched on Angkor and somewhere in

the vicinity or Pra Khan a great battle was fought. Thonnit, defending the town, was having all the better of it until in one foolish sally he encountered the king who cut off his head with one of the neatest full-arm swings seen in Cambodia in many a day. The army of Thonnit turned to flee but the king rallied the minor officers and told them that he would take the late general's place. He was unanimously elected to the office, after which he turned upon Vayvonksa, routed his army and killed him. He rode toward the North Gate once more master of Angkor, but just at the moment of his triumph his horse took fright at an old woman in the road and he was pitched to the ground. The old woman threw herself on him and embraced him before anybody thought to have her killed. Almost at once the king knew that he had been kissed by a leper.

When he rode into Angkor he rode alone.

His people shunned him. The guards of the palace ran away from him. The ministers of state and the minor officers of the army held a hurried meeting and decreed that he must live in isolation at the north end of the royal terrace. And there he lived alone until one day the four wives dug a tunnel to the place of his imprisonment and remained with him till he died. He knew at last the meaning of the prophecy that in the mire he would find unsuspected jewels. . . .

The names of the wives as the story is related

around Angkor are not familiar except in the case of one who was called Roum-Sey-Sack. This lady in another folk-tale was found floating as an infant in the bud of a lotus flower and figured in a quarrel with a pet crocodile. What more natural than her appearance in the affairs of Angkor as a self-sacrificing heroine?

There is a statue on the terrace of the Leper King. . . . At present it is believed to be a conventional figure of the seated Siva. But at one time it was identified as the image of the king who had fought well against all but the dread infection.

So much for legend. Tradition, which is something else again, has held for hundreds of years that the king who founded Angkor Thom was a leper. And it is historic that Yaçovarman was the builder. The King of Glory died before he was forty years old, presumably of disease inasmuch as inscriptions show his eldest son to have succeeded him without trouble. It is significant that his name, despite its glorious connections in the history of Angkor, was never taken by any of his successors.

Chinese records of the thirteenth century mention the leprosy of the first king of Angkor Thom as a matter of common knowledge and to-day natives point out a spot in the forest where his body is supposed to have been cremated after he had renounced his throne and died in seclusion.

Aymonier who reviews all of this evidence without attempting a judgment closes with a comment on the career of Yaçovarman which after all is more to the point than any mere study of his possible physical debilities:

"Leper or not this young and boastful king, who celebrated his glories in tablets with marvelous epithets, is a striking example of the vanity of human grandeurs. His name is one of the first which I read . . . the date in figures of his arrival, 811 of the local era, was the first which I deciphered. But if I have been able to aid by my feeble efforts in his emergence from the oblivion in which he has slept for centuries I have seen with my own eyes the disruption of his grandiose masterpiece—the ten square kilometers of his capital invaded by the forest and given over to the wild animals and the serpents."

CHAPTER XIX

Necromancy at Pra Khan

THE REASSEMBLING OF A SKELETON

There are always weird noises in the jungle—gibbons leaping in the treetops, insects droning across the shafts of light where the sun strikes down through the green, birds with querulous whistles, and the rustling of leaves where unseen animals go about their unclassified business. The formidable chaos of the forest is terrifying at first because it seems to be rooted in death. Later it is doubly terrifying because of the life that shimmers momentarily in its sun spangles and whispers incessantly from its shadows.

After a while one becomes used to the consciousness of spying eyes and to the murmurs that filter through this graveyard of time. The ghosts of the forest seem harmless enough in daylight whatever may be their activities at night. One does not begrudge them their odd little moans nor their incessant and unfriendly surveillance. And yet . . .

There are voices in the groves of the Sacred Sword. Iron clinks on stone. And there is a rumble as of falling debris. . . . Ghastly sounds in this loneliness . . . more awesome than the crashing progress of the elephant or the furtive passage of the tiger, for the animals have a right to be here and human voices should have ceased to echo in this jungle hundreds of years ago.

So it is with some trepidation that one pushes through the curtain of bamboo and comes at last to the threshold of Pra Khan. Nor does a mere sight of the long causeway, strewn with wreckage, and the brown temple spilling its tiles through the snaky enceinte of the trees, tend to alter one's presentiment that he is about to intrude upon some unholy rite. Something is amiss here. Men are moving beyond the causeway. Artizans are chiseling rock and coolies are hauling huge blocks into place with ropes of vine twist. It is an incredible scene. There is no explanation for it save that possibly in wandering about through the trees one has strayed from the path that leads to automobile roads and the twentieth century, and, in some occult fashion, has stepped back through the hoary cycles of years into the days when Angkor was young.

Here, moving about as they did a thousand years ago, are the Khmers directing their slaves in the uplifting of a temple to the high gods. Their tools are unchanged. Their methods are the same as when their race set out over the south countryside to die.

The men, so far as dress and poise and facial contours are concerned, might have stepped directly out of the bas-reliefs.

It is almost with surprise that one discovers them to be flesh and blood. Perhaps, after all, the magic in this is less potent than one might imagine when one comes upon it suddenly after a plunge through the echoing forest. Come to think about it, the French have something to do with this and the French had nothing to do with the Khmers in their prime. This is not exactly a view of the life of the temple builders, however close may be the approximation.

Here stands Pra Khan, the Pra Khan of Angkor as distinguished from the Pra Khan that lies almost a hundred miles to the east—city of the sacred sword and perhaps the capital where the culture of the Khmers was nourished until it burst into full flower in the city and temples that lie to the south. The Pra Khan of Angkor is a ruin so extensive, so desolate that it seems to be the product of high explosive rather than ambitious verdure, but a ruin whose beauty, triumphant over chaos, has led science to attempt here a work of restoration.

So these men who stand half naked in the cool depths of what was once a temple basin are not the Khmers but their dismal sons. They are not wraiths come back from their ashes to carry on interminably the task they once performed so well in the erection

PRAH KHAN
To the east of Angkor Thom, a building whose vault was supported by massive columns

PRAH KHAN
One of the towers of the north part and a spandrel showing Vishnu lying on the monster, Çèsha

of a great shrine. They are laborers whose only interest in the work is thirty Mexican cents per diem and whose only ambition is to reach the cool shadows that lie at the end of the long afternoon.

With great reluctance they go about the simple engineering incident to the slinging of rocks to bamboo poles and carrying them up to the causeway. They loiter with ultra-modern skill over such details as the scraping of moss from a sculptured fragment or the sweeping of a leaf-strewn block.

Even so the visitor can not behold them without feeling that he owes them a debt of gratitude for they have done something that not even the enchanted figures of the bas-reliefs could do in bringing back for one moment and in one small corner the life of Angkor. They may be like the individual actors in a pageant only slightly aware of what the plot is all about and less than a little concerned with it. But in the ensemble they are the Khmers as the Khmers were when the step pyramids began to blossom in the plain of Cambodia.

The work of reconstruction somehow gets itself done—as one may gather from the careful assemblage of components that once fitted together and will be fitted together again as stone giants carrying a long serpent across a temple causeway. Toward the end of this causeway the pavement ends in a little mound of earth but one sees a trench recently sunk at the side of the mound to reveal an avenue of lanterns buried for hundreds of years in the loam. The drifting earth, product no doubt of forest decay, has served a purpose here, for the sculptures on the sides of the stone lanterns are as legible as they were when first carved. Perhaps, eventually, they will divulge the secrets of Pra Khan and no district in the neighborhood of Angkor is more in need of a revelation.

Pra Khan lies a few kilometers to the northeast of the North Gate of Angkor Thom. Nothing remains of it now except its temple cloisters, and they are in a state of ruin that closely approaches annihilation. But there is plentiful evidence that at one time an important religious center occupied this site. It is within reason, as Aymonier suggests, that it was the great capital of the Pre-Angkorean period in the history of the Khmers . . . that here in these root-clothed halls Yaçovarman dreamed the dream that became Angkor Thom.

The temple itself is of a period probably much anterior to that of the Bayon, but there are portions of its structure which reveal its alliance to the same school that produced the masterpieces of Yacodhapura. The groups of giants and multiheaded cobras along its causeways are the same as those which guard the gates of Angkor Thom and probably in no worse state of collapse here than in the great capital. The scheme of the temple grounds might well be that of one of the later shrines although Pra Khan was not a pyramid. The decorative friezes are well executed and if the shrine of the Sacred Sword fails to find a place in the era of magnificence described as Angkorean it is only because the restraint was greater in this northern shrine. Its architects were less daring, less original perhaps . . . but who can say that they did not achieve a closer approach to beauty?

The temple area of Pra Khan is rectangular, nearly a thousand yards in length on its east and west dimension and something over eight hundred yards in width. It was surrounded by a moat, now dry, and a wall, most of which has fallen away. The south wall was only about three hundred yards from the moat of Angkor Thom.

In construction the temple was a nest of galleries connected by cross corridors. Save that it was built on level ground instead of on a cone of rock it was much the type of shrine from which the three-step ziggurats were derived.

Massed walls clustered about it. The galleries themselves were arranged as for a defense of the faith whose fires burned before the holy of holies at the center. . . . One encircled the other, and moats and artificial ponds possibly lay between. Pra Khan, when it was completed and the priests walked into it chanting the litanies of Siva, must have seemed invulnerable and yet not once in all its changing history was it able to keep out the evil ones that sought its sanctuary—neither the heretics who effaced the emblems of the Destroyer and planted in their stead the cuckoo symbols of Buddha, nor the ultimate Conqueror whether Thai invader or Angkorean rebel or shadow of plague. And in its final weakness it was not able to withstand the trees that clutched at it amorously and tore out its heart.

Pra Khan is second in extent only to the Bayon and Angkor Vat among the great temples of Cambodia. It was as much a thing of intricate detail and gauzy carving as either of its rivals. It is second to none in devastation.

One who would penetrate its galleries to-day is constantly balked by the piles of stone that have fallen from the shattered vaults. Tree roots, white as bleached bones and ubiquitous as serpents, writhe in impenetrable masses through the cloistered openings. From the tops of its galleries rise the inevitable fromagers which by some old inconsistency are now holding together the walls and lintels and gables that in an earlier day they pried apart.

Four causeways led into the temple area, across the moat and through the cinctures of chiseled masonry straight to the heart of the sanctuary. Only one road is now practicable to the visitor—the highway from the north, and it follows a haphazard course along the broken dike where once walked the kings. The eastern causeway is the one on which the Cambodian laborers are now carrying out their long slow work of reconstruction, and some day it will be fit for traffic once more. It was the road of honor to Pra Khan when the temple was new, at once a via sacra and a highway of triumph. To-day, though its pavement is intact, it is useless, for one end of it lies in a tangle of jungle and the other is smothered abruptly in the rubbish heaps.

Iron clinks on stone. There are whispering voices in the old basins that flank the causeway. Half-clad coolies set their shoulders under a bamboo pole from which is suspended a square of rock. Bodies of men slip through the green-toned shafts of light. Temple builders are erecting a sanctuary to the god Siva and will call it the shrine of the Sacred Sword. . . . But the pageantry is somehow less convincing than it was before one looked into the broken cloisters. One can not see the builders in what is left of Pra Khan but only the destroyers, grim, relentless and terribly efficient.

Two kilometers east of Pra Khan's eastern moat is a square depression with a chapel at the center— the strange little temple of Neak Pean. Its basins are dry now save when the rains of the spring fill them to a depth of two or three feet. But when there were temple votaries to see that pond levels were maintained this shrine to the coiled cobra must have seemed like a vast and beautiful fountain.

The outer enceinte of this sunken garden was about four hundred and fifty yards on a side and very nearly square. Dikes of masonry, narrow at the top and widening toward the base, separated the pool into a number of lesser pools. It was at the point of convergences of these dikes that the shrine rose up from the embrace of the Nagas carved about its foot.

The Nagas have survived the ordinary ravages of time and tempest fairly well and take their part in an odd group of masonry that recalls the Laocoon with the exception that instead of Man struggling with serpents the home of a god struggles with them. The Khmer designers themselves probably would be thrilled to-day to see how nature has improved on their plan. A fromager tree sprouts from the middle chapel and the long roots crawl down the terrace, more snakelike than the Nagas themselves, more godlike than Siva in their powers of destruction.

Still onward through the jungle wanders the old road of pilgrimage.

As one follows it from shrine to shrine, moving farther and farther away from the enceinte of Angkor Thom, one realizes the logic of the archeologists who held that the suburban population of Yaçovar-

BANTEI KEDEI
Eastern portal of the inner wall

NEAK PEAN
The shrine of the sacred Naga is now the sanctuary of the cobra roots of the encompassing trees

man's capital must have been very nearly equal to that which dwelt inside the walls.

Pra Khan may have ceased to function as an imperial city when Yaçovarman moved out of it. But there is plentiful evidence that its temple remained in use, supporting hundreds of priests and votaries and consecrated dancing-girls, well along toward the time when Angkor was snuffed out. One may suppose that the Khmers were not basically different from other races whose civilization and state religion have been closely linked. In this case it appears to be a tenable theory that large numbers of people—particularly the poor who had no good reason for moving into Angkor—remained to serve the servants of the temple.

As for the other great shrines and monasteries scattered about in this region beyond the walls one can explain them only as integral parts of a great metropolitan development. Dozens of them are encompassed by the highway—some twenty-five kilometers in length—that leads northward from Angkor Vat through Angkor Thom and returns through the native village of Siem Reap well to the south of the Khmer monuments.

A little more than a mile from the fountain temple of Neak Pean is the scattering ruin of Bantei Kedei, the "Citadel of the Little Cells."

Legend in great variety clings to this labyrinth of

stone. Native guides assert that it served as the principal crematorium for Angkor Thom.

Archeology contributes nothing to this theory. It, too, is put to much guesswork concerning the origins and uses of the temple but develops its conjectures along independent lines. Aymonier himself admits that there is nothing in the inscriptions to justify the verdict of scientists which makes Bantei Kedei the work of one of the two sons of Yaçovarman who in turn succeeded the King of Glory on the throne of Angkor. He says merely that the architecture and ornament of the ensemble shows that it probably was an erection of a later date, but not much later, than Angkor Thom and the Bayon.

In construction and design Bantei Kedei is similar to Pra Khan and in the extent of its park it is very nearly as large. It was surrounded by a moat and an exterior wall, and was itself a series of cloistered galleries set within other squares of galleries so broken by cross passages that it well merited its Cambodian designation as the "Citadel of the Cells."

It appears that this temple was given over to the service of Buddha at an earlier date than was Pra Khan. Perhaps it was a Buddhist monastery from the very first, for, as has been seen in Angkor Thom, the sovereignty of Siva did not prevent the erection of temples to his rivals.

Like Pra Khan, its bewildering passages, difficult

of access when they were unimpeded, now are almost impassable because of shattered masonry and wandering verdure. To-day one enters the temple area through a breach in the wall near its northwest corner and picks a precarious route through tumbled porches and wrecked chapels toward the eastern portal. Save for the pathways carved by the feet of hundreds of natives marching through here on their way to places where the French directors are conducting the legions of the ax in their almost vain attack on the forest, one might well get into this place and remain for ever. A few turns through the darkened galleries, a few struggles with the mazes of fromager, and he could face the prospect of adding another handful of human dust to a supply already beyond need of further enlargement.

The outer wall encompasses an area about half a mile square and most of the enclosure is cut into a checker-board pattern by the withered arms of the temple. There is nothing in the visible ruins to support the theory that the bodies of the dead were brought here for cremation. As a matter of fact, one would be more likely to look for traces of a crematorium on the banks of the river where the disposal of the ashes would be more simple. But one does not quarrel with the assurance of the natives. In the Bantei Kedei there is a desolation that seems to be the twin brother of Death. The dense black clouds of the funeral pyres settling over its low-lying vaults would detract none from its atmosphere.

One emerges from the depressing mazes of Bantei Kedei to plunge at once into the most beautiful spot in all the region of Angkor: Ta Prohm ("The Ancient Brahma"), legendary treasure-house of the Khmers, and undisputed capital of the Kingdom of the Trees.

Elsewhere the zeal of the French archeologists and their hardy axmen has made some headway against the destroying jungle. Here the legions that lifted Angkor Vat back into the eyes of the world stand baffled. For this is a sadder ruin than Pra Khan and a more impenetrable labyrinth than Bantei Kedei. Trees eight and ten feet in diameter rise out of the pavements on the terraces. Roots pursue a snakelike course for hundreds of feet across the ruined courts seeking moisture and nourishment. Great trunks press down on the weakened vaults and tear massive friezes apart to pile their wreckage amid the splinters of earlier destruction.

Ta Prohm in the ensemble—if one could ever look at it so—must appear to be the abandoned toy of giants who tossed it here from an unbelievable height. It is impossible to conceive that such thoroughgoing wreckage could have been accomplished a little at a time.

TA PROHM

In the grasp of the serpentine roots the chapel of the royal treasure house lies suffocating

And yet Ta Prohm is beautiful in the chaotic mélange of its trees and in the isolated glimpses of desolated gods who peer out of its walls through the infrequent clearings.

The conservators of Angkor have come upon a new problem amid the endless colonnades of the conquering fromagers. Elsewhere they could halt destruction with destruction and feel a pride in their work as hidden cities emerged once more before the eyes of the world. Here is another temple to be saved, a work as important in its architectural conception and lacy detail as any of those which have been found in the neighborhood. But they dare not proceed. Ta Prohm, facing a definite and inevitable end like Kambu in the halls of the cobras, is more majestic than pathetic, a thing apart from all the other works of the Khmers. Denuded,—transformed into another group of carved galleries,—its wounds laid bare and its broken back exposed to the arid sun, it must become merely another Raknarök of slabs, another whitening churchyard.

If the trees are left to work as they will with Ta Prohm the destruction must go on and on unceasingly. New fromagers will rise up beside the old. New roots will creep down like tendrils along the walls, entering the crevices and strengthening their grip. New shoots will expand to gigantic trunks piling their weight on the trembling vaults. New creepers will pry the great blocks apart until the stones come tumbling down.

And yet were the axmen to come in here now and seek to arrest this slow march to annihilation there seems to be a reasonable doubt that they would accomplish anything. The fromagers that are bringing Ta Prohm to its ignominious end are at present one of the chief influences holding its walls and arches together.

Native legend has identified Ta Prohm as the royal treasure-house but one gathers that in this sprightly idea fancy may have followed a misunderstanding of fact. The French savants in translating the inscriptions of the temple found a list which may have been an inventory of the materials stored there and again may have been merely a record of the pious gifts of the king.

The bill of particulars mentions among other articles quantities of paddy, beans, millet, butter, cheese, honey, syrup, oil of sesame, camphor, wax and pepper. In addition to these groceries the treasure or the king's donations included six hundred and forty pairs of vestments, and forty-five veils of "Chinese material" to be hung about the pedestals of the divinities "on account of the mosquitoes."

A more interesting inscription is one which mentions the progress of medical science among the Khmers.

M. G. Goedes, commenting on the tablets, says:

"Through one of the inscriptions we learn that there were one hundred and two hospitals distributed through the different provinces of Cambodia. It is not stated that all of these were founded by Yaçovarman but it is very likely. The great movement for the aid of the sick in the year 1186 did not consist solely in the founding of new hospitals but in the conservation of institutions of that kind already in existence. The list furnished in successive inscriptions is a sort of budget of expenses incurred in the upkeep of all of these hospitals for it is impossible that the great quantities of materials itemized could have gone to one institution alone."

Some authorities believe that isolated buildings in the Ta Prohm area and Pra Khan were given over to the treatment of the sick. It seems likely that in all instances the hospitals were closely allied to the temples.

There is plenty of argument about the part Ta Prohm may have played in this beneficent work. Most authorities contend that it was just a temple consecrated to the service of the dour gods. But one who looks at it in the green pall that it will presently carry to its grave prefers to see in its shades the phantoms of humans whose lot was made a little easier because of its existence.

CHAPTER XX

The Lesser Temples

CLUES IN THE LENGTHENING TWILIGHT

Wherever one walks in dim avenues of Angkor he comes upon traces of Yaçovarman, King of Glory. Sixty years ago his ashes drifted with the breezes in the jealous and uncommunicative forests. Came Mouhot to look, unrecognizing, at his ghost and to exclaim hopelessly:

"Sad fragility of human affairs! What of these centuries that generations which succeed them shall be able to tell us nothing of their history. What of the illustrious men, artists, sovereigns, warriors, whose names, worthy of preservation to posterity shall never be able to emerge from the heavy pall of dust which covers their tombs!"

To-day the name of the founder of Angkor takes rank with those of Cheops and Nebuchadnezzar on the roster of the world's great builders. The marvel is not that he should have emerged from oblivion but that he should ever have been forgotten.

Angkor Thom, of course, must always eclipse his

other works, but it is manifest that he did not finish his program of construction when the chiselers completed their work on the Bayon.

If only for the works which he sponsored outside the walls of Yacodhapura, he must always be known as a great man. There is some possibility that he gave the inspiration to the designers of Bantei Kedei and Ta Prohm. It is certain that he sponsored the odd developments east and west of the capital known as the barays.

The barays were artificial lakes, probably the largest basins of their kind in all of Indo-China. They were about two miles long and a mile wide and reached a depth of some thirty feet. Striking in their way as the other engineering feats of Angkor Thom, they had no part in the ornamental scheme of the capital. They served as vast reservoirs to insure the irrigation of the rice fields and possibly to supply the town with water during the dry season.

To-day much of their original outline is gone. The eastern end of the western lake, which probably was the shallowest portion, is now a marsh planted in rice. The eastern baray is similarly divided, and a road runs past a temple that was once an island in its center.

The Mebon temple, also accredited to Yaçovarman, was in itself a considerable work. The records tell that he did not decide to erect it until the baray was completed. However, engineering difficulties meant nothing to the King of Glory. He caused the lake to be drained and the rivulet which fed it dammed.

After this preparation rock was sunk in the soft ground until a foundation solid enough to support the weight of a shrine was completed. Then the water was allowed to flow once more.

The island itself was square and the temple a pyramid which, while small, was a definite architectural mile-post in the direction of Angkor Vat. It was ornamented with the lavishness that characterized all the art of the Khmers and the inevitable Nagas railed its approaches. However, it boasted one bit of decoration entirely new. At each corner of its lower platform stone elephants, virtually life size, stood peering out at the lake. They were not, as were the others of their tribe at Angkor Thom, mere bas-reliefs clinging shadowlike to a wall, but complete sculptures anatomically correct and well executed.

The elephants have withstood the rains and the sun and the invasion of the forest much more successfully than the temple they decorated, for one sees them to-day as lifelike as when they were placed there, still looking off into the distance as if in search of the vanishing waters.

One discovers here that the entire baray is overgrown with forest and underbrush. The thick loam

TA KEO

Smooth, hard rock that defied the carving chisel gives a dominant quality to a shrine said to have been dedicated to human sacrifice

of decay has filled it virtually to the level of the first terrace of the Mebon. Only in the wet season does this important engineering work of Yaçovarman give hint of the purpose for which it was designed. Even then the island of the Mebon is no island at all inasmuch as the road that crosses the reservoir is diked to prevent inundation.

All the countryside hereabout is strewn with temple buildings, sometimes triumphant against the forest with towers that stand clean and beautiful in the light, sometimes mere rubbish heaps out of which the fanned heads of the cobras and the dismembered arms and legs of the guardian giants protrude with horrible effect. Men have given lifetimes to the study of these groups and yet have not penetrated to some of their disrupted galleries. The traveler can visit only a few of them and retain a definite mental picture of only about half of those he explores. For the most part his memory of those back areas beyond the east wall of Angkor Thom will be a formless vista of desolation sunk in roots and greenery.

However, in the days before the phalanx of the forest broke across the northern moats, and when temples stood as monuments in open spaces or lifted their pinnacles out of calm blue lakes, this region must have been the scene of a pageantry hardly less magnificent than that of the capital. Sitting by the elephants of the Mebon, for instance, one can imagine the plain swept clear of its trees—a wide garden of greenery checkered with the turquoise of reservoirs and the cruciform pools of the sanctuaries. One can see the temples standing out of it, their towers visible for miles across the terraced fields. White roads spin through this vision like the veins of a leaf and lean brown men and their dark-eyed wives move in a nimbus of silvery dust.

It is the night of a feast—the birthday of a king, or the holiday of a god. Fires are burning in Pra Khan and in Ta Prohm and Bantei Kedei. There is a ruddy glow in the sky above Angkor Thom and the pyramid of the eastern Mebon is an inverted flame in the still water of the baray. And the close-packed millions of the people of Angkor are on the roads with torches in their hands. Patterns of light weave across the blackness of the plain. Streams of fire are flowing in weird channels, welding at the unseen crossroads and spreading out in dazzling tapestries in the temple courts.

Religion was the poetry of these people and it was more than that . . . it was the sublimation of art and the drama. The temples were the esthetic soul of the nation.

Near the Gate of Victory of Angkor Thom—that oddly placed arch of triumph in the eastern wall—are to be found two symmetrical shrines, Thom Manon and Chau Say—alike in design and structure and twins also in ruin. They seem to have been little pavilions erected on platforms that were lifted above the ground level by pillars.

Adjacent to them is the majestic ziggurat of Ta Keo, most enigmatic of the minor fanes, stepping up toward the sun with a dignity and power suggestive of Angkor Vat. It is dripping with green and crowned with trees but is still supreme over the forest. Its rocky masses rising above the tops of the coconut palms convey the impression that it only recently emerged from some cavern underground, carrying the forest with it in its rocketing ascent.

It prefigures the final temple of Angkor in more than its size for it has a chastity of design that sets it apart from the school of thought represented in the Bayon. It is built of a rock much harder than that which is found in the other temples of the district—a material that did not lend itself readily to sculpturing as the incompleted chisel marks of the builders present plentiful evidence.

These same chisel marks were given an entirely different interpretation when the early investigators began the classification of the Angkorean ruins. The archeologists who first saw the unfinished work took it for granted that the temple itself was incomplete at the time when the Khmers departed. A translation of its inscriptions later tended to show that it was in existence in the middle of the tenth century.

The outer enciente of the temple park was about

seven hundred and fifty feet on a side. The pyramid rose in three stages to a central platform supporting five towers, the highest of which reached an elevation of something over one hundred feet. Ta Keo's lack of ornament makes it distinctive among the works of the Khmers who were so prodigal of decoration. But its very simplicity gives it architectural importance. Its basic design—the three-stage pyramid surmounted by five towers—is precisely that of Angkor Vat. Its plan shows the development of a new spirit in the people, the growth of good taste, a commodity for which the young and boisterous builders of Angkor Thom will never be celebrated.

What carvings there are in the galleries show Ta Keo to have been another shrine of Siva but legend gives the place a definite individuality. Here, it is said, were the altars of human sacrifice. Here congregated the masters of black magic, dispatching hecatombs of slaves and reading auguries in mirrors of blood.

One feels that there might well have been some such dark shrine in Angkor. Voodooistic sacrifices to destroyer gods seem not at all inconsistent with the spirit of the place. It is probable that the collapse of the Khmer capital was in itself as terrible a human sacrifice as the world has ever seen. But admitting all that, one listens to this tale of Ta Keo with some skepticism.

BENG MEALEA

The adjuncts of ecclesiastical murder did not differ much in shrines separated by seven seas. The altars of the druids and the courts of Kali are quite alike. They show that they were designed for the purposes of sacrifice by men who had given some thought to the apparatus required. One finds them arranged for the convenient binding of the victim and slotted with drains. If Ta Keo were the fane of such an industry one would naturally expect to find in it some relics of the priestly axmen. But there is none. The galleries are quite like those of any other Sivaistic sanctuary and the steps of the pyramid rise up to the usual climax in a chamber which probably housed a linga.

From Angkor Thom the road that passes Ta Keo strikes eastward and loses itself in the bamboo. Once it was a royal highway crossing the country like an arrow-shot to shrines long forgotten. It disappeared like the men who built it when the blood-weary gods got down from their pedestals and departed from the land. Out at the end of it is Pra Khan of Kampong Sveay which will be considered later. Fifty kilometers east of Angkor Thom the talons of the jungle have been loosed from Beng Mealea, another capital city whose discovery startled the world hardly less than the finding of Angkor itself.

French engineers to-day are preparing to follow

this road to its terminus—to connect it with a north and south highway out of Kampong Thom, and to open to the traveler new and startling vistas of the Khmer civilization. But at the moment they stand face to face with the forest, deep and impenetrable and conscious of its power.

Beng Mealea can be reached—has been reached—by expeditions overland but it is still as far removed from Angkor Thom as if half a continent lay between it and the Gate of Victory. Few travelers have ever heard of it—a mere handful of adventurers have ever borne the hardships necessary for a sight of it.

One may smash through the forest overland as Groslier did in 1913, marching in fear of the tiger and aware that the wild elephant is not far off. Or one may sit cramped in the steaming heat of a sampan and gamble with the deadly fevers as he moves slowly and miserably up the little stream that connects the region of Beng Mealea with the Tonle Sap. In the end he will see a sight that the gods looked upon when they decided to breathe a soul into the people of the Khmers.

Beng Mealea is worth the visit. It is something more than a kingly city. It is the crystal cavern of the Naga monarch. It is the hall of the wonder-workers out of which came the djinns of the lamp to toss up the towers of Angkor and to write in scrolls of gold the culture of Cambodia.

CHAPTER XXI

The Dead Capital of Paramacevera

HERE LINGERS THE AURA OF LOST GLORY

The sampan men, nearly naked and glistening with sweat, lean on their oars like figures out of an Egyptian frieze. Against the slow current, against the tidal wave of heat that flows down through the jungle, the little boat moves steadily onward.

It is water that slips away under the keel and past the cumbersome rudder, but it seems like metal out of a cauldron—yellow glowing metal that stuns the eye and portends destruction. The sky that comes down like the blade of an adze fresh from the forge is yellow white where it cleaves the trees—hazy orange where it touches the stream.

The air is still and unbreathable and scented with the humus and decay of the jungle that goes on for ever and ever to the north and east and west. There is no rest inside the tent of matting arched over the boat amidships . . . no room to sit up, no space in which to stretch out if one lies down. Food is loathsome, the drinking-water so warm that it is hardly palatable. Sweat streams unceasingly into one's eyes. Clothing was wet hours ago. Now it is plastered against tingling and protesting nerve ends, irritating and unbearable.

The rivulet seems hardly to be a stream at all. It curves with maddening indecision through the flats of the forest, dallying about little promontories of verdure, turning back and veering sidewise until one doubts that it ever came from anywhere or will ever lead anywhere. Save for the fact that the position of the sun is constantly shifting, the scene over the side of the sampan is always the same—a matted tangle of bamboo and fromager. For all visible signs of progress the straining Cambodians might be attempting to move a craft at anchor.

And there are miles and miles of this. . . . Hours and hours during which the ghosts of the fever touch one's cheeks and hell seems to be close at hand.

The rowers never tire. Standing, they clutch their prehensile toes about the gunwale and the edges of their meager supports, and they push forward with that peculiar jerking stroke which is the heritage of Cambodian river men from the days when the Khmers dragged their nets through the Tonle Sap. Onward, foot by foot against the stream. Onward through tunnels of trees to the headwaters of a civilization.

There comes an end to this . . . an end that one is hardly able to comprehend when at last the boat is grounded and aching legs are apprized that they may once more be of use. One stumbles into the water and out again and lies panting on the edge of the forest. And so at last one comes to Beng Mealea.

Paramacevera, also known as Jayavarman III, was a restless monarch. It was he who built Bantei Chmar far to the north of the great lake where the plain of Cambodia rises up to meet the ridge of Pnom Dangreck. Inscriptions in Sanskrit, taken from Bantei Chmar and preserved in Bangkok, testify that he was the patron of a cult that combined Brahmanism and Buddhism and that the arts of both religions prospered in his ubiquitous capitals.

There is logic enough in that. It is known that he spent his youth in Java where, no doubt, he was deeply influenced by the Buddhist temples of Borobudur and Prambanan. Something of what he learned there manifestly found its way into the art of the Khmers and it is perhaps through him that the puzzling link between the Javanese and the Cambodian schools of architecture was established.

Archeologists ascribe to him the erection of Pra Khan of Angkor, pointing out the numerous points of similarity between that ruin and the temple near the Pnom Dangreck. But it would seem that he was a builder whose work never satisfied him. He moved his wives and elephants and chattels out of Pra Khan just as he had moved them out of Bantei Chmar and journeyed eastward to do a finished bit of art work in the planning and construction of Beng Mealea.

The capital proper was at Pnom Koulen a butte lying northeast of Angkor and known in the records of his day as Mahendraparvata—"Hill of the Great Indra." And the removal of the royal residence there from Amarendrapoura, as Bantei Chmar was called officially, was an epic undertaking. The astonishment of the people at the building of the new city is reflected in the stone poesies of Paramacevera's contemporaries.

It is easy to see why the king picked this region for his building site. Pnom Koulen is an uplift of sandstone some sixteen hundred feet high, and, aside from the picturesque novelty that it gives to a landscape table-flat all the way up from the delta, it is an almost limitless source of building material. From this hill came no small part of the stone that went into Angkor Vat and probably the great bulk of the slabs that were transformed into the city of Angkor Thom and the minor shrines beyond its gates.

It is wooded and craggy and creased with ravines from which torrential cascades leap down toward the plain to form the little river that enters the great lake below Angkor at the little village of Siem Reap. At present the plateau adjacent to the mountain is inhabited by an isolated tribe which seems to have little in common with the Cambodians of the great river. These poverty-stricken people carry on a ceaseless fight with the forest, burning out squares of underbrush to plant their pitiful crops of rice. Their villages are plunged in savage squalor.

Somewhere in the district, in which living is now as difficult as one may discover in all of Indo-China, was the great capital of Paramacevera. But one will seek vainly for a trace of it.

It may be that somewhere up on the mountain is another of the hidden cities which the Khmers have left to startle inquisitive posterity. Some day it is possible that another Mouhot may stagger through the brakes and come upon another maze of golden towers and sculptured palaces. But we may take the word of Aymonier for it that no such miracle has taken place as yet. He says:

"Without doubting at the time the historical matters brought up by this Pnom Koulen, I explored the region completely, not only through a sense of duty to my profession and an archeological zeal, but because I was attracted and interested by the pleasant and agreeable aspect of a mountain in a district where such things are exceedingly rare. I am qualified then to say that the ruins are insignificant and that there is nothing to indicate the establishment of a royal residence which was a prodigious event."

However, Beng Mealea, in the plain south of the

mountain, comes close to satisfying the requirements of a Khmer capital and may well have furnished a site for the royal city as well as for the religious center that flourished about its great temple. Aymonier fixes the classification of this area among the works of Paramacevera and in an interesting study of the religious thought of that day explains away the mystery of the shrine on the mountaintop, while he establishes the chronological order of the three capitals, Pra Khan, Bantei Chmar and Beng Mealea.

He points out that the ancient cults as transplanted in Cambodia and the land of the Chams out of India demanded that their shrines be erected on elevations. He suggests that the temple pyramids of Cambodia were built in an effort to compensate for the natural deficiencies of a flat countryside.

"Inasmuch as the rule demanded the erection of temples on heights actually inaccessible for such works," he says, "fiction came into play eventually to reconcile the conflict of sacred rite and practicality. Situated on a plain the monument was borne by a sort of mystic association to the distant summits and the less its real position conformed to the rites the greater was the necessity for affirming its fictional situation." From this one gathers that the inscriptions describing the city of the heights of Pnom Koulen were written for the purpose of deceiving the gods who, had they been able to tell the difference between a plain and a hill, would undoubtedly have put more mountains in Cambodia.

Aymonier also points out the similarities of the three towns built by this peripatetic king and finds a significance in the lake shrines which were common to all of them.

Neak Pean, the shrine of the serpent at Pra Khan, was the largest of its type. A similar Mebon temple is found near Bantei Chmar but it is smaller. At Beng Mealea the Mebon of the pool that lies to the east of the principal temple has shrunk until it is scarcely more than an altar. This he takes to indicate that the cult of the female serpent, patroness of Cambodia, had become less and less popular during the reign of Paramacevera, until at the time of the building of Beng Mealea it had virtually disappeared.

Beng Mealea as one sees it now resembles Ta Prohm in its complete submission to the trees. The jungle has not merely hemmed it in. It has crushed it down and the highly ornamented galleries parade through a limitless pergola of trunks.

But once it was the Cambodian Venice, jeweled with artificial ponds and garlanded with sparkling moats. When the king came here questing for a place in which to build his city he found, no doubt, a semi-arid region. Gardens blossomed in this land which so nearly conformed to the legendary description of the home of the Nagas. And there is something pathetic in the possibility that the irrigation projects of the Khmers which softened the baked surface of the soil may have prepared the way for the forest that now is choking the city and scattering its remains.

Beng Mealea was a place of many projects aside from its principal temple. Even amid the trees one can still trace out the walls of six secondary shrines and miles of banked roads and causeways that connected them.

The royal shrine was in the midst of a square park whose outer enceinte measured more than seven hundred and fifty feet on a side. Monumental gates, similar in position at least to those of Angkor Thom, pierced the walls. Paved roadways led across the moat and under the arches toward the temple terrace.

Basins lined with masonry formed an important part of the ground plan. The causeway crossed a system of ponds on the east. Other such works were symmetrically arranged on the sides. On the west were two detached buildings set in courts made by the junctions of galleries, and Aymonier has pointed out that they may well have been human dwelling-places.

The temple itself was, like Pra Khan, a system of concentric galleries in the center of which was a great square sanctuary surmounted by a tower. The tower is gone although enough of its remains have been found to indicate where it stood and what it looked like.

The beauty of Beng Mealea is to be found not only in its site and in the setting which glorifies while dismembering it, for the works are on a scale almost without parallel in Cambodia. The cloisters are high and wide and perfectly planned. And the material is a bluish sandstone, cut and set and polished and chased with much greater care than is to be found in other buildings of the Khmers of the same period.

The sandstone came no doubt from quarries to be found to the west of the temple area. Only one sort of material was used and that seems to have been carefully selected.

The city must have been a splendid sight before the dying lichens changed the tinting of its masonry and before the mirror surfaces of its lakes disappeared to make way for the gluttonous fromagers. One can imagine it with the waters rippling along the sides of its roadways and reflecting the polished walls of its enceintes. It was a place of incredible whiteness rising like the home of the peris out of a man-made sea . . . and situated unlike any other temple group in Cambodia with a wilderness of rock about it and the misty reaches of the mountain for its background.

It probably was the serene capital . . . the shrine of perfect peace . . . for all that warrior gods came here to worship and to pray for success in their carnage. But the hint of peace is gone from its ruin. The setting sun brings back to its gaunt towers little of the gold that is spilled each evening on the spires of Angkor . . . instead it sets alight the flaming torch of an enemy conqueror. The echoes that shiver through the jungle are the ghostly cries of men and women who fell under the feet of savage invaders. Elsewhere in the land of the Khmers one feels the loneliness of an empire deserted and envisions a people in flight. Here one walks as in a graveyard and feels the imminence of Death.

The hand of the vandal has left broad fingermarks on the walls of Beng Mealea. It is conceivable that the lianas and fromagers worked their ruin unassisted in Pra Khan and Ta Prohm. One sees them carrying on their parasitical advance even today. But this shrine was constructed with an engineering skill that should have baffled them. Their presence in the wreckage can be accounted for only if one admits that man opened the gates for them and fertilized with malice the ground that nourished the jungle.

There was no rough construction in this region. The stones, as one is able to judge from structures still fairly intact, were put together so skilfully that their joints were barely visible. The material itself was hard as marble and polished to a degree that should have made it impervious to weather. The most eager root could have found no crevice in the vaults of Beng Mealea as they were when the builders finished them. The temple was without those flaws which elsewhere made fulcrums for the leverage of the trees. So one is forced to see in the flattened loveliness of the buildings the deliberate intent of crazed warriors who pried them apart.

Beng Mealea shows much in support of the theory that the Thais rode down out of the North not only to conquer the Khmers but to satiate a puny spite in the destruction of their buildings. One can not look at the depression where the lakes made a sparkling highway to the horizon without seeing the elephant men and horsemen and leg-weary infantry spreading out in a great shapeless horde over the plain. One must hear for ever the crash of iron on iron at the gates and listen with tortured ears to the shrieks of the unfortunates who clustered in the temple galleries awaiting death. . . .

And one watches this scene go on to the horror of corpses piled in the chambers of the gods while vultures fill the gray sky of a dismal morning.

Beng Mealea was one of the outposts of the Khmer civilization but it was erected virtually without fortifications, indication that it came of a period when the nation had little thought of war. And so it must have been engulfed in the first of those tidal waves of massacre that broke for years upon the stern coast of Angkor Thom.

Groslier who explored every known corner of the land of the Khmers was astounded at what he found in Beng Mealea in 1913 and deeply moved.

"It is sad to see the ornamental bloom of the temple pitilessly destroyed and prostrate beneath the living bloom of the earth. Of that art which nothing equalled an incalculable number of manifestations are gone—broken, formless blocks.

"Of that temple which the constructors erected of a bluish sandstone fine as marble with a science and skill never surpassed, of that temple almost as large as Angkor Vat which was to the architecture of the Khmers what the Sainte Chapelle is to the Gothic and which leaves nothing to the eyes of the beholder but masterpieces of fineness and variety, of that temple four-fifths are nothing but debris. . . .

"The galleries neglected by the vandals remain much as they were, between massive walls in which one cannot detect the joints between the rocks. In the shelter of their vaults neither vines nor mosses have been able to find life. Humidity alone has pried off a little of the stone at the base. . . .

"The sanctuaries on the other hand are almost entirely overthrown from bottom to top, precisely because the rage of war or revolt would look to them above everything else."

When scientific excavation is begun in the region of Beng Mealea it is to be expected that the work will bring to light numberless treasures of stonework such as may be found nowhere else about Angkor. Ruin itself has preserved them—a paradox of conduct worthy of the great god Siva himself. For where buildings have tumbled down, the cornices, which fell first, and the chiseled blocks of paneling which followed them, were buried alike in the final avalanche of the walls and so have lain protected from the weather through the centuries. Some of these stones already uncovered show a delicate etching that might have been contrived day before yesterday instead of a thousand years ago. There are finely wrought ornaments that seem almost to be the work of goldsmiths instead of stone-masons. There are friezes of figures bent in prayer and long ranks of dancing-girls which have been classed as the greatest pictorial effort of the Khmers. And all of this in a variety without end.

Archeologists have found more reason to regret what has been lost in this temple than the vanished chambers of the Angkorean shrines inasmuch as the artizans of Beng Mealea did not repeat themselves. In the sanctuaries northeast of Angkor Thom one finds a motif of one chapel carried out similarly in another. But it seems more than likely that no two corners of this "garden of rock" bore any resemblance to each other in their decoration.

The principal charm of Paramacevera's city of the

gods is to be found in its restraint and dignity . . . a fact that adds a little to the puzzlement with which one looks at the Bayon, efflorescence of a later generation. In Beng Mealea beauty was sought before grandeur, and the mere vastness of the temple is something that one does not comprehend until he has fought his way through the forest and made a circuit of its ruins. It becomes apparent that art underwent some radical development between the time of Paramacevera and the rise of Yaçovarman. It is delicate and lovely in Beng Mealea, arrogant and mighty in the Bayon, assured and triumphant in Angkor Vat.

The sun has set. But night brings no new shadows to Beng Mealea already immersed in an impenetrable darkness. A sunset here is anticlimax since that long-gone day of the red twilight. . . . The faggots are gathered. One strikes a match to cook a simple meal and for the moment the sacred fire is rekindled before the sanctuary and the wavering flame weaves a pattern of weird shadows on the vaulted ceiling. But one realizes sadly that all of this is an empty gesture. Beng Mealea is dead and there is no necromancy in the night nor in the white magic of aromatic woods and lazy smoke.

CHAPTER XXII

Angkor Vat

A NATION'S SPIRIT IS MADE CAPTIVE IN STONE

"They builded a tower to reach to the throne of God and so were confounded for ever...."

One sits on the curb of the moat and watches the thin little ghosts troop across the causeway into the temple grounds of Angkor Vat.... A simple matter on a night like this when the sun has dropped through the trees into the great lake and the moon has not yet risen. One sees them drifting through the cloisters of the enceinte, a pitiful company dusty with the ashes of forgotten pyres, their heads lifted proudly, their diaphanous bodies swinging to the measure of the unheard drums. One sees them advancing toward the shrine of their jester god, a sleazy re-creation of a pomp that had its being in blood and iron. And one is surprised to discover that they are making no pilgrimage of sadness and tears. Rather they are smiling and self-satisfied, seizing upon this brief respite from death as a gift of the high ones in recognition of greatness.

For a moment one feels indescribably sorry for them and then one realizes that they crave no sympathy. As they lived they died and their wraiths retain their pride of accomplishment.

The Khmers on their march from a great to a greater mystery were undoubtedly the supreme artists of their age and just as manifestly a curse to the other races that sought a place in the sun on the edges of their dominion. When the first armed host moved northward out of Fou Nan the doom of Angkor was already written. It was not in the ghastly frenzy of the Thais or an uprising of goaded serfs that the culture of the race came to its finish, but in a national arrogance that fostered hatreds without the walls while storing magnificence within. The frosty towers of Cambodia were carved not with the chisel but with the sword and even the most transparent of the ghosts can not deny that the climax was logical. The Death that rode through the four-faced gates of Angkor Thom did so on an invitation of long standing.

Who were these people?

The old question hurled into the abysmal silences for the first time, no doubt, from the lips of Mouhot, comes back again as the shades are marching across the ancient flags of the via sacra. Who were the Khmers? History—even the history put together in startling mosaic by the archeologists, a history writ-

ANGKOR VAT

Where the precipitous stairs leap up to the Holy of Holies

ten in Sanskrit character and illustrated with a million stony portraits out of the bas-reliefs—gives no satisfactory answer.

What does it matter that we know now how a race, strengthened by Aryan blood or imbued with an Aryan culture founded a kingdom that was called Fou Nan, conquered the peninsula and settled down to make a literature out of architecture and engineering? What difference does it make that the name of one kingly builder was Paramacevera and that another was called Yaçovarman? In past times there was a city called Lyonesse and there were princes whose names were Aladdin and Hercules. Classification of this civilization has made it less real than the courts of the gods who dwelt on Olympus.

We do know that at one time a people dwelt in this valley of the great river and that they tore down the jungles to plant their fields of rice and that they worshiped the gods of deadly fear. They mated and had children as is the fashion with humans, and in time there were millions of them living on the Cambodian plain. They tamed the elephant and rode with him to war, and they brought back nations in chains to quarry and carry the rock that they worked into shrines for the gods that had favored them. And so for a thousand years they were the marvel and the scourge of the Orient. And in the end they stepped out of Angkor into the night.

So much for the physical aspect of the Khmers. It involves no great amount of detective skill to translate that story out of the stones one finds scattered on the path up which they came to their glory. As for the soul of this race one does not touch it as he pores over inscriptions or fixes the period of a jungle-throttled nave. One may catch glimpses of it when the sun is shimmering on the open square in the middle of Angkor Thom or when the twilight brings a touch of realism to the still figures of the Bayon's friezes. But there is one place in the region of terrible ruins where it can not escape, where it is caught up and imprisoned in an aureole of stone. The Khmers can never die while the white towers of Angkor Vat step up to their heights among the low-hanging stars. . . .

Angkor Vat is the apotheosis of the Khmer people. If nothing else remained of all their works it would be enough to mark them as one of the great races that time has produced. One could read in it all their arrogance and cruelty, their poetry, their love of art, their craft and intelligence, their skill as engineers, the fear that they deified as a faith, their surge upward out of the muck of the rice fields and their striving to be demigods.

As one looks at the temple, whitening against the moon, he can not but feel that it was fitting for them to disappear after its completion. Life must have seemed something of an anticlimax to them when the stone-masons came down from the pinnacles and stood back to survey their work. Probably man never contrived a monument to compare with it. Certainly it is without peer in the world's antiquities.

It is difficult to fix the date at which the temple was built. It must have come more than a hundred years after the erection of the Bayon. It has a clean definite plan that seems to be lacking in the temple that Yaçovarman built, and it has a chastity of outline and a pleasing symmetry of ornament suggested in the Baphuon of the royal terrace but carried out on a scale that bespeaks the rise of the people to the zenith of their glory.

One gathers from some of its inscriptions that it was completed sometime in the reign of Souryavarman II who came to the throne of the Khmers in 1112 and left it in 1145. But there is nothing at all to show how long a time was required for its erection or what starry eyed figure stood sponsor for its plan.

After all, the name of the king or the kings who caused it to be built is unimportant for manifestly the temple was something more than a regal monument; it was the expression of a culture.

Angkor Vat stands in a moated park south of Angkor Thom. The temple area is square and a little less than a mile long on a side measured along the outer edge of the moat. The moat is broad and filled with water so that, as J. Commaille expressed it: "Angkor Vat is isolated like an island in the middle of a lake." The façade of the temple proper is five times as wide as the Cathedral of Notre Dame de Paris. The central tower is more than two hundred feet high.

The inner side of the moat touches an enceinte like that of Yaçovarman's capital except that on its west side which was pierced to form "the gate of honor" the wall is decorated with an elaborate colonnade similar to the medieval cloister. A causeway built of massive blocks of stone leads across the water to the wall and strikes through it toward the temple pyramid under a towering portal.

Archeologists have spent much time in the discussion of why this temple came to be built with its principal entrance toward the west instead of east as in the case of the Bayon and other important shrines of the Khmers. That question now seems to be definitely settled.

A hundred years after the completion of Angkor Thom the road that led from the South Gate to the great lake through what is now the native village of Siem Reap was fixed and widely used. A highway followed the eastern shore of the lake down toward Kampong Thom, but for the most part the traffic of Angkor was carried by water. Fishermen who followed an age-old calling on the Tonle Sap brought their produce to market through the South Gate. And up from the delta came merchants and pilgrims and the thousands of casual visitors that flow in and out of any city where the population totals more than a million.

The region immediately north of the capital and the suburban districts to the east were already filled with temple areas. When the designers of the new shrine came to look for a site there was little left save a portion of the plain between the little river of Siem Reap and the road that led to the lake. West of the road were marshes such as are still to be found there. The builders had virtually no choice but to remove the population that undoubtedly had settled south of the walls, drain the rice fields and lay out their square. The size of the temple area was determined by the road on the west and the river on the east.

The orientation of the pyramid then became a matter of no option. The temple was manifestly a royal work, hence the convenience of the king and his court had to be considered. Had the gate been placed on the east side of the enceinte the parades from the royal terrace would have been long and tedious. The natural decision, of course, was to set the temple so that its court of honor faced the highway that passed the royal palace as it came down from the North Gate to the south. Ingress to the sacred park was thus simplified and the ultimate work of the Khmers stood where it could be viewed in all its stupendous grandeur by the travelers who streamed in from the outer world.

The construction of the pyramids of Egypt was a task of minor importance compared with the building of Angkor Vat. For the works of Ghizeh it was necessary to haul the stone only across the valley of the Nile from the quarries beyond the present city of Cairo. Some of the rock used in Angkor Vat is believed to have come from points more than forty miles distant, part of it by water, much of it overland on rollers. And there is no group of structures in Egypt, not excepting even Karnak, as intricately carved as was this.

The causeway leading to the western gate of the temple enceinte is an oddity of engineering. It would be enough to excite the wonder of the modern visitor had the huge stone blocks of its construction been squared as were those of the old Roman roads. But the builders of Angkor cared nothing for expediency. The slabs were cut in irregular shapes which meant that each had to be chiseled to fit the one adjoining. The effect as seen under the noonday sun when all of Angkor is shaking with heat waves is like that of a long strip of watered silk.

Cobra balustrades lined this bridge, lifting their fans where the broad stone stairs come up from the

ANGKOR VAT
Ceremonial basin in the first stage of the great pyramid

royal road to meet the somewhat higher level of the via sacra. Little lions squatted at intervals all along the route to the first steps of the ziggurat. Some of them remain on duty. Some are mere fragments. But the causeway itself is in a remarkable state of preservation.

One passes through the high vaulted gateway where bats are squealing overhead and enters the park where grass plots and a few scattering coconut palms have taken the place of the jungle that had moved inside the walls when Mouhot first crossed the moat.

Ahead, the pyramid of the temple mounts skyward—not in the fashion of the Egyptian pyramids which are definitely geometrical in design and achieve their effect by sheer overpowering mass—but in three ornate stages suggesting the terraces of Babylon and Assyria. One is conscious instantly of a strange combination of delicacy, finely wrought detail and terrific immensity, a conception that is peculiarly typical of the Khmer arts. Here is at once a rocky uplift, whose very bulk is potent thaumaturgy, and a hanging garden whose banks of flowers are chiseled stone.

Never, if one looks at it for an hour or for a day or repeatedly for weeks on end, does Angkor Vat seem real. It shivers in the tropic sun and the rivulets of light that drip over the galleried façade impart to it the phantom quality of an image on a shadow screen. It has no part in the jungle which it has defied for centuries. Its intricate mass—crystallization of thousands of lives—has no place in an empty desolation.

Midway between the outer enceinte and the entrance to the first stage of the temple, one on either side of the causeway, are two symmetrical chapels, jewel boxes of the Khmer art, now slowly falling to pieces. In the local terminology these buildings have been called "libraries" for what reason one might be hard put to say. They are one-story structures with scrolls of the Naga on their façades and colonnaded sides. Their roofs are corbel vaults as are those of the other temple buildings, and, in keeping with the scheme of design, are finely fluted.

Of themselves the two "libraries" are of no great importance, particularly if one has been seen the hundreds of other structures of their type in the shrines north and east of Angkor Thom. But here they are worthy of consideration as a definite part in the general plan of Angkor Vat. The architects of the great temple were masters of their craft, but first of all they were close students of the human eye. They set out to build not only a tremendous pyramid but an ensemble which would instantly seize upon the vision of one who entered through the West Gate and carry it irresistibly in a direct unwavering line to the climax of the central tower.

Angkor Vat is built up from the fan of the multi-headed cobra at the end of the causeway through a series of buildings of increasing importance and cumulative effect. Without the twin libraries the eye might be distracted by the reaches of open space on the sides of the road of honor. With them it is caught and centered. The pools that sparkle in the park are merely decorative fringes to a picture whose essential values are never for a moment in doubt.

It is one of the strangely fascinating features of Angkor Vat that a person must go about the work deliberately if he is to study the building in detail. So long as he stands on the causeway before the first staircase he is conscious only of what lies ahead of him, a vision so ethereal that it might well be a mirage or a thing of moon-dust dropped from Indra's heaven.

CHAPTER XXIII

March of the Demigods

A LIGHT GOES OUT

High up among the stars they placed the symbol of Siva, the Destroyer, and while the flares of the altars transformed the great pyramid into a cascade of flame they chanted in pride that they had made an everlasting shrine to an immutable god. And Siva smiled here as he had smiled at Angkor Thom, complacently, convinced of the truth of what his votaries said. For neither he nor they could foresee the end. Nor could they possibly have guessed that of the two, mortal worshipers and eternal deity, the god would be the first to go.

Angkor Vat was not well served in its gods. Siva vanished and it is significant that with his banishment the forces of destruction ceased to concern themselves with this his principal shrine. Vishnu paused for a moment on his way out into the twilight and there is little to mark that he was ever honored here save for an isolated statue or two falling to dust before the ravages of white ants. In the end came Buddha to overthrow the linga in the holy of holies and to rule over decadent people whose fate he was powerless to avert and whose exile he shared.

It is significant, however, that Siva never could be completely eliminated from his shrine. His ghost, a bit thinner than other ghosts as the ghost of a myth is likely to be, but just as recognizable on a moonlight night, was one of the first of a large company to wander about the shadowy terraces. His ownership was only half-heartedly disputed even at the time when yellow-robed bonzes were chanting the litanies of Gautama here and hundreds of gilt statues of Buddha were being hauled up the hill to repeat the image of self-satisfied detachment in every niche of the long galleries.

Whatever the votaries of Buddha may have wished to do in the way of revising Angkor they found the task beyond them. The motif of the sacred Naga was as much a part of the building as it was of the Khmer spirit and tradition. It could have been removed only with the total demolition of the towers. The derivation of the temple from the Bayon and Baphuon and Ta Keo, and other constructions which were typically Sivaistic, can not be ignored. One feels that here the Khmers succeeded almost in reaching the deity which they had worshiped and feared. For they worked their miracle and through it remained alive long after the gods were dead.

It was no mere detached engineering project that lifted the tall tiaras of Angkor Vat out of the rice fields and into the sky. A whole nation was involved in it . . . possibly two whole nations—the one captive and the other free. The little river that passes to the east of Angkor Thom and then turns toward Beng Mealea and the district of Pnom Koulen was virtually roofed with barges bringing down building-stone from the distant quarries. The overland road was a continuous pageant of naked brown men marching up and toiling down. And steadily out of the east came the immense blocks of rock too large for river transport,—white masses on rollers,—so close together that the highway itself seemed to be in motion.

Brown men in harness hauled the stones. Other brown men picked up the rollers left behind and placed them ahead. The sun was hot as only a Cambodian sun can be. And when it ceased to shine came the rains that made swamps of the roads and lakes of the fields. And still the tide of stone flowed down out of the hills to pile its breakers higher and higher on the promontory of Angkor Vat.

The records of the Khmers are disappointingly meager on the subject of such works as this. One finds plenty of pictures of the life of the man in the street except that portion of his life in which he earned his living. Engineering work possibly had

ANGKOR VAT

The weakness of the corbel arches and centuries of struggle with jungle and weather have not effaced the beauty of the towers nor their connecting galleries

become such a commonplace to this civilization that it seemed hardly worth a stroke of a chisel in the bas-reliefs where the nation's history was compiled.

Aymonier, among others, comments with amazement upon the methods of construction (now a lost secret) by which these people hoisted blocks weighing as much as ten tons to the very heights of their works.

He mentions that at Ko Kher, one of the ephemeral capitals of the early Angkorean dynasty, he saw a slab thirteen feet long, four feet wide and three feet thick on the very summit of a lofty erection. It is within the possibilities that the Khmers covered their works with earth as they ascended and thus had the advantage of a gentle slope to points where stones were required. Removal of such a mass of earth after the completion of the work would have been in itself a stupendous task but somehow just the sort of unveiling that would have appealed to the dramatic sense of these people.

At any rate, however they hoisted their blocks, they must have developed a system whereby such handling was simple and rapid. Had it been otherwise no such temple as Angkor Vat could have been completed between the earliest recorded date in the Khmer history and the time when Mouhot arrived at the head of the great lake.

In general plan Angkor is a typical Khmer

temple. It is a three-stage pyramid as was the Bayon which preceded it by at least a hundred years. Its cruciform central structure was surrounded on each stage by a square of cloistered galleries. Four stairways marched up the sides of the pyramid at the points of the compass. And all of this is typical of no great originality. Yet one does not look at Angkor Vat ten minutes without realizing that here is a building as far removed from the Bayon as Notre Dame de Paris from Cluny.

The difference is largely in the effect of the ensemble. For were the Bayon intact it seems likely that its mass appearance would be much the same as that of the vast pile to the south. But the difference in effect is the difference that lies between the self-satisfied pride of youth and the tolerant, orderly thought of one who has lived his life and profited by his experience. Angkor Thom in a way was the capital of the nouveau riche. Angkor Vat is the accomplishment of culture.

The Bayon even in its ruin is a striking bulk which dizzies one with its ornament. It falls just a little short of true beauty in that the application of the ornament was a bit too lavish—just a little ill-considered. Angkor Vat, which is one great expanse of embroidered stone, does not seem obtrusive in its decoration. Mere embellishment is made subject to general effect and the whole is entirely symmetrical.

One rises from the causeway to the gate of honor of the temple proper, a sort of cloistered porch on the level of the first stage. The rocky stairs are rounded smooth—polished by bare feet that went their way hundreds of years ago. There is some evidence that elephants came up to the portico on a ramp at the side. But there they must have stopped. From the vaulted portico to the shrine of the holy of holies in the distant summit even the kings of the Khmers must have journeyed afoot.

From the gate of honor a causeway leads through the galleries surrounding the first stage and into a court which is unique. Here, midway on its march to the steps that lead to the second stage of the pyramid, the causeway is crossed by a second causeway. The squares thus formed were once ceremonial basins with steps leading down into them on all sides. Even nowadays the rains of the wet season fill them but they are generally kept pumped out by the department of conservation lest seepage destroy some of the foundations of the galleries.

Beyond the court of the pools another staircase goes up to the second stage which is quite the same as the first except that it is perfectly square and lacks the ablutionary basins. From the second stage a third staircase, steep and almost forbidding, leaps up to the heights.

All travelers have conceded that the steps of the

third stage are the steepest in the world. In addition to that they are so narrow that one can obtain little more than a toe-hold on them. One shod in modern footwear must make the ascent sidewise, from which point of vantage, as he looks down upon the tumbled steeps of the temple, he realizes the vastness of the work.

At the top is the third square of galleries with the usual cruciform system of side passages centering in a dim, cavelike room beneath the central tower. This room is the focal point of the monument—the sanctuary where stood the linga of Siva as now stands the weather-pocked image of Buddha, the Usurper.

It is from this stage that all five of the towers start on their way to the sun. The four minor spires are built over the corners of the outer cloister. Under each is a chapel open on two sides to the communicating corridors and on two to the cascading roofs of the lower stages.

From the top galleries one obtains an impression not only of the extent of the temple but of its solidity. The Khmers either knew nothing or cared nothing about cement. Their work is similar to that of the Romans which one finds scattered about the valley of the Rhone, in that the weight of the component rocks was the chief factor in holding the masonry together. Nothing short of an earthquake will dislodge these stones.

True, some of the lower courts present a scene of bewildering wreckage as one sees them from above. But one discovers swiftly that the bits of sandstone are mostly pieces of frieze and ornament which in their original state had little or no part in the support of the building. The curators have gathered them up and placed them in piles for possible classification. But they could be thrown away, and the casual observer would have to look closely to see that they had ever been there.

Fromager and banyan and liana and bamboo were in this area just as they were in the other temple parks of Angkor. But they remained merely on sufferance. Angkor Vat had been built to stay. No wandering root ever succeeded in prying one of its pillars apart. The joints between its stones are quite close despite weathering. The roofs are still serviceable, and this despite the fact that the Khmers did not know the secret of the arch and keystone. The inscriptions on the columns of the upper stages give no indication that they were not completed only last week. The life expectancy of the ziggurat—galleries, towers, terraces and all—may well be another thousand years.

The four faces of Siva, decorative motif of the Bayon, are not to be found in Angkor Vat. There is no end of sculpturing about the walls, inside and out, but it is subdued. Dancing-girls—millions of them—step lightly through the corridors and along the narrow parapets at the edge of the pyramid. They give a gladder note to the decoration than is to be found elsewhere in the Angkor area. In the Bayon Siva was a god, and only the gods could pay him homage. In Angkor Vat his deity was still considered worthy of all that man could devise in the way of a shrine but its elevation above mere humanity was not so well defined. The female figure, endlessly repeated and delicately contrived, is the chief ornament of the work which was left to the world as the Khmer masterpiece.

It is significant of the culture of these people that the pornographic note is entirely lacking in all of their constructions. The Apsaras and the sculptured images of the dancing vestals are quite decorous in all their poses and are dressed, as were the noble women of the time, with a sarong or sampot draped about the waist. The costume is still to be found in vogue in some of the villages away from the zone of French influence. In more civilized centers it has changed by adding a scarf or a loose-fitting shirt.

Angkor's "goldsmiths in stone" were given every chance here for the display of their art. The columns and cornices of doorways are carved in complicated patterns of flowers and vines and in geometrical scroll works so fine that they might have been the product of knitting-needles.

Angkor Vat

The profile of the temple suggests the work of Titans, but the detail of the outer walls might have been contrived by the shuttle of a lace-maker. Tireless chisels made this place a tapestry of stone

The sculpturing along the inner side of the gallery about the first stage suggests that of the Bayon, in that it is the pictured history of the Khmers from their mythical antecedents in the heaven of Indra to the day of glory which came after they had obtained definite mastery over the Chams. Like that of the Bayon it is nearly a mile in length, and also like that of the Bayon it consists chiefly of a pictorial presentation of the Râmâyana, the epic that the progenitors of the Cambodians brought with them out of the Arya Deca. It differs from that of the Bayon in the greater delicacy of its workmanship and in its excellent state of preservation. Of all the hundreds of thousands of faces in the bas-reliefs of Angkor Vat less than a dozen are so chipped or worn as to be unrecognizable.

The Râmâyana, as found in India, was composed of twenty-four thousand verses or slokas, and detailed the adventures of the demigod Râma, his struggle with the traitors who would bar him from the throne of Dasaratha, his alliance with the monarch of the monkeys, and thousands of stories concerning the conduct of his war and his ultimate triumph. Added to that are long panoramas of the Khmers marching to battle, routing the Chams, and bringing home slaves amid exploits of valor hardly less incredible than the episodes out of the history of the gods.

The Râmâyana is supposed to have been written

by the poet Valmiki who set a style in meter that became classic among the Hindus. The date of its composition is some time prior to 2000 B.C., and it is without adequate translation in English. Some scholars take it to be a more or less historical account of a raiding expedition undertaken by savage hill tribes who lived somewhere in the district about the headwaters of the Ganges River and who penetrated down through India as far as Madras and Ceylon. With the celebration of the actual expedition in folksongs, the leader of the raiders attained great honors as an epic hero with fictional qualities that later deified him. Similarly the hairy hill men whom he led were identified from more or less accurate descriptions of their physical appearance as an army of monkeys.

It is not at all surprising to discover one of the world's finest pictorial treatments of the Râma legend here in Angkor. The Khmers who must have received the legends of the Brahmans together with their religion, if indeed one may differentiate one from the other, were the best qualified of all the peoples under the influence of the missionaries from Arya Deca to translate poetry into stone.

So in Angkor Vat one follows the early life of Râma and sees him leading the monkeys in the war that was to bring him back to the throne which he lost through treachery. One sees unfolded the love-story of the beautiful Sita who was coveted by many men but gave her heart only to Râma, and one follows the machinations of Pushkara, the lovely Apsara who made trouble for the gods by tempting the ascetics consecrated to their service. The Apsara was a water nymph in whom one may see a prototype of Undine and the river goddesses of the Greeks and all the lovely creatures of fountains and pools with whom the imagination of man has concerned itself since the so-called Aryan forebears of the Western peoples spread across the European continent toward the Atlantic.

If any minor deity may be said to share with Siva the honors of Angkor Vat, Pushkara, then, would be the temple familiar. For it is she, undoubtedly, who has given the impetus to the chisels that cover the walls with her smiling sisterhood.

There are many other miraculous affairs in the bas-reliefs. One great section of wall is given over to the churning of the sea of milk by a group of demigods who use for this purpose the body of a Naga. There is little in the method to excite surprise. If one sets about churning a sea of milk it is reasonable to suppose that the body of a Naga would do as well for the purpose as any other tool. But in the picturing of the event one discovers a clue to the identity of the giants who stand at the balustrades of Angkor Thom and Pra Khan. They too are holding

Nagas, and apparently, as one realizes after a study of the friezes in Angkor Vat, are holding them for purposes quite aside from the prevention of accidents in moats. The churning of the sea of milk was an affair that appealed to the imagination of the Khmers as well it might, and so it was frequently included in the decorative motifs.

As one blends into the other, the Râmâyana and the warlike history of the Khmers are strikingly similar. True there were no supernatural influences at work in the subjugation of the Chams . . . at least none of the gods who followed the standards of Cambodia showed themselves as picturesquely as they did when Râma was mobilizing his army of monkeys. But there is a fairy-tale quality in the drive of fighting elephants across the screens of sandstone—the mazes of spearmen—the charging of cavalry. . . . And the ultimate dénouement, still unwritten when the poets of Angkor threw down their writing implements and took up carving tools, is the same in both epics: the parade of the demigods into the mysterious shadows.

CHAPTER XXIV

The Tale of the Hidden City

FAIRY-STORIES SOUND TRUE BY MOONLIGHT

To the rest house at Kampong Thom came a Cambodian with the story of another Angkor.

"I have been working on the new road that goes north from here to the border of Siam," he said. "And I have seen many of my people who know of a hidden city northwest of Pnom Dek. They tell me that no white man has even seen it . . . that it is just the same as it was when our ancestors, the Khmers, gave it back to the jungle hundreds of years ago." . . .

Probably Cambodia is full of such tales of buried cities. Subsequent experience would tend to show that the story of Mouhot, told and retold as the men of the villages encounter their brothers in the wilderness, is constantly changing in characters and locale until it seems like something entirely new. There will always be buried cities in Indo-China even after the last of the jungle is cleared and the last tiger is killed and rice fields extend all the way across the peninsula.

The whispers that preceded the rediscovery of Angkor will always remain in circulation even though in time they take on a character of legend.

But there was no denying the sincerity of this road-worker. There was the light of faith in his eyes. He himself had never seen this city. He had not ventured any farther into the jungle than most Cambodians will venture. But the stories he had heard had evidently made a vivid impression. As he talked one could see the temple towers of another Bayon thrusting their gray tiaras out of the entangling green. . . . And it becomes singularly easy to listen to fairy-tales when one has looked for a time at the glorified myth of Angkor Vat.

"The new road is not a very good road yet," he said. "It goes from here straight into the forest to the mountain of iron that is in the north. That is why the French have built it. There will be a mine up there and supplies have to be taken to it and the iron will have to be brought back. Some day—maybe next year—the road will be like the one that goes to Angkor, smooth and hard and paved with rock. Then many people will see this city. But now the road is new and difficult and nobody follows it who does not have to." . . .

Monsieur Albertini, manager of the hotel, heard the story of the hidden city without surprise or great concern.

"He probably means Pra Khan of Kampong Sveay," he said. "Monsieur Groslier was in that region some years ago and reported a temple group of considerable size. . . . But on the other hand it may really be another lost capital. It would not be surprising.

"The ruins of Sambour, up the river a short distance from here, were hardly suspected two years ago. Recently more than fifty temples have been located and possibly there are others still to be found in the bamboo. Just because the maps do not show any extensive remains up near Pnom Dek one need not suppose that there aren't any. . . . And against that is the imaginative instinct of the native.

"The Pnom Dek is a butte about a hundred kilometers north of here and the road- and mining-engineers who have stayed at this hotel have told me that the trail is practicable for a small car to that point at least."

The Cambodian road-worker was definite in his description of the region in which the hidden capital was supposed to be located,—which in itself gave his story a quality lacking in most legends of the district.

He told of a depression running westward from Pnom Dek and said that the lost town would be discovered at a point back in the jungle where a second depression ran north and south.

"A road has been laid out toward the west," he

said. "Why it is there I do not know but I have been told that the engineers cut into the bamboo to get timbers for bridges. If the stories are true—and I believe that they are—then you should be able to go by automobile to within two or three miles of the place. . . .

"Why do I not go myself?" He smiled at the thought.

"My people must have had some good reason for leaving these cities. I have a wife and family in Kampong Thom and I have no business with ancient temples." . . .

And that attitude of mind did not seem at all strange when one remembered how Yin, product of the Saigon schools, had felt the age-old curse of the Khmers as he stood at the gates of Angkor.

Day after to-morrow a boat would be sailing from Ream on the Cambodian coast for Bangkok and in Bangkok a train would be waiting to carry one down through the jungles of Malaysia to Singapore, the world's crossroads. Angkor, with all its beauty and mystery, was back there in its forest, a poignant memory beside which all other secrets of the Cambodian plain must seem matters of no importance. The journey of an inquisitive pilgrim was finished and the sky-line seemed filled with a mirage of clean cities with snow in the streets and holly wreaths in the windows.

THE TALE OF THE HIDDEN CITY 295

Here in Kampong Thom the white stars were pressing down on the roofs. Xylophones were trickling the same old tunes in the native huts along the river. Brown men and naked children in the streets. . . . Masculine women in gaudy sampots shopping in the open-fronted stalls of the market or slipping like shadows through the half-seen dust . . . A hint of a warm night in the still fragrant air . . . Fans whirling in the high-ceiled dining-room of the hotel . . . Mangosteens piled in compotes on the tables . . . And near the door a calendar whose red lettering blazoned forth the irony that in a week Cambodia and the rest of the world would be celebrating Christmas . . .

If there were the potent ingredients of nostalgia in all of this where is there any inconsistency? Anticlimax, in the person of the Cambodian teller of tales, was manifestly worthy of no consideration. Half across the world lay home. And at Singapore would be many ships with smoking funnels, their prows turned toward the west. . . .

However, there are influences stronger than nostalgia and one of these is curiosity. What if this tale of a hidden city should be true? What if the prince of the fairy-tale had laughed at the reports of the sleeping beauty who lay enchanted in a capital girt with lianas? What if one were to obey a momentary impulse and dash half across the world only to rediscover a civilized monotony and substitute for the memory of Western cities a vision of splendid towns beyond the curtains of the jungle?

So an impromptu expedition was organized overnight. The heavy motor that was to have gone on down to the sea was shunted into a semi-permanent berth beneath the sheds of the rest house. The ship that sailed northward through the Blessed Isles of the Gulf of Siam slid out into the opal waters beyond Ream with a vacancy in her passenger list. A little automobile, smaller than the smallest of the American products which courtesy designates as automobiles, was hired from Monsieur Albertini who had some faith in the car and more in the luck that favors the inquisitive. And dusty maps were produced from somewhere in the residency to show a routing in pencil-marks toward intriguing white spots that made a phalanx along the upper edge.

"The trail will take you within four kilometers of the city," the Cambodian road man had said. So preparations were quite casual. There would be little walking—so canvas shoes would do well enough. There would be virtually no quarrel with the shadowy jungle—so firearms would be merely an incumbrance. Water supplies could be kept in the car—hence no need for canteens. Save for the long empty miles in which a broken steering knuckle or a damaged axle might be disastrous the expedition seemed no more

THE TALE OF THE HIDDEN CITY 297

complicated than a ride through the streets of Saigon.

Enough food for three days was stowed away in a box in the tonneau, a Cambodian chauffeur who had worked on the road was impressed into service as chief engineer. Another Cambodian with some knowledge of the upper country was hired as a guide, and the caravan was ready for the journey.

One morning shortly after midnight it got under way. . . . A cool night for the tropics, with a north wind that became genuinely chilly when the highway turned over the river to meet it.

The dipper was hanging upside down in a dark sky. The manager who had retired early came down to the driveway in his pajamas to give some words of cheer. He looked into the blackness and shivered, remarking that warm clothing would have been a desirable addition to the equipment. It was too late then to profit by the advice. He shook his head and waved farewell, expressing the hope that no one would be brought home frozen to death and the little car swung out of the gravel path and into the main highway.

Birds sat huddled in the road and took sleepily to flight as the lights struck them. Sometimes they cleared the hood in their lumbering ascent. Sometimes they crashed against the wind-shield. Rabbits proved more agile but just as numerous and just as careless in their choice of sleeping quarters.

A short distance from Kampong Thom the road branched to the right from the course that leads along the Tonle Sap to Angkor. At about ten kilometers it shut its eyes and dived into a dense forest where lights were flickering like will-o'-the-wisps. Here and there close to the highway one could see natives building fires under their elevated huts or huddled together in their doorways.

At twenty kilometers came the end of the pavement and the car struck a road that was fairly hard but not graded. It was one long procession of hillocks and thank-you-ma'ams for the next sixty kilometers. The composition was sand, sometimes packed, sometimes loose. The little motor whined through it in low gear with a vibration that threatened to disintegrate it.

There were indications that some real highway engineering had been done along the route. At twenty-five kilometers came a definite mark of civilization: a detour sign: *"Route Peste, Pas Ouverte Pour Circulation."* And one smiled at that. There was genuine naïveté in the thought of designating any particular section of this road as a *"Route Peste."* It was all *"peste"*—as bad a road as automobile ever attempted to negotiate.

Obeying the instructions on the sign the driver turned west. The route as a matter of fact was no worse than it had been save that the scenery was a bit of wilderness with a quite chilly fog floating over it.

At thirty kilometers came a clearing that looked like any section of the Argonne in 1917. Possibly a forest fire had visited the region. More likely the open space represented some of the outposts of culture as represented by the invading rice fields. It was too dark to make any investigation of the landscape.

Almost immediately the forest closed in again and the road pinched out at a gateway beyond which a group of barracks stood in a grove of bamboo. This turned out to be a police post whose usefulness up there in the wilderness must be largely conjectural. A sleepy-eyed Annamite sentry rested his rifle, hitched up his sampot and grudgingly gave the information that the caravan was on the wrong road.

Followed a back-track seemingly without end, a turn to the east and then a narrow slot in the jungle. The Cambodian scout had said that the iron mine trail was not a very good road. This lane, to which the darkness gave the appearance of a moraine between the trees, answered the description to the letter. It was hardly a road at all. Some one had chopped down the trees. But here and there the stumps stood out of the sand and in numerous places the logs lay where they had fallen.

One could only hope that this time the driver had guessed correctly. The grass was growing two feet high in the so-called road and there was no room to turn around in the event of a mistake. The Cambodian at the wheel kept sounding his horn. . . . This may have been the result of habit or merely the yearning of an elementary nature to make a noise.

Eventually this lane led to a kilometer post marked twenty-eight, where it joined another road—probably a continuation of the *route peste* from which the detour had been indicated. The old highway had been blocked off at this point. The new veered into a district that seemed to have been purposely corrugated.

And so the protesting motor shivered in its slow journeying—always in low gear, always threatening to fall apart. Progress so far had been made at a rate of about fifteen miles an hour.

At forty-seven kilometers a string of natives came out of the forest. The lamps showed that they were carrying the wicker sieves used in the working of rice fields and apparently they were turning out ensemble for some sort of community service from a near-by village. It was still three hours before dawn which indicated that their fields must be at a considerable distance from their town.

Their dogs, apparently, had never seen a motorcar. Instead of loitering as do the stupid animals about Kampong Thom, or taking two thoughts about which direction they had better choose in leaping to safety, these started to run along the highway in front of the car. It never occurred to them to get off the road at all.

At fifty kilometers the road was white with floury sand, and along it ranged the gaunt, bone-white trunks of the fromagers. Beyond this stretch, which was very nearly impassable, the trail sidled up to a ravine with a bridge across it. The bridge was made of bamboo—matted and tied together with liana and anchored at the corners with stakes.

To test the crossing, ropes were attached to the rear axle and snubbed about adjacent trees, then as the guide allowed an inch or two of slack at a time the car was pushed out on to the bridge. The structure sagged perceptibly but it held. After that one ceased to pay much attention to such engineering. The jungle seemed full of it.

At sixty-five kilometers there was another bamboo trestle with a road crew at work on its supports. Here the end of the trip seemed to be definitely in sight. But the road-workers scoffed at the idea that their shaking death-trap could be any more perilous than those to the south. A coolie, picked up as a sort of auxiliary guide, stood on the running-board and shouted what may have been prayers as the chauffeur let in the clutch and rolled the car out on to the quivering mat.

The crossing here was almost a bit of tight-rope

walking. There was a sickening elasticity in the middle of the bridge and a side sway that promised momentarily to drop the whole structure into the bottom of the ravine. The sag created a serious gradient at the far approach, but the little car found traction and lifted itself back to solid ground.

Beyond the ravine the woods seemed scrubbier. There was no bamboo tangle and one saw few ferns and virtually no underbrush. It was apparent that this must be the spot from which the road crews had taken their timbers.

At sixty-five kilometers the trail bore off to the left. A sign-post announced that Pnom Dek lay some thirty kilometers ahead. But instantly the chance for getting to it seemed remote. If the road had been bad before, it was now unthinkable. It was hardly a trail—merely a shell-shocked forest where somebody had cut out a few trees but had paid no attention to the grass.

The next fifteen kilometers were accomplished only by dint of continuous wrangling with the chauffeur and the guide from Kampong Thom. The driver could not rid himself of the thought of what might happen to him if anything went wrong with the car. The guide was nervous for some reason which he did not explain. He kept glancing at the woods on both sides of the trail and paid little attention to the plaints of his companion.

In one spot the driver stopped and turned off his switch.

"It is impossible to go any farther here," he said. "The grass is too high. There are rocks and stumps in this place and we may break a spring or even an axle."

The argument was true enough but on the other hand it might have been advanced at almost any time or place during the last fifty kilos. The driver gave in at length,—to threat rather than logic,—and proceeded while his passengers walked ahead seeking out stumps. The high grass belt extended only for a kilometer or so.

Real trouble came when the car passed the marker at the fifteenth kilometer and stopped in front of a camp of coolies who were tying saplings together to make a bridge. A gully running between steep walls of black rock stretched at right angles across the trail. And that was the finish of the route so far as motor travel was concerned.

The coolies averred that there was no other way across and that there was no real object in looking for one inasmuch as nothing but jungle lay beyond. The chauffeur shut off his motor, leaned back in his cushions and looked about with an expression that told eloquently his opinion of amateur adventurers.

A crazy quest had come to the finish that he in his superior wisdom had foreseen. . . .

The forest seemed deadly silent now that the motor had ceased its plaint. But one's spine still tingled with the vibration of those weary miles up from Kampong Thom. . . . The dawn was streaking the sky with tiger stripes above the fromagers. . . .

CHAPTER XXV

INTO THE WILDERNESS

PROGRESS OF A FOOL'S ERRAND

THERE was deep disappointment here. . . . A weary journey come to nothing. . . . A maddening complacency on the part of the natives who plodded on about their work only slightly concerned that any one might wish to cross the ravine—less concerned that the crossing could not be made possible in less than three weeks. From the point of view of one who stood looking back at events from the brink of the gulley it seemed childish to have listened to the folk-tales of a starry-eyed savage, stupid to have stepped out of the trodden highway that would have led eventually to Bangkok.

The world seemed an incredible distance beyond this wilderness. Its very existence now appeared as dubious as the magic cities of the forest so glibly described in Kampong Thom.

"Shall we go back now?" inquired the driver.

It was not until afterward that one learned of his recent marriage and of the young bride who mourned his absence in the civilization that lay to the south. . . . Taken merely at face value his question savored of undue haste.

True, an immediate return seemed to be the only logical course in the situation. But on the other hand no mere logic had had any part in the expedition so far. Its intrusion at this point seemed unwarranted.

The coolies were questioned about the condition of the jungle beyond the ravine, about the location of Pnom Dek and the possibility of reaching Pra Khan of Kampong Sveay.

They were dubious in their replies to all the queries. They had seen little of the farther jungle—enough to make them distressed at the thought of penetrating it. Pra Khan, they thought, lay farther south—fifteen or twenty kilometers farther south. As for Pnom Dek they were divided as to whether it lay on the right or the left of the road or whether or not it existed at all.

As against this was the tale of the Cambodian— one attached less significance to it now than it had seemed to merit night before last under the stars at the rest house—that the ruined capital lay only a short distance from the end of the trail. The trail, according to the foreman of the road-workers, normally went on for another six kilometers. And here in the cool of the morning that did not seem to be any great distance.

The foolishness of experiment in a bamboo forest where the visibility is close to zero and one has no equipment for its exploration seemed apparent enough. And yet . . .

To return to Kampong Thom for proper equipment meant an immediate ride of close to ninety kilometers in the spine-jerking vibration of low gears. To complete the object of the trip would mean another journey north and south under similar conditions, and the soul rebelled at the thought of it. Better the quick completion of the work at hand. Better the jungle than the delay which after all might end in another disappointment.

The guide was summoned from the car. He came reluctantly. The suggestion that the trip be completed afoot struck him as another of those humorous vagaries that one may expect in all of the Pale Ones. He shook his head.

"There are tigers in the jungle," he said. "There are many tigers there, and wild elephants, and jungle cats that creep up from behind and kill you. . . .

"And then, too, there is no road. You get lost in the bamboo and nobody ever finds out what happened to you."

It was suggested that the tigers would be finishing their night's hunting and that the elephants probably could be heard approaching from the distance. But he found no solace in that.

"No matter where you go in the jungle beyond the ravine you are in the home of the tiger and elephant," he demurred. "I think it would be wise to let the tiger sleep. We have no guns and I have heard it said that the tigers up here get very hungry."

There was no moving him. Fear of the tiger—hardly less than a claustrophobia born of the forests—was his racial heritage.

Man could not fight the great cats barehanded nor could he rely on his dim wits in competition with the mazes of the bamboo thickets. Moreover, there seemed to be a long walk in prospect and the Oriental soul of him was saddened at the thought of a walk for no better purpose than the search for a hidden city.

So in the end the motion-picture equipment was unloaded from the car and mounted. Its usefulness was carefully weighed against the possible need for water. And in the end the water was put back in the box.

One manifestly can not carry a liter of water in a glass bottle very far through a dense woods, especially if he must carry it in his hands. Moreover, it did not seem to be a thing of any immediate necessity. The morning was cool. The objective seemed near. With ordinary luck one might get into the bush and out again before the sun had marked noon.

And thus started a trek whose only excuse lies in

the haphazard information that prompted it—the tricks of imagination that got the better of sane judgment.

One might have thought, for instance, that beyond the ravine would be traces of a road similar to the one over which the car had come . . . at its worst a trail blazed through the forest. One might have expected tall trees and deep shadows and a refreshing breeze stirring through the bamboo.

Instead there came more gullies and black stagnant pools with rotten logs to clamber over before one could take the risk of crossing them. . . . And rutted paths where water-buffalo had marched in the wet season . . . And, where the trail persisted, it was merely a dim opening in the woods with the reeds growing up in it so densely that it could hardly be followed. . . . And low marshy flats, open as a desert, where hot humidity was in the air and lumpy going underfoot . . . And dusty snake grass beating across one's face . . .

There was plenty of animal life in the forest. Red birds circled overhead, screaming at the sight of a white man. They sounded a sharp whistling call of two notes and their fellows farther back in the trees picked it up and carried it on until the whole jungle was echoing to their fluting. It was easy enough to see how one bird might be alarmed into a vocal performance by the note of another. But when one stopped short in the brush the whistling ceased instantly. And that was not so simple of explanation.

The cessation of sound was not gradual. It came as suddenly as if the leader of a trained orchestra had lifted a baton—as if some one had pulled out the switch of a radio set.

One might guess that the birds near at hand were guided in their conduct by what they could see. But manifestly birds hundreds of yards back in the forest can not see farther through bamboo than other animals. The only solution to the problem was that the birds acting as spies on the movements of the interloper conveyed some sort of a signal to the scarlet cohorts under cover. What the signal was and how it came to receive such instant obedience was a mystery that accentuated the fear of the jungle.

Gibbons hurled themselves through the treetops, and now and then came down into the open spaces to examine this new specimen of their kind—this sorry specimen that wore white things about his legs and a white covering on his head and did not seem to know much about climbing trees.

Four times in the tortuous maneuvering through the grasses cobras slipped silently across the path, paused long enough to swell out their hoods and decided to give no battle. Once a little green viper came to provide a tense moment. But he, too, went on about his business.

The jungle had ceased to be merely a region of close-growing trees and luxuriant vegetation. One had hesitated to enter it because of what seemed to be its depressing loneliness. The imagined loneliness would have been preferable to the whispering presences that one could not see . . . the consciousness that millions of eyes were spying from the brush.

The ravine at which the road had come to its unfortunate end wandered about aimlessly but pursued a general course toward the west. So far, at least, the Cambodian's information had been correct. It was impossible, however, to follow its vagrant progress, the more so since pools of water stood in it and snakes had chosen its graveled banks for a convention. A course was laid out with a pocket compass, bearing directly on the spot where the pencil-markings on the map showed its junction with the depression that came up from the south.

The sun came up. In an hour the day was what might have been expected in the land of the Khmers—as hot as it had ever been at Angkor, plus the asphyxiating calm of a region into which breezes can not penetrate, and the stifling humidity of lush lowlands.

Less than an hour after the start of the trek the most poignant desire was for water. In two hours the water had become a genuine need.

But still there was no turning back. Only a few

more paces ahead would be an open space and in that open space would be a city with high towers and massive gates—a city upon which man had not looked for six hundred years. . . . Only a few more paces . . .

And, counting the paces, one presently realized that the eighth kilometer had been passed. The road, if it ever could have been called a road, had disappeared. And there was no golden city on the horizon. There was no horizon. Nothing but the wall of bamboo—inscrutable, baffling.

The sun was getting higher and, if possible, hotter. The metal case of the camera had become so hot that one could not touch it. There were rocks in quantities beneath the reeds and grasses, all of them with upturned points that speedily made shreds of canvas shoes and a bruised pulp of feet.

Back in the jungle were crashing noises—falling trees, perhaps, or elephants. Now and then, over the flats, came the smells of the cat house at the zoo—dense as a cloud, a choking, unpleasant wave that recreated every atavistic fear of the tiger and his lesser brethern.

At dawn it had seemed a simple thing to strike into the jungle and out again . . . an enterprise involving nothing of the adventurous and suggesting no more hardship than a walk along the stone road out of Angkor. It had seemed a matter of only a few hours. And now, with the road gone and the bamboo barrier closing to the west, there was serious question if the round trip could be completed before sunset . . . or if it could be completed at all.

An occasional glance to the east revealed the fact that the freshly broken trail was ill defined. That it could be followed back to the car was by no means certain. But it was not yet time to worry about that. It is virtually impossible to quell the spirit of curiosity once it is aroused. Here as the flats gave way to the bamboo groves and the bamboo thinned out into reaches of elephant grass and the elephant grass broke like a surf against the bone-yards of the fromager trees it was a simple thing to recall the ancient story of pocket mining: A pocket miner was a miner who spent his time boring one shaft in search for a single pocket of gold that would pay him in a lump sum for all his labor. And once he had started such a quest the miner must continue it until he came to the pot of gold or died; for, if he sank a shaft a mile without finding anything he never could be sure that the pocket was not waiting at a depth of a mile and one foot.

And so with an investigation such as this. Each succeeding fruitless mile made it more necessary that the next be traversed. . . . On and on, despite a constricting throat, bleeding feet and the increasing weight of camera and tripod, ever toward the west—possibly straight on to the gates of Angkor.

Walking became a mere automatic performance in which one foot was picked up and another set down. A mind numbed by the insufferable heat was conscious merely of the needle on the compass and a hazy recollection that at some time past there had been some reason, now not worth recalling, for the inception of a fool's errand such as this one.

Still the going was not so bad. Jungle, as envisioned by the Occidental who has never seen one save in the moving-pictures, is an impenetrable mass of liana and fern and scrub palm with morasses underfoot and garlands of moss swinging overhead. The Asiatic jungle is seldom so dense that a man can not walk through it. The trees are straight and clean with little foliage about the roots and the curtain of foliage at the summits is so thick that there is sufficient shadow to discourage any entangling growth of underbrush.

Low visibility is the most discouraging factor in any casual jaunt through the bamboo, and the greatest physical discomfort, aside from the heat which is not indigenous to the forest, is caused by the tall grasses that set their traps for bruised feet in the flat open spaces.

With plenty of water, a few bearers and some axmen, and no necessity for driving into the stifling humidity at a speed which would tax one's strength on a boulevard in any tropical city, the trip from the end of the trail into the Pra Khan district would be no more worthy of mention than a boat trip from Saigon to Pnom Penh. This expedition was of consequence only in that it seemed so likely to end in the disaster that its lack of preparation merited.

The counting of paces became as much of a routine matter as the paces themselves. It was probably no very accurate measure of distance. But even a dizzy brain was capable of realizing when the steps had shortened and so after a while a count that would have indicated a normal thirteen hundred meters was registered as a kilometer. Hence it would seem that there was basis in fact when, as the ground took a gentle rise and dipped again to meet a north and south depression, a hasty calculation set the point at the end of the twentieth mile.

Here, then, in an area close bound by the forest and palpitant with the sun of high noon, was the spot that the Cambodian had designated that night at Kampong Thom which might have been night before last and then again might have been a hundred years ago.

There was no sign of a hidden city. No sign of anything that remotely suggested any activities of human beings in this region since the King of the Nagas dwelt here with his lovely daughter shut off from all the rest of the world.

Once more disappointment, this time coupled with an overwhelming consciousness that the way out of the jungle might never be found.

CHAPTER XXVI

The Phantom Capital

A GHOSTLY METROPOLIS LIES AT JOURNEY'S END

The back trail had been a matter of only an occasional thought as the zest of exploration and the drive of curiosity commanded the advance. Here with the objective vanished and the vastness of the wilderness everywhere apparent it became a matter of poignant concern. The pace that had been maintained on the way in could not possibly be expected on the way out even if the course laid out partly by guess and partly by compass could be picked up again.

Lagging feet turned wearily down toward the bottom of the depression and eyes blinded by the glare and a smarting flow of sweat sought for the broken reeds and crushed grasses that would give a clue to direction. And then, suddenly, a misstep into a hole, a fall, and a painful finish on top of a piece of carved rock.

Carved rock!

The quest was on once more. . . . This time at increased speed despite the treacherous irregularity of the ground hidden by grasses and bamboo. Rock does not come ready carved from the outcroppings of Cambodia however much one might be led to think so from the oversupply of it in the temples to the west. It was manifest that this piece had been brought down from some point above by the rushing of flood waters after the rains.

And so another three miles were smashed into the jungle to a terminus that compensated at once for all the suffering of the journey so far and for all that was yet to come. . . . The climax of a red wall threaded through the green . . . the thrill of somnolent towers sticking up among the fromagers . . . a dead city come to light as Angkor rose before the eyes of Mouhot . . . The fairy tale had come true.

Marshy ground which may have been a moat or merely a scum-covered backwater of the rivulet that had brought the piece of carving southward lay under the wall. Still, greenish objects that may have been logs or may have been crocodiles, broke the oozy surface.

As at Ta Prohm the forest had come into this place from all sides and all angles and had covered it. Vision was obscured save for such little patches of masonry as could be glimpsed through masses of tree trunks and tangles of roots. A hurried inspection of the eastern enceinte conveyed no definite idea as to whether this was actually the boneyard of a dead city or merely a large temple area. But it was evident immediately that the walls and towers belonged to a work of major importance.

A walk to the north along the eastern side of the marsh ground furnished some information after a wearying struggle with the bamboo. About a mile from the south corner was a gate which apparently had been ornamented with a tower. Fromagers had taken root on the vaults and roots were draped down in a tangled mass that defied penetration even had it been possible to cross the green ooze. Probably a causeway had given access to the place at this point but there was little enough left of the masonry to show where it had stood.

It was manifest now, however, that this was no mere temple ground. On the supposition that the Khmers built this monument as all their others were built, then the gate marked the mid-point between the south and north corners of the wall. That would show the eastern side of the enceinte to be two miles long. Presuming the enclosed area to be square or nearly square, one might place the total length of the wall at eight miles. Manifestly this was a city and a city of a size only slightly less than that of Angkor Thom.

It was a fascinating place with its temples only suggested by bulking masses of fromager and its spires glimpsed piecemeal through the trees. Here

THE HIDDEN CITY
The trail drives blindly through the bamboo to nowhere

THE HIDDEN CITY
Telescopic view of wall detail as viewed from across the moat

walked kings whose ghosts by now must be ancients even among the ancient company of phantoms. Here came slaves to die in toil. Brown children played in the streets beyond the gate now blocked by trees. Dancing-girls of temple and court walked abroad under crimson umbrellas. And a population of nearly a million (if one reckons on the opinion of archeologists with regard to Angkor Thom) lived in its clusters of houses, begat its babies and fought its wars.

There was a sadness about it unequaled even in Angkor. A greater mystery than is to be found on the banks of the great lake . . . a more uncanny desolation . . .

Possibly a white man had never looked upon this place before. Possibly no one had penetrated its dismal streets since the Khmers went out from here as they went out from the western capitals into the silence of the centuries. . . .

A great detective story may still await solution inside the walls. It is possible that the temples may reveal a treasure of information if not the gold whose lure has brought so many adventurers into these parts.

One doubts that the shadows of this Hidden City hide objects of more tangible value than those that were discovered at Angkor—which is to say none at all. For whatever this town was, however the

Khmers came to place it here, its fate seems to have been merely a ghastly repetition of that which overtook the other towns. It seems hardly likely that a city which did not escape the Death could have escaped the looters.

But there is no time for such ruminations here. Verification of the Cambodian workman's impossible story has not changed the circumstances of its proof. There is still no drinkable water closer than twenty miles. There is still no assurance that a white man who has looked on these red walls will ever live to tell anybody about it. The back-trail is no clearer than it was two hours ago. And by seven o'clock at the latest there will be darkness. . . .

Some day men will come in here as they came to Angkor. There will be a stone road out of Kampong Thom along the route which now is so close to impassable. Tourists will be sitting on the screened veranda of a government bungalow looking across the moat, as they look across the lily-covered water, at the gate of Angkor Vat. And they will be complaining bitterly about the hardships of automobile travel and the arrangement of the bathing facilities and the quality of the food. Some day, and that not so far in the future, aged ladies from Iowa will come here to contrast this city unfavorably with other cities of the jungle no longer hidden. They will be unable to realize that any fool could have undergone the tortures of thirst and bone-racking fatigue to see such a place when he might have waited a few years and come by *char-à-banc*. Such things will come. The destiny of the Hidden City is in the white stars. But for the present the objective of this expedition is attained. It would be humanly impossible to go farther. . . . .

So in a red haze began the long trek back out of the wilderness toward water.

Water! Once one set his back to the Hidden City and faced the east again the Khmers and their works ceased to be matters of importance or interest. Long miles back beyond the fromager and the bamboo and the elephant-grass of the flats there would be water.

The air was dank and damp and blisteringly hot even in the shade. The smell of celluloid hung like a nimbus about the camera. Even light linen clothing—torn long ago to rags—was an insufferable burden. But such things were minor considerations as compared with a swelling throat.

The first few miles were the most terrible of the trip. In those miles lay the lowlands and the patches of snake-grass and the open spaces where the temperature was somewhere around one hundred and twenty degrees Fahrenheit. With physical discomfort was coupled the uncertainty of the trail. And in time the two produced a dizzy lassitude, a willingness to lie down and rest indefinitely. Only the urge to reach water prevented what would probably have been a monumental and permanent error.

Possibly instinct, possibly a trick of the eye in catching such signs as crushed grass and broken twigs made it possible to find the trail. But there was no assurance that the course was correct for hours after the Hidden City had been left behind.

Hope kept recurring that the change in the sun's position might have cooled some of the shaded spots where the bamboo succeeded the grass. But there were no cool places. The expected breeze through the shadows proved to be a mirage of memory.

There were some elephant tracks in the lowlands. But they were old and received little attention. The cat smells of the brush were still pervasive and easily recognizable. Toward three o'clock a parade of peacocks came out of the denser thickets to walk along like guides, pausing now and then to look back and make certain that they were being followed.

They preserved their distance but showed no haste and did not seem to be at all concerned at the presence of a man.

Probably half the distance back to the road had been completed when there came a collapse. At the end of a fainting spell that lasted possibly twenty minutes, returning consciousness discovered some new characters worthy of their place in the nightmare of the jungle.

They were two Cambodians, totally naked, squatting on their heels and awaiting developments with polite interest. When they discovered that they were observed they fell to their knees and put their clasped hands to their foreheads. The gesture might have seemed totally outlandish save for the fact that previous experience identified it as a sort of salute given by natives to their white "protectors."

They made no answer to questions in French and English but pointed back along the trail and said something. Their manner seemed to indicate that they had been following for some time.

The march was resumed. The elder of the pair walked ahead. His companion brought up at the rear of the file. Both were fresh and apparently in no need of water. Their pace was difficult to follow but there was consolation in the thought that every fifteen minutes at that speed meant fifteen minutes of real progress.

So in a silent *cauchemar,* as unreal as anything that ever plagued human imagination, the dizzy procession went on for another five miles. There the trail came to one of its numerous barriers in a crossing of the ravine. The bank was steep, which presented some difficulty. The old stream bed was filled with stagnant water which could be crossed only by wading, and that presented a greater difficulty.

On the opposite side was a bluff perhaps fifteen

feet high and it seemed impossible that human ingenuity could ever devise a means for scaling it. The men walked into the little river and began to dip up the water in their cupped hands and shower themselves with it. By means of gestures that could not have been misunderstood they indicated that a bath—even a haphazard bath—might have a refreshing effect. There was merit in the idea but it had its defects.

The temptation to court cholera and black-water fever by drinking out of this semi-stagnant stream was strong enough without getting too close to it. And the problem of removing clothes and getting them back on again after removal was too complicated.

There were voices in the air. They seemed to be coming from around a bend in the ravine. But one could not attach too much significance to that. Such things are always the part of delirium. Before any decision could be reached as to their actuality there came another fainting spell.

This time the feverish mists dissolved to reveal two women who apparently had been bathing in the creek around the curve whence the voices had come. They had forgotten their sarongs and made a startling picture. Two brown Eves attempting to drag a reluctant Pale One into the water and give him the bath he no doubt needed. The men stood apart directing the operations after the fashion of the male wherever and whenever there is work to be done in the Orient.

The women seemed disappointed when their ministrations were brought to a sudden halt. It was manifest that they and the men were simple kindly people attempting to show kindness to a stranger from a world that they never would see and in whose continuing existence they could not possibly have any interest. They accepted an Indo-Chinese piaster long enough to look at it, then gravely handed it back. It was manifest that they had never seen a silver coin before. And this within a few miles of the spot where civilization—as represented by iron—is cutting out the axis of its most important advance into the forests of Cambodia.

. . . The trek went onward. In some fashion the creek was crossed and the opposite bank ascended. But that is merely a hazy memory.

Light was fading. The sun had gone down long ago . . . or at least had passed below the tops of the trees. And, though the heat was hardly less, night seemed to be well on its way.

In another hour the jungle would be in darkness and then there would be nothing to do but sit in a silence as deep as that which fills the black halls of Angkor, and build a ring of fires as a protection from the prowling cats until the return of the hot dawn.

But the traveling was easier. The poorly blazed trail had opened into what remained of the old road. Stumps and logs and a wide slot through the trees made a course which could be followed even in the forest twilight.

Somewhere ahead axes were ringing as coolies cut the timbers for their bridges. Trees were crashing down and there was a smoky smell of balsam from unseen fires.

There came suddenly a turn in the road and down at the end of the corridor of fromagers stood the car. The Cambodians had not bothered even to turn it around. . . .

Water!

The jungle folk, who looked with amazement at the bridge coolies and were received by them with no less interest, were given a jar of conserves out of the food box and a little can of sugar which they promptly traded for rice.

The Cambodian driver let in his clutch. . . .

Hours later out of a sound sleep emerged the unbelievable reality of the hotel at Kampong Thom.

CHAPTER XXVII

The Shadows of Babylon

SAMBOUR WRITES ITS STORY ON DUSTY BRICKS

The identification of the city that lies to the east of the trail from Kampong Thom is to-day as much of a mystery as it was when the Cambodian brought word of it to the moonlit courtyard of the inn. It may, of course, be a part of the Pra Khan that Groslier visited some years ago. As against that is the fact that the maps of the district show Pra Khan to be considerably south of the region where this capital flourished. And in rebuttal is the undeniable truth that the maps aren't very good.

The chart which was carried by the impromptu expedition out of Kampong Thom was in error to the extent that it showed Pnom Dek to be on the right-hand side instead of the left of the trail as one faced the north. Manifestly if the cartographer could have been in error in the placing of the tallest point in the district there is at least an equal chance that his guesses were no better in the orientation of other landmarks. The contours of the ravine and the last ten miles of its course show no signs at all that an actual survey of the ground had any part in their design on the map.

The next two years will determine definitely whether the Hidden City is really another of those works of the Khmers which retained their secrets despite exploration in districts near them, or merely some group of monuments already known and improperly mapped. In two years, at the most, the drive of the French into the north will have brought stone surfacing to the trail, and archeologists will be able to study at their leisure this latest chapter in the mystery of Cambodia.

Whatever may be the ultimate decision with regard to this capital, it seems hardly probable that it was ever penetrated from the eastern jungle before. And there rests the excuse, if any, for the great adventure. To-morrow many men will be traveling northward through scenes that probably will match those of the south for monotony. And they will cover in two hours the present harrowing route between Kampong Thom and the moat of this dead metropolis. But there is compensation for smashed feet and a swollen throat in the thought that they will never experience the thrill that comes when the thousandth chance proves worth the taking . . . the bewildering surprise of seeing a fairy-tale actually come true.

When the archeologists started to work in the Angkor region on the heels of Mouhot sixty years ago there was little belief that the Khmers might have had other cities besides those at the headwaters of the Tonle Sap. The mystery of these people was deep enough without further complications. It seemed to be a bit of lily painting to suggest that these great builders might have done more than the titanic work which taxed one's faith in his own eyes at Angkor.

And yet each succeeding year saw new names added to the list of royal residences . . . new towns whose architectural dissimilarities were a more vivid history of the Khmers than the Sanskrit tablets carved to glorify their kings: Beng Mealea, Ko Kher, Bantei Chmar, Pra Vihear . . . a whole procession of cities any one of which would have startled the world had it been discovered before Mouhot started his trek up the valley of the Mekong.

That the end has not yet been reached is made credible by recent investigations about Kampong Thom, where Sambour has come to light after twenty years or more of security from civilization behind a screen of bamboo a little more than a mile deep. One can not see far in a jungle and if one is a native he does not venture far into thickets where he fears the tiger. So monuments forgotten by the Cambodians and so long unknown that they have no place in the local legends are doomed to lie in their green tombs until accident brings the stranger up to their gates.

Sambour is about twenty miles from Kampong Thom—less than that in a direct line. It is near the banks of the little river that runs through this region to join the outlet of Tonle Sap on the way to the Mekong. Its empty temples and walled courts have echoed for years to the sound of steamboat whistles. But it is now only a matter of months since a coolie, more venturesome than his fellows, went into the jungle and came out with the usual tale of a hidden city.

Came the usual mobilization of archeologists and Sambour was snatched back from the fromagers. To-day more than fifty temples line the haphazard avenues that modern axes have hewn through the jungle, and the city is once more identifiable as a city, in some respects more interesting than the masterpieces of the Golden Age of the Khmers.

Here at least is evidence of what the Khmers were before they became the architects of Angkor. Here is material for the reconstruction of their life when the Kingdom of Fou Nan had gone and the scourges of the North were just beginning to taste their power.

Sambour is as unlike Angkor as Angkor is unlike Saigon, and yet one does not need to be able to translate the inscriptions to see in it the beginnings of greatness. There is no swashbuckling design here, no lavish display of ornament, no tremendous massing of building material. The temples are small and of uniform design and the walls of the central portion encompass no such areas as were sometimes allotted to a single shrine at a later date. But it is unlikely that any territory so far explored or still to be discovered will show more of a zeal for building.

Even Aymonier in his *Histoire de l' Ancien Cambodge* makes no mention of Sambour, and reports of investigations about Kampong Thom are few and difficult to find. But it is manifest that the Sambour group was the product of some king of the Pre-Angkorean dynasty. The city, according to the French people living in the neighborhood, was a royal residence. Probably it was the capital from which the policy of Cambodia's expansion in the north received its greatest impetus.

For one thing the temples are built of brick instead of stone and are entirely free from the corbel arches that are to be found all across the upper valley. It is not surprising that vaults should be lacking. Their construction in brick without the use of a keystone would be difficult engineering. All of the Sambour remains are constructed in the form of towers surmounted by pyramids. They are from twenty-five to fifty feet square and seldom rise higher than fifty feet. But in them the parentage of the corbel arch that so closely approximated a true vault in Angkor Vat may be easily traced. The ceilings of the temples slant upward to a point closely following the outline of the pyramid.

There is a decided hint of Babylon in all of this. It does not require much imagination to see in the conventional rise of straight walls and the acclivity to a central peak a relationship to the ziggurat. There is further hint of Babylon in the sculpturing of the brick. Some of the carved wall panels if set down in the Mesopotamian plain, beside the gate at the end of the sacred way that led from the temple of Ishtar, would seem like the work of the masons of Nebuchadnezzar.

Apparently at one time the town stood on the edge of the river. But, as in the case of the Euphrates, the course of the water changed and the town was left facing an area of silt that proved to be fecund soil for the propagation of the jungle. The mud of the river or the humus born of the rotting forest covered up many of the surface works of Sambour, much to the benefit of explorers who now come to look for architectural finger-prints that will enable them to classify the ruins. Excavation has revealed wall after wall of carved brick, and it becomes evident that the burial has preserved the etchings in their original values.

One door-post of stone had fallen flat on its face and was lying in the muck, broken, when the French savants resurrected it. The inscriptions are just as legible as they were when some forgotten chisel man put them there.

Such discoveries as this eventually will divulge as much information about Sambour as is now available with reference to Angkor Thom. It will at least serve to identify the period of the kings who kept their court here. At present the status of this remarkable group is about the same as was that of the monuments about the Tonle Sap when science first became interested in them.

It is possible of course that the appearance of age so manifest in the tower temples as compared with the freshness of Angkor Vat is due to the more rapid disintegration of brick. But any guess that would date the building of Sambour later than the ninth century would seem on the face of the evidence to be in error.

Conceding that there might be some good reason for the establishment of a metropolis in this region, one can admit that brick structures were a logical development. There is no supply of stone near,—a fact which scientists take as an explanation of the lack of ruins in the southern delta where Fou Nan laid the foundations for the greatness of the Khmers. Whatever rock was used in building operations had to be brought from quarries at least a hundred miles away. Hence it is with some surprise that one finds occasional lintels and friezes of rock and at least one shrine made completely of stone.

A carved block that once graced a gateway or temple portico was found recently and propped up under a canopy of bamboo to be protected from the rains. It appears to be sandstone of the type used in Angkor Vat; but there is nothing Angkorean about its carving. The middle of it is given over to a human head with a peculiar coronet and spreading hair, carried out like the lines of a fine etching to the extremities of the frieze.

There is none of the placidity of the Sivaic visages in this piece. Nor does the head-dress seem familiar. This image, save that it was found in a buried capital of Cambodia, might well be mistaken for a picture of an American Indian.

Nor is this the only puzzle in the array of buildings upon which one stumbles every few hundred feet in that empire of trees. There is one little monument in the classification known as "Group A-Gauche" which might have been copied with considerable fidelity from the Doric. It is hardly larger than a modern cemetery vault, probably because stone was used in its construction and there was a scant supply of stone. It seems to have been transported directly out of Greece and is the first indication in long travel through the works of the Khmers that these people ever moved farther afield than India.

Its plan of construction is Greek. Its shape is Greek. The arrangement of its pillars is Greek. The cornice above the door is Greek. But the carvings on the wall and the arrangement of decoration are nothing if not Khmer.

The trees have done their part in the destruction of the ruins—just as they have done at Ta Prohm. But as one looks up through the holes in the towers from the inside, one realizes that destruction here has been aided by the monkeys. Verdure and the rains have made small openings at the summits. Monkeys looking around for missiles to hurl at one another have taken what bricks they needed.

Even now, when pathways have been cut through the ancient town and occasional visitors stop long enough in Kampong Thom to spend an afternoon here, these monkeys carry on their important work of hurling brick.

Hordes of them sweep through the treetops and cluster on the pyramids pausing in their removal of tile only long enough to inventory the wandering humans. As in Angkor, they are nearly tame and do not consider the presence of amateur archeologists as a serious handicap to a profession of wrecking that no doubt has been a tradition in their tribe for centuries.

Cambodian chauffeurs and guides fear the tiger in these woods as they do in the deeper jungles of Kampong Sveay. They will not venture on to these paths without armed escort, and even then walk with obvious nervousness.

Monsieur Albertini was openly contemptuous of this panic.

"I have hunted in this forest ever since I was given the management of the hotel three years ago," he said. "And I have never seen a tiger here. The tigers may have been here once but they have been pushed back farther and farther from human habitation.

"There is little wild animal life left here now except the birds. But because there were tigers in this region a generation ago none of these Cambodians will believe that they have gone. . . . Odd lads these Cambodians. They will pick up a cobra without hesitation or fear and I have seen two of them carrying a live python fifteen feet long. But they will not forget the stories the ancients told them when they were children."

Certainly there is no denying the native fear of the place whatever its origin. One can not go deeply into the feelings of Cambodians. There is a possibility that the tiger is merely a figure of speech covering a much greater if more intangible fear. Yin quaked before the gates of Angkor and was unable to fight off a mental depression despite the fact that he was able to analyze the pscyhological processes involved.

SAMBOUR
The tower of the lions

SAMBOUR
A Greek temple whose presence among ruins of early Khmer architecture is by no means the least of the region's mysteries

The native has no taste for mystery and there is plenty of mystery in Sambour. Perhaps at the back of his cowardice is a taboo that persists although its causes are no longer remembered.

However, if one carries suitable armament and permits them to travel in pairs, native boys can be persuaded to drive the cars over the trails of the rice fields and up under the tall arches of the jungle. They will not stay behind when it becomes necessary to travel afoot over paths too narrow or too soggy to permit the passage of an automobile. But they display none of that reluctance to keep with the expedition which they showed in the journey to the Hidden City. A taboo or a tiger may have definite uses.

Few of the temples of Sambour have received any names other than a letter to identify them with marks on a map. The Tower of the Lions—so called because of the conventional sculptures that flank its stairs—is one of the exceptions. This tower stands in an enclosure that probably was the royal center of the city.

Close by it is what remains of a brick-lined pond now so overgrown with roots and vines as to be almost unrecognizable. It is apparent, however, that this pool may possibly be one of a class with Neak Pean and the Baray of Beng Mealea . . . one of those serpent shrines which marked the deference of the Khmers to the Princess of the Nagas who married Kambu.

The shrines of Sambour are fairly close together and so there is no great difficulty in seeing them. At least there is no difficulty after one has made the jolting passage over the road from Kampong Thom. Within a few months this road will be surfaced. . . . It is graded now to within a mile or so of the lane that leads to the Tower of the Lions. . . .

Just now it has that inaccessibility which makes it seem doubly worthy of a visit and that wild aspect which adds so greatly to its beauty.

CHAPTER XXVIII

SHRINES OF THE VASTY DISTANCE

PARALLEL MYSTERY IN JAVA

ONE can not leave the mystery of the Khmers without considering its connection with the Hindu civilization in Java. There was more than a surface similarity between the two. The hills about Djokjakarta are covered with the ruins of temples, and like the monuments of Angkor they are all that remains of a well-developed culture.

If there were no Angkor the world probably would come to look with amazement upon these shrines and would count them among the architectural marvels of antiquity. But even so Borobudur and Prambanan would lack the human interest of the Cambodian ziggurats. For Java is lacking in the dramatic elements which, even more than the great buildings, give the hazy history of the Khmers its importance in the chronology of peoples. There is no great mystery here.

The Khmers are almost godlike in their legendary backgrounds, and they went out as demigods should in a total and permanent eclipse. The Hindus of Java clung more closely to their parent culture. And when it came time for them to go as all nations must eventually go, their passing was a sort of official execution, conducted by known forces and witnessed by historians competent to write the record.

The Moslems, carrying on their iron-handed crusade through the East, were the principal cause which underlay the collapse of the kingdoms which the immigrants from Madras founded on this island. And in that respect the story is no different from that of scores of other communities. Change the place names and one finds it in the Mesopotamian plain; with slight variations it becomes the tale of the Moors in Spain. The very nature of their destruction seems to identify the Javanese kingdoms as parts of a civilization already quite well known to the Western World. The kinship with Angkor is overlooked in the kinship with other countries all over the face of the earth that heard the voice of Mahomet.

To appreciate them one should see the temples of Java first and then take the long trail toward Indo-China. The Hindu remains along the equator furnish a logical starting-point for such an adventure inasmuch as it seems more than likely that the culture of the Khmers received its impetus from the civilization that developed in this island.

If one accepts the theory that the intellects which

made Cambodia what it was came from the south of India, then one faces the corollary that all or a part of them first stopped here. There is some discrepancy in the fact that the chief work of the Hindus in Java was dedicated to Buddha, whereas the gods of the Brahman cults ruled in Angkor. But that would be simple of explanation if one were to admit the possibility of parallel migrations linked by ties of race and artistic training if not by a community of religious interest.

One takes the red road down from Pnom Penh to Ream on the Gulf of Siam, the threshold of Cambodia, and thence sails northward among a thousand misty islands to Bangkok. From Bangkok he may travel by rail nearly a thousand miles through the jungles of the Malay peninsula to Singapore. Out of Singapore a line of Dutch mail-boats goes to Batavia. Thence railroad or automobile complete the journey to Djokjakarta and the great temples.

There are two distinct temple groups in this neighborhood: Borobudur, a Buddhist shrine and outstanding as the supreme effort of the Hindu colonists in Java, and the monuments about Prambanan where the deities of Brahman India were worshiped until the day when the emissaries of Mahomet arrived to carry on their work of conversion with sword and torch.

As one comes across Java from Batavia by motor-car, Borobudur is the first temple one sees—a shrine whose silhouette suggests Angkor although its details are in no way similar and its decorative friezes portray the story of Buddha rather than that of Râma and the Princess of Nagas. It stands not far from the road, this temple, another ziggurat whose size would seem majestic were it not subjected to instant and disparaging comparison with the memory of Angkor Vat.

That Borobudur belongs to that transitional period of the Hindu religion, so marked in the multiplicity of gods about Angkor Thom, is evidenced in its decorations. It was primarily a temple to Buddha whose story has inspired most of its art. But the other deities whom Buddha superseded and by whom Buddha was later absorbed were not left without suitable representation.

R. Friedrich points this out in his book on the antiquities of Java.

"The mixture of Buddhism and Brahmanism is best seen in the three upper and inner galleries of Borobudur. In the first we see the history of Sakyamuni from the annunciation of his descent from the Heaven of Indra till his transformation into Buddha with some scenes of his life. The thirteen first scenes of the second gallery likewise represent Buddha as a teacher with his pupils; after that it would seem as if a concordat had been formed between the different cults. We have first, in three separate scenes, Buddha, Vishnu, (Batara Guru) and Siva, all together, and other groups follow, Buddhistic and Sivaite without distinction. It is only in the fourth gallery that we again find Buddha dominant. . . .

"Already in the first gallery we also see Brahmanic divinities—Garonda for example—but not in separate scenes. In my opinion the cupola is the principal part and the most ancient part of the temple of Borobudur. It must have been intended to serve as a dahagopa (dagoba) i. e., a place for the enshrining of relics. I do not as yet know of any other dagoba in Java but I should not be surprised at their discovery. The dagobas of Ceylon have an exterior resemblance to the Borobudur cupola but I prefer to classify it rather with the topes or stupas of Afghanistan."

There is logic in this when one considers that Borobudur was not erected—as was Angkor Vat—out of a level plain, but constructed about the summit of the butte already dominating the landscape of the Praga Valley. So there is nothing incongruous in the idea that the top spire of the temple was built first, the lower galleries coming later as a sort of graceful drapery down the slope.

At any rate, the most careful workmanship, the finest carving of the vast shrine, is to be found in the top galleries. The lower tiers are successively worse and the bottom stage of the rising pyramid is haphazard in some spots, unfinished in others.

It is manifest also, from the very design of the

temple, that it had only one shrine of any significance—the bell-shaped stupa which is its crown. Unlike Angkor Vat which it resembles to a certain extent in general plan, it has no cloistered galleries between its entrances and its topmost stage. From beneath the baleful gods who peer down from its gateways the stairs mount upward in a straight and terrifying sweep with no hesitation at any of the four terraces till they come to their breath-taking finish high in the blue. The galleries of the terraces are unceiled tunnels hung on either side with a lace-work of stone and apparently had no place in the religious rites which must have made Borobudur the spiritual capital of Hindu Java.

The carving on the walls is better if less intricate than that of Angkor. Whatever the period at which this shrine was constructed its artists had learned something more about the technique of bas-relief than their brothers among the Khmers. Here the chiseling went deeper—so deep that sometimes the sculptures look more like statuary mounted in niches than relief work. The anatomy of the figures is excellent and feet are presented at their proper angle. Hands are well executed with that attention to detail that comes only after long development in art. Even after the erosion of centuries, one may still distinguish markings at the knuckle joints, folds of skin and the outlines of finger-nails.

In one of the scenes in this panorama of rock, visitors marvel at a full-rigged ship of the high-stern variety used by the first adventurers who journeyed out of Spain and Portugal and Venice into the East. There is solace in the picture for those who hold that the civilization of the Khmers was carried out of this district and into Indo-China by boat, for it shows that these temple builders of the volcanic uplands were not strangers to the sea. It is something more than traditional, this ship, otherwise it must undoubtedly have suffered as the decorative lion suffered through conventionalization of design. The sculptor who carved this galleon had not merely heard of tall-masted ships. He had seen one.

The entire group of bas-reliefs—from this patently European boat to the coy little elephants that never have had an existence in Java—marks the shrine as the work of an alien people. The ziggurat is as plainly Hindu as if it were somewhere on the Deccan Plateau instead of here on the nether side of the Straits of Malacca.

Indian wisdom may have flourished here as one may gather from the mighty ruins of the table-lands and the familiar genealogy of local deities. But it developed no such indigenous culture as that which sprang from it in the valley of the Mekong. The disappearance of the builders of Borobudur seems to have been merely the disappearance of a religion and the abandonment of its shrines. Buddha—whether as a dominant deity or merely as another incarnation of Brahma—fell before Mohammed; but, though the priests changed their garments and their ritual, there is no proof that the people suffered any such extinction as is evidenced in the silent halls of Angkor. The clerics walked out and volcanic ash rained down out of the sky to cover this shrine and others of its kind in the neighborhood with a protective coating that preserved them from fanatic destruction for hundreds of years.

To-day as one looks upon the cupolas of Borobudur he sees it as it was in the beginning, a monument to the gods of an alien land, planted here by aliens who remained aliens to the thought and culture of the country of their adoption until the day of their disappearance.

It has been said by many a traveler that Borobudur is a finer temple than Angkor Vat and there is a wide-spread belief that it is larger. Local pride would classify it as one of the wonders of the world—as in a way it is. But for all that it represents a finer development of the culture that reached its zenith in the building of Angkor, it lacks the spirit, the extent, the grandiose conception of the Cambodian monuments.

A butte of volcanic rock, rising above the flats at the right bank of the Praga River, made a natural site for a terraced shrine. At the time when the Hindu conquerors came into Java the countryside must have been strewn with lava blocks and so there was no lack of building-stone. Eventually the entire hill was encased in carved stone to a height of one hundred and fifty-four feet, with seven terraces marking the successive stages from the floor of the valley to the stupa or dagoba—the bell-shaped spire at the summit.

The three lowest stages are unornamented and seem to be a base for, rather than an integral part of, the architectural design of the temple. The four topmost stages are elaborately chiseled and show some of the most beautiful specimens of Hindu art to be found outside of India.

Fifty feet above the river level a gentle up-slope of ground comes to a square rampart, four hundred and ninty-seven feet on a side, the enceinte of the first terrace. Five feet higher is a second terrace, three hundred and sixty-five feet on a side, and eleven feet above that is a third step whose retaining walls are about two hundred and fifty feet along each face. From this point ascends the ornamental pyramid of the temple through four other stages, each with a carved rampart supporting it. The crown of the structure is a bell-shaped stupa fifty-two feet in diameter surrounded by sixteen smaller cupolas of similar design. There is a wide-spread belief, based on a tradition the source of which has long been in doubt, that part of the ashes of Buddha were brought here from Ceylon and enshrined under the great central spire. The smaller cupolas are not solid but made with a basketry of squared stone through which one can see the Buddhistic image which each contains. There are two other circular terraces of dagobas between the central spire and the floor of the top stage.

If Borobudur lacks the magnificent spread of Angkor it has compensation for the eye in the richness of its ornament. Its terraces are populated by a vast assemblage of legendary characters made vivid in stone . . . the petrified ghosts of a mysticism which vanished from these shores hundreds of years ago. There are about the second enceinte alone five hundred and sixty-eight bas-reliefs, picturing, with troop upon troop of sad-eyed little people, the life of Buddha. Above the bas-reliefs are one hundred and four niches, each of which contains a statue of Buddha. The statues appear to have been chiseled out of cubes of rock five feet on a side.

As at Angkor the general shape of the temple pyramid is square with a stone staircase on each side. But where the stairs cut through succeeding terraces the ramparts jut out perceptibly on either side. There is a second break in each stage midway between the stairs and the edges of the pyramid, and thus the straight line between the corners is effectively and artistically broken. Seen from the air the stone butte is like a great square wedding-cake, with round ornament at the top—a ghostly gray against the yellow and green of the rice-paddies that surround it.

The countryside about Borobudur has become a panorama of rural prosperity since the Dutch occupation of the East Indies. Water steps—the amazing cascades of the rice-paddies—rise out of this valley, as they rise everywhere in the rugged uplands of Java, beyond the treetops and up into the mists that veil the mountaintops. Coconut palms line a magnificent avenue to the temple's west approach.

But it was beautiful here long before man knew anything about landscape-gardening, for there must always have been forests where soil and climate combined so readily for their propagation, and behind all were the ragged fringes of the volcanic peaks. Today these peaks, swimming in the heat of the morning or lost in the clouds that gather every afternoon, are still the most impressive thing in all the region about Borobudur. The landscape at their feet is yellow with new rice, or deep green with cane, or silver where the paddies are covered with water in preparation for a new crop. But there is never any sameness about the color of the mountains. A tropical atmosphere, always misty with rain, gives them a continual iridescence . . . and as one looks at them they turn from black to gold and then to purple.

They have seen many gods come to this lovely valley. . . . And they have seen them go . . . the wooden gods of old Java . . . the pantheon of India . . . the upstart Buddha. And they saw these gods go out again and stared with placid unconcern at the crumbling of the eternal temple.

There is no inscription on Borobudur to show at what period it was erected. But the imagery in the galleries and certain elements in its architecture have led archeologists to place it in the middle of the ninth century. Its construction then would seem to date back to the period when the strong-backed slaves of Yaçovarman were tearing the heart out of Ko Kher for the building of Angkor Thom.

About 925 A.D. the Hindu principalities in central Java suffered reverses, while those in east Java continued to prosper. Borobudur, of course, shared the fate of the government that had cherished it.

It probably retained some importance as a shrine until after the Mohammedan invasions. Then, when the old gods fled from the land, it was forgotten. Trees grew in its galleries and decayed. Volcanic eruptions covered it year by year with tons of ashes and presently the sacred hill became much as it had been before the Hindus cut steps in it to make a pyramid.

BOROBUDUR

The great Javanese temple near Djokjakarta which was the prototype of Angkor Vat

Unlike Angkor, however, its story was never completely obliterated. Always in Java there were tale-tellers who passed on the tradition of its grandeurs, and when, after centuries, the English came under Governor Raffles they heard the whispers. Raffles ordered that the hill be excavated and that the temple, parts of which were visible, be restored.

To the governor its mystery made it the most interesting monument in Java. He was personally concerned when foot by foot the magnificent carvings emerged once more to daylight, and when the odd treaty was completed, by which Java was traded to the Dutch, Borobudur looked as it must have looked when the Hindus left it.

Legend that had been circulated by word of mouth during all the lost centuries back in the jungle came out of its shadows to explain this sculptured miracle. And strangely enough, the old wives' tales fitted in very well with what the archeologists were able to reconstruct from the appearance of the temple itself. To begin with, the shape of the central spire and its encompassing cupolas identified Borobudur at once as a shrine of the type where relics were housed. In the second place, its design was obviously centered in the principal stupa. As a third consideration, it was too lavishly ornamented to have been a work for the aggrandizement of any mere prince. To this was fitted the story from the hinterlands:

When the body of Gautama Buddha was cremated his ashes were distributed among eight towns so that his followers might not have far to go on their holy pilgrimages. At a later date seven of these tombs were opened at the command of Ashoka, the Great King, and the ashes were redistributed in eighty-four thousand stone jars. These jars were placed in the hands of missionaries going out to spread the wisdom of the ultimate negation among the spiritually arid peoples of the Far East. . . . And eventually one of them came to Borobudur to find a resting-place on the lava hill and to bring about the erection of the great shrine.

A dagoba of the usual design was constructed on top of the hill and surrounded by the rings of smaller dagobas displaying the image of the dead leader. Whereupon came a great architect to seek the fulfillment of a dream in stone—to make a ziggurat of the hill and to deck its encircling galleries with a tremendous cyclorama of the Buddha legend.

And so was built the top terrace and then the others stepping down from it, until eventually, seven stages from the top, the designers came to the gentle slope of the valley. It was the intention of the great architect to make the entire hill a thing of lacy ornamentation, but when work was just getting under way on the bottom terrace the lower masonry began to crack. The hill, shaken by seismic disturbances not at all uncommon in the valley, was beginning to slide. Consequently all thought of artistic decoration was abandoned and the two bottom stages were made buttresses of stone to bind the pyramid at its base. . . . So much for legend. Not the least amazing thing about Borobudur is that its traditions fit in so well with the tangible facts.

About three miles to the northeast of Borobudur is Tjandi Mendut or Mendoet, a Hindu shrine whose shape recalls the recent discoveries about Sambour in Cambodia. Like those hoary brick piles it is a cube surmounted by a pyramid—a design more typical of the Hindu arts than the Assyrian step pyramids of Angkor or Borobudur. But despite its kinship in shape it differs from the relics of Sambour just as all Javanese monuments differ from those of the Khmers. It is made of stone instead of brick and shows the work of artizans whose skill the northern builders had not yet attained. It seems to be in a remarkable state of preservation but here one must not pay too much heed to outward appearances. Some years ago an earthquake knocked a large part of it down and its present aspect is due to painstaking Dutch archeologists who probably had more trouble piecing it together from its remains than the Hindus had in erecting it in the first place.

Its preservation up to that time was due to volcanic debris which had piled up on it during centuries of disturbance in a region of active craters. Hartmann, resident of Magelang, found traces of it in 1832 and it was uncovered some years afterward.

The temple is about sixty feet high with an inner sanctuary about fifteen feet square. The exterior walls are finely sculptured. The sanctuary which is reached by a series of stone steps from ground level contains three well-executed statues, life size. The middle one is supposed to represent Buddha, the accompanying figures are princes or disciples.

Mendoet is no more definitely placed chronologically than Borobudur except that most archeologists believe it to have been built at a later date.

To one who has visited Angkor first this theorizing is quite confusing. In the Cambodian region there is no doubt that the cube and pyramid style of temple was greatly anterior to the step pyramid. Sambour as a capital shows the Khmers in the period of their transition—the time when they were making a culture of their own out of the raw material brought to the valley of the Mekong out of India.

Here the first work of the Hindus, whether missionaries or conquerors, was to outdo Babylon in the erection of a ziggurat and to follow that work, if the archeological evidence be correct, with a temple which, in outline if not in finish, was the twin of the earlier efforts of the Khmers.

Mendoet in profile and treatment is less like a

temple than a magnificent tomb,—which for that matter it really is,—the tomb of a faith that got lost in its own Nirvana. It stands now in the midst of a green park with the palm trees hedging it in and the dark shadow of its tower creeping through the graveyard of stone pieces that have fallen from its cornices never to be replaced.

Coconut palms are about its ancient temple area. The inevitable cone of the volcano fades into the sky behind it and Buddha, its forgotten god, stares out through its open doorway toward the white spire of a Catholic church across the road that leads from Borobudur to Djokjakarta.

There are scores of Hindu monuments in Java. Some of them, like Borobudur, the visitor sees in great number. Some—particularly those in the highlands of Bagelen, the Benares of Java—he never even hears about. If the culture of the Khmers actually came out of Java then the Bagelen region may well have been its birthplace.

Something of the Khmers' magnificent disregard for time and expense and labor and material is visible here—not so much in the temples themselves as in the selection of their sites and the remarkable engineering involved in the construction of their approaches.

The group of temples stands on a point sixty-five hundred feet above the sea, and causeways known to this day as Buddha's roads lead up to them from the lowlands. Between Lake Mendjer and Lake Tjebong are the remains of a staircase that once was made up of forty-seven hundred steps, probably the longest staircase in the world.

And there on the high plateau the Tjandi Bima group spreads out over an area whose very size proclaims its kinship to Cambodia, and Ardjuna the beautiful crumbles to a dust which after all is quite like that of Angkor.

Djokjakarta, principal town of the Borobudur region, seems to have inherited all the old Hindu ghosts as it has inherited the bones of their sanctuaries. Dozens of weak-chinned gods, distorted images from the Hindu pantheon, are to be found at work keeping off evil and promoting good luck in this region. They are impressed for dozens of local ceremonials and their emblems are more frequently seen than the Dutch coat-of-arms or the insignia of the devout Mohammedan.

Djokjakarta is some twenty-six miles from Borobudur and is the capital of an opera bouffe sultanate, one of a pair that lies between the highlands and the sea. Farther north—about midway between Djokjakarta and Semarang—is Solo where another toyshop sultan carries on his "let's-pretend" government in the comforting shade of Dutch bayonets.

One might philosophize here on the collapse of

power and glory if one had not already spent too much time in a similar pursuit. The Hindu kingdoms are less than a memory in Java. The temporal power of these intellectuals who contributed so much to the civilization of this part of the world might never be known were in not for the images of Siva, the thoroughgoing destroyer, and Vishnu, the somewhat ineffectual preserver, and Brahma, the theoretical creator, which peer from the ruins all over the land. The wisdom of India either was brought to Java by, or came there under, the personal escort of the priestly caste, and so culture and religion were indistinguishable. Superior intelligence brought power, and naturally it, too, seemed bound up in the destinies contrived by the hundreds of little gods in Mother India's heaven. But the power and the wisdom are gone and the bones of piety remain—a matter about which one ought to be able to contrive a fine moral.

There must be some solace in this region for the ghosts of the Brahmans if they can ever reassemble enough of their scattered ashes to make a temporary covering for their superior souls. The kings passed. The priests passed. New powers came and Arabia furnished a new idea of a deity. And now these newcomers are going the way of those that went before.

The sultans of Djokjakarta and Solo are the inheritors of the Hindu lands and culture, and presumably are the heaven-born in whom are kept alight the mighty spirit of those who overcome the Indian might and religion. But a disinterested passer-by may find something to stir his thought in that the barrack-like palaces of these princes are less beautiful in their supposed splendor than are the graveyards of the dead gods in their unmistakable ruin. People who come to Solo to-day do so principally to laugh at the funny hats of the court attachés. The Dutch soldiers in the palace grounds do not laugh for the hats have ceased to interest them. They merely yawn across their rifle sights.

Eleven miles from Djokjakarta on the road to Solo and Semarang the Dutch have mobilized all the king's horses and all the king's men in a repetition of the great humpty-dumpty operation. There in the field of Prambanan is a spectacle of tumbled desolation such as one might expect to find after an earthquake in a cemetery. Stones everywhere in chaotic disorder—a disorder the more evident in that their gleaming white under the hot noon sun is sharply contrasted with the brilliant green verdure of a tropic lawn. It is as if a pair of hobbledehoy giants had grown tired of a domino game and scattered their ponderous markers all over the landscape.

Prambanan in its heyday must have been one of the most important temple groups in all the Hindu kingdom of central Java. There were five or six temples in this group—possibly a dozen if one counts the remains still to be seen outside the area fenced off by the Dutch archeologists. If one may judge from the two best preserved of the collection the shrines were something like Borobudur and Ta Keo and the Baphuon in shape—step pyramids with ornamented galleries. The two that remain sufficiently intact to permit inspection are not nearly so large as the temples of Angkor built on similar lines, but they are impressive even in their decay and show closer affinity to the architectural oddities of the Khmers than any other group in Java.

Down at the edge of the temple grounds a Dutch scientist in a cork hat and a suit of pongee is directing a score of sweating Javanese in an endless classification of dissociated stones. Many years ago an earthquake contrived to do what was still to be done in the way of obliterating the works of the Hindus. Two of these pyramids collapsed completely. The others were very nearly buried under the wreckage of their own cornices. So for something more than seven years the patient archeologists have been picking up a rock here and another there, piecing together this or that jigsaw puzzle that was once a bas-relief or a sculptured god or a carved pillar or a curving balustrade. One by one the rocks are carried out of their churchyard surroundings. Each is given a number and eventually carried to a pile that is supposed to contain others of its kind. Some day, probably far in the future, these various files will be ready for assembly and then the patient workers will discover whether Lot 382-A is a portion of the second terrace of Temple 4-North or merely part of a stone road dislocated by ambitious coolies.

In the meantime such gods as are left gaze out upon the world in a variety of moods. They can afford to smile in this region . . . the smile that comes of antiquity and wisdom.

One discovers with something of a shock that a face is peering down from the tower-like erection over the west gate of one of the pyramids. The expression is different, the sculpturing is of a slightly different school, but even so, except for a matter of a few hundred miles of geography, here is one of the human-visaged towers of Angkor Thom—a spire that might have come directly from the Bayon. And as if that were not sufficient connection one becomes conscious presently of a tower at the corner—the linga symbol of Siva and the four sensuous faces of the destroyer god gazing down from its sides.

Only the seven-headed Naga and the squatting giants of the Angkor causeways are absent here. Otherwise this might be the art school in which the architects of the Khmers learned their trade. Arrangements of bas-reliefs, subjects of bas-reliefs, tricks of corbel vaulting—all are here to contribute their bit toward complicating the puzzle of the Angkorean temple builders. If the engineers of Yacodhapura did not come from here they neglected an opportunity to establish an authentic and logical ancestry.

True there are many vital differences between the Angkor construction and that of this wide-spread desolation. The Javanese sculptures are certainly better pictorially than those of Angkor Thom and the Gate of Victory, but few will say that the spirit is better. The Javanese temples are possibly more carefully finished. But no one will argue that they have any of the surprise element which makes Angkor Vat the marvel that it is.

One authority has said that "beside the great temple of Borobudur the labor involved in the building of the Great Pyramids fades into insignificance." And if that be true one can barely imagine the toll of human energy and human life that was exacted before the towers of Angkor rose to their magnificent heights. The engineering skill, the patience that had to rely on a stone-yard more than forty miles distant, the constant procession of naked slaves toiling under the whips to bring the cut rock down from Ko Kher to Angkor Thom, are almost beyond imagination.

Prambanan is worth a visit in the blistering heat of high noon. It presents a series of façades and galleries and vaults that conjure up pictures of temple cities on the Nile, or Baalbeck or possibly Palmyra.

But after all, its significance seems to lie not in its tawny masses but in the Four Faces of Siva that look down from the corner tower. It is chiefly remarkable because it looks as if it might have suggested that great capital of the dead in Cambodia.

CHAPTER XXIX

The Long Trek to Nowhere

THE KHMERS WALK INTO THE GREAT SILENCES

One might look upon them almost as oracles, these lofty temples of Java,—oracles with a single message: The Doom of the Khmers.

The Fate that overtook the builders of Borobudur and Prambanan may have become a bit weary in her work of mapping destruction but she was not long deterred from its accomplishment. The Javanese civilization was independent of that of the Angkoreans and in its way as great. But always to one who has made the pilgrimage to Cambodia it must seem to have had no purpose in existence, save as a red reflection foreboding the wrath of the gods in the dawn that was breaking over Indo-China.

Always the memory comes back from Borobudur to Angkor Vat . . . Angkor that had made a pact with Siva in the blood of shattered nations, and saw the day when the Destroyer played his last sardonic jest. The tragedies of Java are those of other nations that took their chances in battle and went out to an end which, if irrevocable, was at least in the sunlight. The tragedy of Angkor lies in its mystery . . . the dread enigma of a grave without an epitaph. There is something about the monumental works of the Khmers that stirs the imagination, some tenancy of ghosts that serves to make these remains different from any of the other stony footprints that man has left on the face of the earth. It is in the valley of the Mekong that one finds the Ragnarok where the exiled gods of the Hindus went down into the shadows.

Sunrise on Angkor Vat . . . a touch of color on the topmost spire, then a nimbus of light, outlining the towers. The silhouette of the pyramid against a sky which for this brief moment of the day is cold and flat as a sheet of silver . . . Sunrise on Angkor—a repetitious miracle . . . Two hours ago it had seemed that the sun would never rise here again.

Some one is moving in the haze that is lifting off the moat . . . Yin. . . . He has passed the night as always, asleep at the wheel of his car. Now he walks the stone quay like a somnambulist or a votary driven to a sacred rite by forces over which he has no control.

He is an unreal figure in the gray sarong of the mist . . . the wraith of a great sorrow . . . a Cambodian Marius before the ruins of the Khmer Carthage. And in the sorcery of the dawn he is looking across the yesterdays of half a dozen centuries. The wan little ghosts are astir once more, marching down from the ziggurat presumably on their way back to the ash clouds from which they came . . . the kings and their elephants, the dancing-girls and concubines, the brocaded priests and the half-naked commoners.

Hordes of them are slipping across the causeway— a throng which for all its numbers stops no light and makes no sound. The road is filled with them—the people not of one day but of the centuries during which men and women and warriors trod this highway. They are hurrying past—toward the towers of Siva in the wall of Angkor Thom, toward the south where if one theory be true the national life of the Khmers was spilled out upon the broad plain.

The sun has set alight the altar fires and the pinnacles are smoldering. But in a moment this flame will be extinguished and Angkor Vat will stand, as it has always stood in the early morning, a black mass with luminous shades floating behind the gratings of its cloisters. By that time the phantoms will have retired to whatever bourne they occupy by day and the long halls will have been plunged once more into their baffling loneliness.

What happened to these people?

Sixty years of study and research so far can offer no satisfactory answer. The known history of Angkor ends with the death of a king called Jayavarman, the ninth of his line, in the year 1201. Undated inscriptions and documents of the Chams, ancient enemies of the Khmers, have contributed a few clues that offer little toward the solution of the mystery.

Aymonier believes that a cultural migration into Cambodia out of India continued until the Moslem activities of the twelfth century left the mother country sorely wounded and closed the routes of travel through the Straits of Malacca. He sees in the decadence of Angkor a rising tide of native barbarism deprived of the restraining influences that had been maintained by a steady movement of colonists from Madras.

Certainly something happened to the culture of the Khmers during that dark night which begins after the year 1201. Sivaic Brahmanism ceased to be the state religion and Buddhist bonzes set up the statues of their master in the old temples.

Up in the north the Thais, a coalition of races in which the Siamese were a principal factor, was gaining power, rebellious as it had always been against the Brahman gods and the castes which served them, and irked to the point of desperation by the government of a race, which, like Rome before its fall, maintained its domination only through the fear that its merciless might had set about it generations before.

Over toward the east the Chams were preparing for revolt. And in Angkor was that lackadaisical atmosphere of nothing to do, whose existence is proved by the negative testimony of the unbuilt temples. Artistic development ceased in Cambodia with the erection of Angkor Vat. It may have been that military reverses cut off the supply of slaves so essential to the massive constructions of the Khmers. It may have been that the artizans in their pride of accomplishment decided that they could do no better and laid down their tools. At any rate, the day of Angkor was done. The night was already advancing although the twilight lasted perhaps a hundred of years.

Here is a new picture: A phalanx of elephants thrown about the approaches to Angkor . . . spearmen and archers on the causeway . . . cavalry riding out to death from the North Gate of Angkor Thom. And then the roads suddenly molten with men and women and children fleeing panic-stricken from the doomed city, the young and the old and the palsied and the strong striking southward along the great lake. Some fall and are trampled under foot never to rise again save as dust tossed by vagrant winds. Some are hurled into the moat by the crush on the highway. And they too die—perhaps a more merciful death than awaits those who stay behind and those who push on.

Warriors man the walls of Angkor Vat but they have no heart for their jobs. Bleeding messengers have been coming back for days from the advanced positions in the country of the Thais and they bring no encouragement. Siva, the Destroyer, is paying his account to those who cast him out for Buddha. Out of habit the troops of the king are going through the motions of defense. But they know that there will be no defense. Not for hundreds of years has Angkor been compelled to fight on its own thresholds and the fact that the once mighty army has been smashed is an advance warning of the finish.

To the north a shaking of earth as the elephants and cavalry take the road out of battle . . . To the north a highway strewn with broken bodies . . . And farther along the highway the victorious Thais, no longer mere soldiery but butchers whose prey is already in sight . . .

The press of fugitives at the North Gate increases. Despite their haste, not half of the retreating warriors can find ingress through the tower of Siva. The elephants block the portal. The foot-soldiery, now completely routed, throws away its weapons and spreads out east and west to go around the town, or risks the horrible menace of the moat filled with crocodiles, and, surviving that peril, scales the walls.

Angkor Thom is emptying rapidly. . . . But not rapidly enough. The gates which were large enough for the normal traffic of commerce during hundreds of years are so congested that the crowds stand motionless as far back as the Bayon . . . crippled ancients, women with babies at their breasts, nobles and artizans and low-caste laborers . . . merchants, priests, soldiers and slaves, are parts of this mélange. Already the south road is hidden by the tide of brown bodies moving slowly between the rice fields ten or fifteen miles beyond Angkor Vat. But more than a million souls must find egress from the capital. They fight one another before the gates and Angkor Thom is already a shambles when the advance guard of the Thais comes crashing down along the avenue before the royal terrace.

The Siamese—an Asiatic army come to a decisive victory after years of subjection—the picture is almost complete . . . Snub-nozed yellow men turned loose in the finest city of the Orient . . . and presently the gutters are running red. The wooden residence district is afire. And corpses—hundreds of thousands of corpses—lie strewn over the temple terraces and in the streets and in the sodden courts of the ruined gardens.

Ghouls have looted the houses and the sanctuaries, and murder one another for their spoils. There is no discipline save in a systematized vandalism which is directed with futile though painstaking earnestness at the destruction of the Brahman shrines.

And the sun goes down but not on Angkor. There is no more Angkor.

That is one view of the great anticlimax of one of the most remarkable civilizations the world has ever produced. Once it was widely accepted as the authentic picture of the Khmers' collapse. It is augmented by some horrifying details of a second day during which the hot sun came to look upon the dead and the vultures were a dense cloud in the sky. One has to imagine it repeated in more or less similarity of detail in all the inhabited cities of Cambodia, but that is simple enough. If the Thais were strong enough to conquer Angkor they could have had no great difficulty in overrunning the lesser capitals.

This theory that Angkor, the Glorious, was blotted out after thirteen centuries of national existence by a single day's slaughter is not at all unreasonable if one considers the parallel cases in Oriental history. But it has points which complicate instead of explain the mystery.

Why, if they succeeded in taking the most magnificent capital in the East, if not in the entire world, did the Thais abandon it? Why, if this theory is correct, did not the refugees, who had escaped to the south before the butchers reached the Bayon, come back to the town they had left? Why did a civilization vanish merely because a group of cities had been put to the torch?

Groslier has produced a quantity of proofs— mainly photographs compared with the bas-reliefs at

Angkor—to show that the present-day Cambodians are actually of the same race as the Khmers. But, admitting that, one does not arrive at any solution of the real problem. The Cambodians of to-day may be true Khmers . . . in them may flow the blood of Yaçovarman the great builder. But they are no more the people who built Angkor than the rock piles of Verdun are the town that stood by the Meuse before 1914. If any large number of the Angkoreans survived then the disappearance of their culture is all the more incomprehensible. One could envision them weakened and afraid to return to their homes. He could not entertain the idea of a civilized people lapsing into savagery merely because of a change of address.

It has been suggested that the plague obliterated the populations of Angkor Thom and Beng Mealea and Ko Kher and Pra Khan. The theory is more tenable perhaps than that of warfare and slaughter by the Thais. But a plague would not have removed all the metal from the temples and pried apart the walls of Siva's shrines.

Monsieur Groslier, after a long study of the evidence, has come to the conclusion that the Angkoreans, weakened no doubt by wars with the Chams and Siamese, were destroyed by an uprising of slaves in which the intellectual minority was systematically murdered.

The logic of this idea is manifest. It would account for the insensate effort to tear apart the stones of the temples, and for the complete looting of Angkor Thom and its dependent shrines, and would explain at the same time the disappearance of the civilization that had built Angkor Vat.

Certainly there were millions of slaves in Cambodia. Just as surely the educated people even amid a culture as fine as that of Angkor were only a small proportion of the total population. It is well within the probabilities that the slaves could have massacred the intelligentsia, and then, deprived of the brain that had directed their handiwork, their quick return to the primitive life of the jungle was an inevitable detail.

In other parts of the world the reconstruction of ghosts has been aided materially by the graves of the dead. Even the tombs of Kish have been productive of much information concerning the manner in which the people lived. But there are no tombs in Cambodia. Cremation is a feature of the Brahman cult, and bodies that were left lying inside the walls of Angkor Thom must have disappeared rapidly in the moisture and heat of the tropics. Only through their works can one arrive at any idea of who the Khmers were, what they were and what became of them. . . . And the longer he puzzles over the matter the more ready he is to accept the local theory that the temples were built by Djinns who tired of their partnership with man, cursed him and drove him out into the waiting arms of Death.

Sunrise on Angkor Vat . . .

The sky is hot now behind the towers. The mists are lifting from the lower galleries disclosing the silhouette of the temple as vaguely unreal as an image on a shadow screen. The ghosts are gone but their memory remains as the elephants come plodding across the causeway. The vastness of the pyramid seems to cover the horizon and for this moment, at least, the Khmers are alive again. A purple shadow, cast by one of the eastern towers, deepens the shade on the central spire. And it takes appropriately the shape of a question mark. No symbol—not even the linga of Siva, the Destroyer—could typify more, clearly the soul of Angkor:

Who were these people?

THE END

SIAM

BANGKOK

BANTEI CHMAR

ANGKOR BENG   PR
        MEALEA   KH
    SIEM REAP
    LOLEI
TONLE BAKONG
SAP
              KAMPONG
              THOM

C A M B

              KAMP
              CHNA

              P

GULF
OF
SIAM

C

SCALE OF MILES
0   50   100   150